WRITING FOR
THE RELIGIOUS MARKET

The Co-Authors

HENRY B. ADAMS, president, Church Broadcasting Associates

ROLAND H. BAINTON, professor of ecclesiastical history, Yale University

MARGARET CULKIN BANNING, author of *Fallen Away, The Dowry*, and other novels

SAUL BERNSTEIN, editor, *Jewish Life* (Orthodox)

GEORGE DUGAN, religious news editor, the *New York Times*

HAROLD A. EHRENSPERGER, associate professor of religion and the creative arts, School of Theology, Boston University

HENRY ENDRESS, secretary for stewardship, United Lutheran Church in America

GLENN D. EVERETT, Washington correspondent, Religious News Service

WINFRED E. GARRISON, chairman, Department of Philosophy and Religion, University of Houston

GEORGIA HARKNESS, professor of applied theology, Pacific School of Religion

HELEN E. HULL, assistant editor, Story Papers, Light and Life Press

CLARENCE EDWARD MACARTNEY, author of *The Woman of Tekoah, Chariots of Fire*, and other religious books

RAYMOND M. RIGDON, editor, lesson courses, Training Union Curriculum Department, Southern Baptist Convention

ROBERT ROOT, head, religious journalism program, School of Journalism, Syracuse University

CHARLES H. SCHMITZ, director of broadcast training, Broadcasting and Film Commission, National Council of the Churches of Christ in the U. S. A.

HELEN F. SMITH, director, New York office of public relations, General Conference of Seventh-day Adventists

FRED D. WENTZEL, director of publications, Board of Christian Education and Publication, Evangelical and Reformed Church

ROLAND E. WOLSELEY, professor of journalism, School of Journalism, Syracuse University

Writing

FOR THE

Religious Market

EDITED BY Roland E. Wolseley

ASSOCIATION PRESS

NEW YORK

WRITING FOR THE RELIGIOUS MARKET

Copyright © 1956 by
National Board of Young Men's Christian Associations

Association Press, 291 Broadway, New York 7, N. Y.

Library of Congress catalog card number: 56-6451
55
Printed in the United States of America
American Book–Stratford Press, Inc., New York

A PRAYER FOR WRITERS

Bless our words, O Lord God, and those who write them, that as Thy Word goeth forth from Thee to run to the end of the world and return to Thee again, so our words may be swift messengers of unity and a just order in the earth. May they be true words, and we be honest writers, knowing that Thou art the true Word, and we Thy servants in truth and love.

—STEPHEN F. BAYNE, JR.

This prayer was written by Bishop Bayne while he was chaplain of Columbia University. It was delivered originally at a Maria Moors Cabot Convocation of the Graduate School of Journalism.

Preface

ALICE HEGAN RICE, the novelist, once called it "a dangerous thing" to give advice to young writers. There is so much to say, she told a correspondent, that "the flood of suggestions is apt to swamp the small craft just putting out from shore." She proceeded, nevertheless, to give most helpful counsel.

Irvin S. Cobb, long after he was established as a humorist, dramatist, and short story writer, also was cautious about telling others what to do. In fact, he refused, declaring that he did not feel qualified, and explaining that he was constantly striving to learn to write good English with "practice, hard work, reading the writings of real master-writers." And Arthur Machen, author of *The Hill of Dreams* and other sensitively written novels, was so downright as to declare: "I can give no advice as to the craft of writing, because in this matter no one man can advise another. Each of us," he insisted, "is faced by a different problem, and has to find the different solutions."

In the light of such statements it would seem futile to continue producing books intended to help writers. Yet, as the bibliographies for the chapters of this volume show, writers like Cobb and Machen have been in the minority. Authors and editors of books about writing have been listening to the scores of equally famed writers who have themselves written articles and books aimed at encouraging authors: Arnold Bennett, Vera Brittain, Somerset Maugham, and many more.

Through two decades of teaching classes in journalism, the editor of this volume has himself seen the merits and values of courses and books on writing. The craft of writing, he believes, can indeed be taught and has been imparted for many years, just as the craft of painting, sculpture, and the other arts is teachable. As Malcolm Cowley has pointed out so clearly in an article on "The Teaching and Study of Writing": "The art, properly speaking, of writing cannot be taught. . . . But the craft of writing can be taught . . . and the craft is a necessary foundation for the art. The craft consists of all past experience and achievement that can be reduced to rules. The art consists of the personal contribution that goes beyond the rules and may some day become a rule in itself." [1]

The *Atlantic Monthly* once carried an article by William Saroyan, the novelist, on "Twenty Years of Writing," in which he asked himself a rhetorical question: "What about courses in colleges and universities on writing?" He answered by writing categorically: "Useless, they are entirely useless." Inadvertently, or maybe they did it deliberately, the editors placed across the page from this dogmatic assertion an article by Professor Roy Cowden, of the University

[1] *Western Review*, Spring, 1950. Used by permission.

of Michigan, for twenty years director of the Hopwood Awards there. His article was entitled "Teaching Creative Writing." The introductory statement about it pointed out that "under his encouragement more than sixty volumes in prose and verse have now been published." It was evident, after reading Professor Cowden's article, that Saroyan, like so many other persons who criticize courses in writing and schools of journalism, simply did not know what goes on here.

It is thus with many professionals besides the author of *The Daring Young Man on the Flying Trapeze*. Sometimes they are self-sufficient and eminently gifted. They do not realize what many others had to learn in order to write well; that the others learned the hard way: by constant practice and study of techniques. Which is not to say that technique is enough, but it is to say that it is essential.

This book, then, is intended to assist those persons who have something to say about religion, directly or indirectly, and want to know of the problems of writing on that special subject and wish to receive assistance with the solutions of those problems. Persons of many talents can be independent of advice from others, but the rest of us must get the best possible guidance.

Some of the most competent craftsmen in religious writing have contributed to this book their best instruction for persons who wish to write on their specialties or in the forms they have selected. All these chapters have been prepared particularly for this book. But these writers, the editor is certain, would not have readers think that all the counsel that can be given is contained between these covers. There are at least four books of more detailed (but usually for secular use) general advice for each chapter. Rank beginners should spend some time with the basic books in the aspect of religious writing that interests them most. Experienced authors, already familiar with what can be learned from books of broader scope, will find in this volume the first integrated and thoroughly planned treatment of the special problems affecting religious writing. Thus this book should be useful to both beginners and veterans, if the beginners are willing to take the prerequisite of preliminary reading.

The co-authors of *Writing for the Religious Market* do not declare that religious writing is entirely different from any other. Because this point is explored more fully and appropriately in the opening chapter, it will not be dealt with here except to say that there are differences that justify not only this book but also volumes needed in several of the forms of writing that use religion as a subject or have religious motivation. A person can be a writer about religion without reading either this book or general manuals, of course. But it is easier to do an effective job by using the help this volume proffers. Some agile lads can climb up the side of a house without the aid of a ladder but most of us would be smarter to do it with one.

The writing dealt with in this book has no denominational or creedal limitations, it should be noted. The co-authors together represent the three principal religious groups in the United States: Jewish, Protestant, and Roman Catholic, in the sense that they are personally identified with such groups and not, most certainly, in any official manner. The Protestant authors together belong to nearly a dozen denominations. This emphasis on religious, rather than particularly Christian, writing is not to invalidate the importance of writing from the Christian viewpoint. Our hope is to influence all religious writing.

Which brings up the subject of all well-behaved prefaces: the ultimate purpose of this book. The desire of the editor is that it will help to create more writers interested in dealing with religion as a subject or in using a high religious motivation for their work, for outstanding religious writing is needed more than ever. He hopes, too, that it will renew the enthusiasm of writers who may be discouraged at the unprofessional methods used by some persons (but a minority) in the realm of religious writing: excessively low and slow payment, doctrinaire attitudes, intolerance of new ideas and techniques, and indifference to high standards of workmanship.

Writing for the Religious Market is not intended to be a how-to-do-it book exclusively. If a reader thinks it will show him, step by step, how to produce every one of the many types of material considered, he will be disappointed. No one book can show anyone how to do all these writing jobs; it is doubtful that a book alone can show anyone how to do even one of them. It can help, but it cannot do the job by itself.

Readers are warned, also, that the contributors have had to shift the market emphasis. For instance, the secular publishing field is virtually no market for religious poetry, but it is increasingly one for the religious novel. The religious short story appears mainly in church periodicals and only occasionally in the secular magazine. It is well, therefore, for the reader to examine the market statements in Appendix I.

This book, therefore, mainly discusses the problems and the methods of religious writing. It is concerned with making distinctions between religious and secular materials and with aiding writers to adjust to the special requirements of the world of religion, the special demands made upon writers. Only with certain topics has it been possible for the author of the chapter to go at all deeply into explanation of techniques.

Whether we define religion as a way of life, a search for an ideal existence, or a set of rites and rituals, in its best manifestations in our time religion is working for the betterment of mankind. Granting this, there can be no arguing that authors who are more effective religious writers than they ever have been before will advance such efforts for betterment. And considering the appalling condition of mankind at this mid-century period, still harried by disease, poverty, ignorance, natural disasters, and the threat of world-destructive war, anything which assists religion to put a check on man's follies is to be taken seriously.

ACKNOWLEDGMENTS

The editor wishes to thank the co-authors for their co-operation. Having been editor of or contributor to a half-dozen other volumes assembled in this fashion, he appreciates the helpfulness of each contributor. Every co-author was responsible only for the production of his own chapter, a bibliography, and a market list or market statement. No author takes responsibility for any chapter but his own. The editor takes responsibility for formulating the plan of the book as a whole, for correlating the contributions of the various authors, for his own two chapters, and for a portion of a third, as well as for some of the biographical, bibliographical, and market statements.

Thanks go from all contributors to the authors and publishers who have permitted quotations and to the innumerable persons who provided information requested by questionnaire, letter, and interview.

Roland E. Wolseley

Contents

Religious Writing
in General

CHAPTER One

What Is Religious Writing?

ROLAND E. WOLSELEY

Now and then someone who knows much about writing but evidently has little acquaintance with the world of religion says blandly: "There's no such thing as religious writing. Writing is writing, and that's that."

To which the writer about religion, especially if he is new at it, sometimes does not know what to say. The non-religious writer's statement sounds pat and seems logical enough, but somehow it does not quite convince. There is more to the situation than the critic realizes, the religious writer is sure, but he is not certain what it is.

Naturally "writing is writing." Similarly singing is singing and reading is reading, and so on. But no one should pretend that all singing is the same. There may appear to be no difference between writing a religious article and writing a secular one, but that is in appearance only. Many authors of competent secular writing have been flat failures when they turned to the religious field. Such an experience should show them and us that writing is not just writing.

Religious writing differs from secular writing in three major ways: in motive or purpose, in subject matter, and in vocabulary.

The Difference in Motive

The religious writer's purpose is to convey a religious attitude or viewpoint to the reader of or listener to his words. He is by function a propagandist, often an evangelist; that goes a long way to explain what is wrong with so much writing on religion. This weakness of religious writing must be admitted at once. But such an admission is something separate from the fact that the religious writer has a special purpose in his work not shared by the secular writer.

What that special purpose may be differs between writers. Because in the United States religion exists in a democratic setting, we have all manner of authors engaged in writing about each kind of religion. Consequently the type of religion or the theology or religious philosophy propounded in the *Moody Monthly* often does not resemble that expounded in *The Christian Register*. A religious novel whose viewpoint religiously is acceptable to Zondervan might not get the same reception at Abingdon. All religious bodies *seem* to have the same motives and objectives: to espouse the cause of religion; in the United States most of them want to support the tenets of Christianity. But the interpretations of each sometimes differ markedly.

As a consequence of his attitude the religious writer frequently does his work in a spirit of stewardship. At his best, his reason for writing, unlike that of the usual commercial writer, is not for personal gain, prestige, or gratification of his vanity. He conceives of himself as carrying out the mission of print (an old expression that neglects the audiovisual media).

Controlled by the zeal to convert and convince, the religious writer cares more for souls than for art. His worst critics say that the quality of his writing reveals that; his best critics point to the lives he has changed.

Religious writers and secular writers, however, are not always different beings whose motives never mingle. There are commercially minded religious writers and there are idealistic commercial writers. Many a commercial writer gladly gives away to religious publications or book firms material that elsewhere might bring him a large profit. Many a religious writer would do the same if he could still pay his bills.

The Difference in Subject Matter

Religion is of course a subject with its own body of information, its own history, its own traditions. Religion, furthermore, is one of the more complex subjects of those a writer may select. That is why effective writing about religion is needed greatly.

Adequate knowledge of religion, for purposes of writing about it, cannot be gained overnight, even for the most popular sort of presentation. Religion, too, must be experienced and lived. To be successfully clear and simple in dealing with so complex a subject as religion requires sound and thorough acquaintance with it. There are two ways of seeming to have mastered a subject. One is by knowing so little about it that you oversimplify it through ignorance. The other is by knowing so much that you know what to leave out to make it clear.

Religion is not business, it is not science; it is possessed of a subject matter that makes it different from all other bodies of knowledge and philosophies.

The Difference in Vocabulary

It follows logically that religion has its own vocabulary. Far too many religious writers remember that when they would do better to forget it. Religious writing intended for the specialists in religion, say the theologians, must be in the language of the specialists. That makes for more efficient communication. Writers about church school operation, religious education curricula, and church architecture who desire to communicate chiefly to the workers in these areas should use the technical vocabulary that is suitable. But here the difference in vocabulary between religious and secular writers should end. For all other purposes the religious writer's job is to communicate with the larger, nontechnical world, to write in the language of the people.

Writing and Religion

Up to this point we have been accepting the expression *religious writing* because it is part of the language. Essentially, however, such a phrase is obviously inexact. Writing, per se, cannot be religious. Other combinations, such as *religious art, religious journalism, religious music,* and *religious publishing,* suffer from the same confusion. What is meant is writing, art, music, publishing, or journalism that uses religion as its subject or has a spiritual or highly ethical motive.

Ronald Wolk, while studying what authors' representatives do about manuscripts dealing with religion (see Chapter 2), evolved a definition of religious writing which may be acceptable for the purposes of this book:

> A religious manuscript is one which is essentially concerned with religion. A manuscript written with the primary motive of evangelism, or of presenting some aspect of religion, qualifies under this definition. . . . Casual mention of religion or God, or merely having a religious figure as a character, does not make a manuscript a religious one. The central theme and motivation of the manuscript must be religious.[1]

[1] "Literary Agents and Religious Writing." Unpublished paper, School of Journalism, Syracuse University, Syracuse, N.Y., 1955.

Such writing also has been called *spiritual*. This term would seem to limit religious writing too much, for *spiritual* connotes the ethereal; religious writing at its best may have certain spiritual qualities, to be sure, but the spiritual cannot and should not, for the sake of readability, dominate all religious writing.

Dr. Benjamin P. Browne and Mrs. Edith Tiller Osteyee, two leading American Baptist writers about religious writing, consistently use the expression *Christian writing* rather than *religious writing*. They do not deny that writing about religion can be done from the Buddhist or Hindu or some other point of view, but they insist that the Christian viewpoint is the most desirable. Their distinction points up the assertion that motive is a distinguishing characteristic of writing about religion.

The Forms of Religious Writing

All modern writing, religious or otherwise, falls into two broad, general areas: fiction and non-fiction. Fiction is invented or imagined material; non-fiction is true or factual. The line between them is less well defined now than it once was, but in general it persists. As an aid to new writers the distinction still is useful.

Within these areas are various forms. Fiction takes the form of the novel, novella, novelette, short story, short short story, the fictional sketch, and those forms that stand more or less by themselves but yet are fictional: the play, scenario, poem, and hymn. Non-fiction covers the fact book, such as history, biography, political analysis; the textbook, article, essay, editorial, factual sketch, news story, feature, column, and the review or criticism.

The audio-visual media have evolved their own subsidiary forms: scripts and scenarios; actually these are adaptations of the older fictional or non-fictional forms, but they have their special problems of writing. In this book, therefore, they have been separated from the rest.

Because religious writing uses all these forms, it appears, on the surface, that the master of forms can write successfully about religion if he desires. But such a master of literary forms cannot write effectively about any subject, necessarily, any more than a master of, say, tennis form can go far on the court on form alone. Good writers understand the forms of writing but they bring imagination, research ability, knowledge of words, and other talents and skills. It makes little difference if an author writes something he thinks is an essay but it turns out to be an article, so long as it accomplishes what he expected it to accomplish.

Forms in Conflict

These forms, which also involve certain media of communication, are somewhat in conflict, whatever their subject. The writer committed to any one form is likely to think that his is the most effective of all in performing the function he desires from writing. The novelist who wishes his work to be more than a vehicle for entertainment of his readers is convinced that this fictional technique puts over an idea or viewpoint more effectively than the didactic article. The professional article writer, on the other hand, often asserts that the novel takes too long to do the job. He prefers to rely more on the straightforward approach of non-fiction.

The conflict becomes sharper when we hear the arguments of those who think that television, for instance, is a more powerful medium than the newspaper or that radio is more wide-reaching than the magazine. This dispute is exceedingly important to the world of religion, for with limited resources and talents the best use of the various facilities of communication must be made. This book presents the view that all media are important to religion and should be put to its use; it is up to the leaders of the religious world to make the choices when they must.

The Public's Demands

The reading, listening, and viewing public makes certain demands of writers. Early in the history of the United States, when the printing press was a scarce machine, the small reading public of the time was grateful for whatever came from it. Because the church was almost as zealous as politics in using the printed word in colonial times, the literate Americans of the seventeenth and eighteenth centuries were exposed to more religious literature than those of the mid-twentieth century, for two centuries ago there was far less printed matter by volume and a greater proportion of it was writing about religion. With comparatively little choice, the colonists made few demands upon the publishers of their era.

Today, however, religious writing is involved in heavy competition. A secular-minded people has a deluge of newspapers, magazines, books, and audio-visual materials to choose between. While by no means feeble, the writing about religion is not dominant, as it was two hundred years ago. Only one religious magazine or newspaper ranks among the sixty U.S. publications that have a million or more circulation. Every religious magazine today except the *Upper Room* has a lower circulation than certain periodicals giving guidance on sewing or television program details.

That portion of the public which now earnestly desires writing about religion makes many demands upon writers. These readers want to know what religion—some sort of religion—has to offer in the way of guidance in solving life's problems. They seek, also, encouragement for survival in an atomic age. They look to religion and religious writing for renewal of waning faith. They expect it to explain religion, to be a missionary, to serve as evangelist, to spread propaganda. Not a few wish authors to entertain them with material having a religious theme or setting. A comparative handful even look to religious writing as a way for them to give to the God of their belief.

Meeting all such demands is impossible for any one writer on religion. Specialists therefore have been developed; these writers have found ways to gratify certain segments of the demand, certain publics, with results of varying quality. As with secular literature, the religious writing that provides easy solutions, spiritual shots in the arm, and escapist entertainment is the most popular. To the disappointment of some authors, readers about religion are hardly more discriminating than are readers about other subjects.

The Place of Religious Writing

Most religious writing in the United States can be labeled Christian, being either Roman Catholic or Protestant in origin,[2] a not unnatural situation, considering the religious history of the nation. Only the considerable body of Jewish religious writing is also of consequence: writing about or from the viewpoint of the Hindu, the Zoroastrian, or other non-Christian is found largely in the nations where such religions are strongest.

In volume of material the writing known as religious appears large. Of the 11,901 books published in the U.S. in 1954, covering new books and new editions of old ones, 875 were classified by *Publisher's Weekly* under the heading religion, an increase over 1953. The increase amounted to 61 per cent, and was double the increase of any other category. It probably is conservative, for a religious novel

[2] Included here for convenience, and despite their disavowal of such affiliation, are the Southern Baptists, the Church of the Latter Day Saints, and other groups.

or book of religious poetry is classified as fiction, not religion.

In sales volume, religious books also have done well in recent years, although not so well as the offerings of book clubs, texts, trade books, encyclopedias, and technical-professional books. Yet here again the *PW* classifiers have put religious encyclopedias with reference books and not religion. At the least, religious books have doubled their sales since 1947. Dollar volume is misleading, however, for religious books often are sold for much less per copy than many other types, especially texts. In numbers of copies sold, in 1947, religious books stood fourth among the eight categories, whereas they were sixth in dollar sales. In the past decade this trend has become stronger.

But it is a different story in the areas of religious journalism and religious radio and television. Among the country's approximately twenty-two thousand journalistic publications of various kinds, religion is the subject of about fourteen hundred, not including the thousands of weekly and monthly bulletins and parish papers. Their aggregate circulation is estimated at ten million each issue. Secular newspapers together sell in excess of fifty-five million daily; secular magazines sell nine million each day. One secular magazine has seventeen million circulation each month throughout the world. Thus there is no exact basis of comparison; all one can say is that the religious press is substantial but hardly comparable in size to the secular.

Religious radio and television are far smaller. Federal Communications Commission staff members have estimated that of the total broadcast and telecast time in the United States, religious programming on both media occupies between 2 and 3 per cent. But even for this small amount, demand for acceptable written material is great, if not heavily rewarded.

Religious writing for all these media has a large enough

public following to command the efforts of the nation's best writers; it has a big enough potential to deserve more attention from skilled authors. Beginning writers should consider it as an end in itself, not only a stepping stone to later literary fame.

Despite its size and potential, religious writing has not won the highest critical respect, however. Ruth Suckow, author of *Iowa Interiors, The Folks, The Odyssey of a Nice Girl,* and other novels, states the situation and its causes well in one of her books:

> I myself started writing at the age of seven, when I sat down to begin a child's novel. . . . All Emma's and my efforts in the arts were encouraged by our parents. . . . But I soon came to feel, all the same, that these literary efforts had little to do with "religion"—at least, with "organized religion." On the whole, it was against them.
>
> From the earliest days, for example, I came to expect that I would find the least interesting stories in the Sunday School paper, and to regard these stories with suspicion, because I could see well enough that they must all reach a predetermined end. Written for edification, they not only failed to edify, but instead contributed to a certain satiric view of "religious" writing. . . .
>
> But far more serious was the fact that I began to think that great writing was not "religious." Only mediocre poems would be considered "religious"—the little verses, well meant but not interesting as poetry, which might appear in church or Sunday School papers, chosen for the sentiment expressed.[3]

Miss Suckow then goes on to say that, at least in her experience, religious people were not encouraged to appreciate high quality in works of art, at least where art pertained to religion. "They looked for explicit subject matter—'sacred art' in painting, in literature, an obvious ethical

[3] Ruth Suckow, *Some Others and Myself* (New York: Rinehart & Company, 1952), p. 235. Used by permission.

teaching." She notes that when a religious novel was selected for review in a church circle, it was likely to be on
subject matter; *Quo Vadis*, she suggests, might have been
selected at one period and later on the novels of Lloyd
Douglas.

Standards Are Changing

A change in standards is taking place, however, in the
nature of both religious non-fiction and religious fiction.
The best of the latter no longer is didactic; religious periodicals more and more are refraining from publishing sermons and annual reports per se; most religious television (if
not most religious radio) is at least inoffensive, if not dynamic; more religious films are being produced with professional éclat.

Evidence of the change of standards is detected in a review of Betty MacDonald's *Onions in the Stew* by Theodore A. Gill, associate editor of the *Christian Century*. He
expresses a view rarely voiced one hundred years ago, when
practically all religious writing dripped with piety. He
wrote in part:

> There is nothing technically or systematically "reli-
> gious" about her account, but there is a high religion in
> the quality of her remembered experience; there is an ap-
> preciation of the world, and a gratitude for what is
> (though that is often not much), and a joy in living that
> ought to be a feature of every Christian life. We can't all
> make it rollick so in the telling but we can all do some-
> thing about the prunes and prim reserve that is too often
> mistaken for piety.
>
> MacDonald should be required reading for all the
> preachers who think the truth has to be pompous. Wis-
> dom can smile, too, and for this author it usually does.
> . . . Positively Pauline, isn't she? And with never a break
> about Original Sin or the Egocentric Predicament.[4]

[4] *Christian Century*, June 15, 1955, p. 709. Used by permission.

Despite the change, far too much material of poor quality still comes from the press and the cutting room. Religious writers need to ponder the statement by Father Harold C. Gardiner, literary editor of *America:* "Authors of spiritual books have owed it to their subject-matter to write well, and readers will find that their spiritual advancement will not be a whit hindered (to say the least) because a book is well written."

Roland E. Wolseley, editor of this volume and author of its first two chapters, is professor of journalism and chairman of the magazine department, School of Journalism, Syracuse University. He is author of *Careers in Religious Journalism* and *Interpreting the Church Through Press and Radio,* as well as *The Magazine World, Exploring Journalism* (with Laurence R. Campbell), *Newsmen at Work* (also with Dr. Campbell), and other books. He wrote *Face to Face with India,* a Joint Commission on Missionary Education study book, while in India in 1952–53, where he helped establish a department of journalism at Nagpur University. Professor Wolseley has done newspaper work in Pennsylvania and Illinois, contributed articles to several hundred magazines, including *Christian Century, Christian Herald,* and *The Commonweal,* done religious publicity writing, had experience in educational radio and film work, been a book reviewer, and written curriculum materials. He speaks frequently at religious writers' and editors' conferences. He was the first head of the graduate program in religious journalism at Syracuse, and also has taught at Northwestern University, Roosevelt University, and Mundelein College.

CHAPTER *Two*

The Practical Side

ROLAND E. WOLSELEY

Religious writers, like any others, use equipment, consult books, deal with authors' representatives, and have to attend to the many other practical details of their occupation. In this chapter there is a quick review of certain essential practices. The bibliography is well stocked with full-length guide books on the practical side for those who have no information whatsoever about marketing, copyright, and the other relevant topics.

The Tools

Writers are more fortunate than most artists. A portable typewriter, a small notebook, a few file boxes, and stationery supplies will set anyone up in business, so far as equipment is concerned. After a while, the professional may add a large, office-model typewriter, even an electric one, a

15

camera, and a recording machine. Soon he needs a small reference library; and, according to his specialty, he may want a travel item in his budget.

Writers who live near public libraries require only a minimum personal library. But they must have that, because town and city collections are not accessible late at night and often not over week ends, especially in summer. Here are the titles of books ranged along the desk-top of a free lancer who writes on religion as well as other specialties. He resides in a large city and has been producing books and articles for two decades.

> *American College Dictionary*
> *Columbia Encyclopedia*
> *Editor & Publisher International Year Book*
> *Familiar Quotations*, by Bartlett
> *An Encyclopedia of World History*, by Langer
> *The Holy Bible* (King James Version, with Concordance)
> *The Holy Bible* (Revised Standard Version)
> *Literary Market Place*
> *A Manual of Style*
> *Modern English Usage*, by Fowler
> *School Atlas*, by Goode
> *Webster's Biographical Dictionary*
> *Webster's Dictionary of Synonyms*
> *The Writer's Market*
> *Yearbook of American Churches*

A biblical atlas might be added to this list by a writer with special interest in writing about the Holy Land. Even better, of course, is travel, which is not always a luxury. Travel is not so essential for religious writers as for some others, but it is useful if it can be afforded and can pay for itself in the long run by an industrious scribe. A trip to the Holy Land gives greater reality to the religious writer's work that deals with historical backgrounds; it also provides him with suitable locale for fiction.

Similar valuable tools are his special knowledge, training, and experience: presumably a writer who has served in the pastorate, priesthood, or rabbinate can write with conviction on subjects related to that experience. The many articles and books possible on religious education come with greater authority from an experienced religious educator.

To gain such experience, a writer must visit the sources of information; if he lives in Des Moines and a Chicago church is the source of a story, the article or book chapter stemming from it is likely to be far more effective if based on first-hand observation of what is being done in that church. Low payment often hampers a writer from making such journeys but if such a trip can be combined with other duties or if several pieces of writing can result from one trip, such travel is worth the trouble.

The Writer's Regimen

Writers are not agreed on the merits of working systematically. But only a few of those who have described their methods (of the many read by the writer of these words) say that they leave everything to inspiration. They say just the opposite, usually. The commercial successful writers generally abide by a schedule. Paul Kearney, a contributor of articles to most of the large national magazines and author of various fact books, records many details about every writing task he undertakes. In *Free-Lance Writing for a Living* he reports that he wrote a book of 36,000 words in four calendar days, a result not to be obtained by waiting for inspiration. He wrote a juvenile book, running to 196 pages, or 48,000 words, on this schedule: "Work begun on May 12; ms. delivered June 4 . . . worked on this only on alternate days . . . job completed in 12 working days, averaging 4,000 words a day."

H. L. Mencken, who may be classed as an anti-religious writer, in his earlier days used to write "in the evening, beginning at 7:00 or 7:30, and stopping at 10. . . . All the writing I do is . . . in three hour sessions, on perhaps 200 evenings of the year."

If he is in "a sensible mood," Carl Van Doren, the critic, editor, teacher, and novelist, once wrote an inquirer, he ordinarily works no more than three or four hours at a time; "but if my material proves resistant I am likely to lose my sense and go on for ten or even twenty hours." Frederick Stuart Greene, the short story writer, advocated writing not less than 1,000 words a day, especially when beginning new material.

Most authors say that writing is hard work. James Harvey Robinson wrote Professor Josephine K. Piercy of Indiana University, when she was preparing her stimulating book, *Modern Writers at Work*, "It is just as hard to write at sixty-five as at twenty-five—or nearly so." William Allen White told her that his 150,000-word novel, *A Certain Rich Man*, was copied entirely three times and each copy revised twice. He added, it should be noted, "Writing is exactly like any other skilled trade; it requires an apprenticeship." Somerset Maugham reports that Colette sometimes spent an entire morning on a single page. Margaret Deland tells an anecdote about Lafcadio Hearn: once Hearn wanted to describe a dragonfly darting about in the sunny air over a swamp. "As I remember that paragraph," she said, "there are only ten lines in it, but Hearn wrote it seventeen times before he was satisfied with it." The editor of this book once was handed a packet of copy paper used by a *Time* magazine writer while preparing the opening paragraph of a short news article for that weekly: it consisted of 123 separate attempts to phrase the start of the article.

The new or the undisciplined writer, then, benefits from producing his work regularly and painstakingly. The mark of the professional, someone has said, is that he works when he does not want to. The professional writer, although he often says that he "loves" his work, frequently has to resist the desire to read, play, or just vegetate instead of working at his typewriter. Regular writing routines assist him in his constant battle with duty.

Especially for the fact writer, such organized work requires files of material, and for the fiction writer, notebooks. Their content must be kept up to date and accessible. It also demands that the writer respect accuracy. He must be patient and thorough in checking statements of fact.

Members of a certain school of religious writers, the sermonizers and speechmakers, have a tendency to use facts loosely. Few persons ever seem to take the trouble to tell a parson when he has made a misstatement of fact. Professional methods require, also, that the writer on religion be tough-minded, so that he is not swept away by emotionalism or the weird magic which seems to solve all problems for some religious folk. It takes a persistent writer, as well, to revise and rewrite that gem he has written.

Professionalism, for most writers, begins with planning their material. Careful outlining is recommended by many successful writers; it is demanded, in fact, by editors for book houses and magazines with high standards. William L. Rivers, a contributor to *Harper's*, *This Week*, and other periodicals, once suggested an article to the *New York Times* magazine. He was asked to send the editor a memorandum of the idea, which he did. The editor wrote: "This is hardly an outline. Send us a two-page outline; block it out in sections." What he next sent, he related in *Writer's Digest*, "covered two pages, Roman numerals followed by single-spaced ABC's, followed by double-spaced Arabic numerals, followed by single-spaced abc's."

Thus there may be differences in these practices between writers of fact and fiction and even between writers of a single form. Yet author after author, in numerous literary autobiographies, describes how he stumbled through his early writing and then became more or less businesslike and systematic about it.

Form and Style

Why do so many books on writing repeat the simple instructions about typescript form? The answer comes from an exasperated editor who wrote a writers' magazine, "It's unbelievable that so many writers are still ignorant of the fundamental requirements of manuscript submission." He had received, he said, "material which must have been dug up from a bottom drawer, some mss. were dog-eared and dated from other editors, others didn't enclose a stamped envelope, some were torn or on small size writing paper. . . ."

The rules are standardized in their main essentials. No editor will reject a piece of work that violates these rules if it contains considerable merit as to ideas, concept, or skill in expression. In general, however, the badly prepared typescript is also a badly written one; the converse is not true, for some writers can master form of presentation if nothing else. No merit attaches, however, to sending out typescripts that connote bad work even in their form and appearance.

Here, then, are the major rules—they may vary slightly if the material is fiction rather than non-fiction:

1. *Paper*. For final drafts, use a high-quality white, 8½ x 11 bond, preferably one easily erased and capable of considerable handling, thus preserving appearance and avoiding excessive retyping. Always make a carbon copy, as a protection against loss of the original or for checking purposes if proofs are returned.

2. *Typing*. All completed work should be typed, double space, with one-inch margins all around except the first sheet, and on one side of the sheet only. Use a well-inked

black ribbon. Keep to the same size type throughout (elite or pica). Submit only typed copy, never printed or otherwise duplicated. Try to keep a consistent width of line, providing about ten words to each line.

3. *Placement.* Except for book-length material, the first page should carry, at upper left, the author's full name and address; at upper right should appear the approximate number of words and the rights being released. In the upper third of the page, centered, should go the title and beneath it the author's name. All other margins should be one inch. Additional pages should be numbered and identified either with the writer's name or a repetition of the title. The typescript can be ended with #, -O-, or "The End." Some writers of newspaper background type "More" at the bottom of each sheet except the last.

4. *Neatness.* A few handmade corrections, if made precisely in ink, are not objectionable, but any typescript mottled with such changes needs retyping. Avoid fastenings, such as pins (hair, straight, or safety), staples, brads, or other such dangerous implements. A clip is sufficient and will not mar the main part of the script if, as with articles, short stories, or poems, a cover page is used at the front and back. This page is prepared much as is the first regular sheet: the author's name and address, the length and rights, and the title and by-line. In the lower half may appear a synopsis or summary of the material; just a few short paragraphs to tell the editor what he can expect.

5. *Style.* Follow the style of the publishing house to which the material is being submitted. A standard guide is the University of Chicago *Manual of Style*, which answers countless questions on punctuation, capitalization, use of footnotes, and dozens of other practices. All major requirements can be met through this book.

6. *Mailing.* Typescripts should be sent out flat or folded, never rolled. They need not be put in a binder or folder.

Doing so helps preserve them, of course, but it also raises the cost of mailing, since such material always travels first class. Copy up to about eight pages can be sent folded twice, horizontally. Up to sixteen pages can be sent folded once, horizontally across the center. Anything larger should be mailed flat. Book-length materials should be put in stationery boxes and can be sent less expensively by express than by mail. Articles, short stories, and other typescripts being sent on speculation (without contract or other assurance of publication) always should be accompanied by return postage; a stamped, self-addressed envelope is preferable. All material should be clearly identified; book-lengths should be sent insured for enough to cover the cost of retyping. Pictures and other art work should go with the typescript, and all material should be well protected with cardboard.

Marketing

Marketing a manuscript generally means selling it. In the world of religious writing, where the ideals of stewardship move many persons neither to charge for nor to pay for writing, or to expect or to pay little, marketing also means publishing. The problem of whether writers on religion should be paid as well as are writers on other topics troubles both authors and publishers. If the laborer is worthy of his hire, as Luke 10:7 puts it, there should be no discrimination. On the other hand, if the writer wishes to perform a service through his work, he should be permitted to do so.

Editors, therefore, should pay the best possible rates, since some writers depend entirely upon their literary work for their earnings. Authors, then, should be free to demonstrate their sincerity about their devotion to their religious ideals by refusing payment, returning it, or using it directly for the aims of religion at its highest, if they can do so.

Where feasible, the authors of the chapters on the various types of writing have indicated what payment is to be received for the material. Generalizations about the returns on religious writing are difficult to make. The literary field in America is not an especially lucrative one, as Malcolm Cowley proves in his *The Literary Situation.* The occasional high figures one hears about go to relatively few authors. One generalization about religious writing can be made, however: rates of payment often are below average for writing in the U.S. No religious paper or magazine pays even a tenth of the amount paid for articles or stories by the best-paying secular publications; even average payments, studies have shown, are far below secular publication averages. Publishers of religious books offer more or less standard royalty rates, but such books rarely are big sellers. This lag is easily enough explained: religious publications can get little high-priced advertising, for they have comparatively small and diffused circulations. Religious books do not usually interest Americans as much as volumes on dieting, the careers of movie actresses, or life in the Tennessee hills.

To say this much is not to say that religious writers are paid too little to make much of the work worth-while. Some are paid well; others are paid about what the material is worth under the best rates. But all should receive more because of the intrinsic value of what religious writers in general are doing and to make it possible to attract more competent writers who cannot now afford to take less than is available elsewhere.

In any case, an author has to find a publisher, whether that publisher pays him nothing, little, or much, and whether the author desires payment. Writers on religion are persons possessed of ideas. They are not content just to write and burn. They burn, to be sure, but they burn to be read and to influence others.

Writers have two ways to market their material: either by doing it themselves or by paying someone else to do it for them. The self-sufficient writer, in order to market his material effectively, must know those markets. He does so by reading carefully the periodicals he wishes to appear in or the catalogs and output of the book publishers whom he hopes to interest in his work. He reads at least one writer's magazine and purchases for frequent consultation a reliable market guide (see Appendix I). He also learns much by direct experience from submitting his material, for editors sometimes take the pains to explain what they need. For instance, Gerald Giving, an editor of Augsburg publications in Minneapolis, sends writers a two-page printed leaflet of carefully stated details about the needs of his firm.

A writer may find it helpful to query editors before submitting material. Because authors are not agreed on the merits of querying, it is well to study what is said on this subject in books on manuscript marketing (see Appendix I).

Literary agents, also called authors' representatives, are sent relatively little religious material. Ronald Wolk learned this in his study of their reaction to the religious writings they receive. Thirty-six reported that less than 2 per cent of what they receive falls into this category. They also told him that both secular and religious magazines are receptive and eager for religious material of high quality, but are unable to get it.

They added, Mr. Wolk wrote, "that most religious writing is poorly done and of too low quality for either editors or agents to bother with." Of the faults specifically named, three stood out: "poorly written, too amateurish, and rely on their subjects to carry them."

The agents declared that "there is a growing need for more good religious writing and a growing desire on the part of the general reading public to read more religious material."

When asked what forms are preferred, the representatives answered: fiction of a religious nature and religious books.

They reported that in 1955 editors were publishing "more personal experience and inspirational material."

Does a religious writer need an agent? How does one learn of a dependable authors' representative? Whether he writes on religion or on any other subject, a beginning writer will not be taken up by a regular agent. The new writer is likely to work at it only part time and to produce too little to make it worth an agent's while. Agents charge a standard fee of 10 per cent for their services (more for placing in foreign markets). Furthermore, the rates paid by many small religious markets are so low that an agent cannot afford to give service.

A productive and capable writer on religion can benefit from the help of a recognized authors' representative. Such a person places his material to the greatest financial advantage of both, obtains writing assignments for him, protects his various subsidiary rights, and acts in general as his business manager. About 125 authors' representatives are listed in the *Literary Market Place*.

Writers should distinguish between authors' agents and critics. Some persons play a dual role by criticizing the work of new writers for a fee, frequently $5 minimum and $3 for each thousand words over three thousand, but charging only the usual 10 per cent marketing fee for professional writers. The majority of agents do not advertise, for most of them are interested mainly in the established professional author or in providing specialized services, such as concentrating on selling writing done for the theater or radio and television.

Copyright and Plagiarism

Religious journalists and authors sometimes are astonishingly unethical in their professional activities. Editors of religious periodicals for decades have been accustomed to helping themselves to the content of each other's publications without either payment or credit to anyone. The incorporation of other people's ideas and statements in their copy by religious writers springs, no doubt, from the habit of many religious workers, who speak in public often, of picking up material as they need it. It is not extraordinary for a sermonizer to borrow wholesale the work of some genius at homiletics. Publishers of books of sermons explain the high sale of such collections by this practice. One might expect religious writers and editors to be meticulous about obeying copyright laws simply because they are religious people. Often, however, their ethical standards as a group may seem low in these matters. Much of the conduct springs from ignorance, not malicious intent.

People surrounded by ideas of sharing, of brotherhood, and of mutual helpfulness see no contradiction in using what others have produced. They are perfectly willing to have their own brain children shared similarly. But they live in a nation with an economic order that makes this sharing impractical; it is noticed, also, that they do not carry out such communal ideas at the supermarkets.

Authors of articles, stories, and other material for print or presentation on radio or television should not use material that has appeared or been used previously without getting permission from the copyright owner, except for a few dozen words usually permitted in quotation. Facts cannot be protected for an author, but his manner of writing and his way of developing his ideas can be. For most casual uses an author can obtain permission to reproduce reasonable amounts of material without making payment, although verse and illustrations are likely to be subject to payment, for they bring so little return to begin with.

Titles cannot be protected under copyright laws, but if an author selects a title that was used earlier by another author and it can be proved that the new use interferes with the sale of the first work, there can be a case because there may have been restraint of trade. A valuable source of detailed information on both copyright and plagiarism is Wittenberg's *The Protection and Marketing of Literary Property*.

Self-Publication

Religious writers, often being by nature propagandists and zealots, long have been susceptible to what are known as "vanity" or "co-operative" publishing houses. Their main business is publishing a book at the author's own expense. In recent years such firms have increased the services to the author for his investment in himself, such as minimum advertising and supplies of review copies. But one standard has not been raised sufficiently: the quality of material published. Consequently, shoddy volumes are being issued, among them numerous collections of religious verse, of sermons, and of other churchly material, little of which is of good quality. Most religious writing of high caliber can find a publisher who either will purchase the material outright (as for articles and stories) or guarantee the author a standard royalty and assume the full publication risk. The only exception is narrowly technical or scholarly work on religion that cannot be expected to command wide sale. Regular houses will share costs of producing such works with an author, or university presses will enter a co-operative arrangement but provide capable editing and agree to publish only reputable work.

Reading and Study

Religious writers should read about writing, but not too much, lest they vitiate their energies better used in producing material and practicing techniques. Lawyers read law journals, doctors read medical books and magazines, and other professionals spend time with their special publications. Authors who produce best sellers from time to time and have the services of one or more literary representatives may not need technical and marketing information from such magazines as *The Writer*. But others find them useful.

Sufficiently experienced writers can apply for membership in the Authors League of America; smaller groups are the Christian Authors Guild, the Catholic Writers Guild, the Mennonite Writers Fellowship, and secular, regional writers' clubs.

Well-conducted writers' conferences and club meetings are a stimulus. The principal secular ones are listed in *The Writer's Market* and the *Literary Market Place*. Most conferences for religious writers are omitted from these lists. These are the principal ones; they meet for a week or two, in summer unless otherwise stated:

> Christian Writers and Editors Conference, Green Lake, Wis., sponsored by the National Council of the Churches of Christ in the U.S.A. and the American Baptist Convention.
>
> Writers One-Day Conference, under American Baptist Convention auspices, held winters in a different eastern U.S. city each year
>
> Writers Conferences, Southern Baptist Convention, Ridgecrest, N.C. and Glorieta, N.M.
>
> Writers Conference, Notre Dame University, South Bend, Ind.
>
> Mennonite Writers' Conference, usually in eastern U.S.
>
> Summer Institutes of Christian Writing, held by *Christian Life* magazine, simultaneously with Bible conferences, in several places in mid-western states
>
> Christian Writers Workshop and Conference, Chicago, in winters
>
> Writers' and Editors' Workshop, United Lutheran Church in America, Gettysburg, Pa.

Writing Religious Fiction
for Print

CHAPTER *Three*

The Novel and Religion

MARGARET CULKIN BANNING

THE MOVEMENT, which is not a drift but a current, of both writers and readers toward fiction that incorporates religious forces is undoubtedly due to many reasons, and it would be presumptuous to be dogmatic about the number of such causes or their relative importance. But to examine some of them is not only interesting but useful, especially to any novelist who contemplates writing a story in which religion will motivate his characters.

One of these reasons may be the perils among which we have come to live and the shocks constantly inflicted by violent and unexpected death, not only during the wars but also on the highways and airways. Few families have not faced up to sudden death among their members or their friends in the past few years. At such times, in trying to sublimate grief, or to be reconciled with life, people often seek sympathy and understanding in the tales of other lives.

31

They can find comfort in a novel when they cannot find it in a book of argument or persuasion or facts. If a troubled or saddened person can find what is called reader-identification in a story, if it offers him an example of spiritual refuge, it is a welcome novel in times like the present. The chances and severities of the world, and its spiritual upsets, are as naturally reflected in novels today as a more peaceful society was truly reflected in the books written by Anthony Trollope and Jane Austen.

Today society is being evangelized. Nearly every sect has devoted "action" groups, and violently partisan as these may be, among them they have stirred up such interest in religion that many readers feel that a novel which lacks religious values is not true to life. If religion is left out, the story seems, to a large section of the reading public at least, to lack thoroughness. The public has stopped being ashamed of faith. Frequently it is front page news. That this trend should affect the novelist and open up new fields for his work is inevitable.

Millions of people have embarked on a frank search for the truth. In this enormous posse are many of our most intellectual thinkers and writers as well as quite a crowd of sentimentalists, some poseurs, and a number who are always around when they think there is a little money to be made by riding on the coattails of a trend. The current has not yet gathered full force, but even now there can be no doubt that, in spite of plagues of comic books and printed trash, the reading public has become more serious, more intellectual, and more spiritually inclined than it has been in a long time.

Religion No Longer Taboo

Religion as a subject is no longer taboo or classified. Time was when in fiction as well as in conversation it was not considered polite—or too safe—to discuss politics or religion. But, as fiction went deeper into reality, writers discovered that it was necessary to involve both politics and religion if the surface of truth was to be pierced, and the nature of man and his struggles fully to be revealed.

Also, the novel can no longer rely on sex interest alone. There is very little—probably nothing—left unwritten in fiction about the sexual act and reactions to it. These descriptions have become so repetitive that they are unstimulating. Both writer and reader want deeper satisfactions. So they constantly search for the most exalting and devastating emotions, for the deepest mystery, the ultimate struggle, and these are found very often only in novels which tie into their narrative of human developments the great impulses of religion.

These are a few of the obvious reasons why religious fiction has become popular. No doubt there are many others. But that it is popular there can be no dispute. I recently asked a bookseller in one of our larger cities what type of book was easiest to sell and he replied, "Those with a spiritual or religious slant. It is as true of fiction as non-fiction." And it is evident that this interest pervades the entire literary hierarchy. While William Faulkner is getting the most erudite attention and the Nobel prize for *A Fable*, thousands of readers who could not understand a page of that novel are building up an enormous public for *The Robe*. Both are novels telling of what happened to various people in the days before the Crucifixion.

The novelist today who deals with some story of God and man does not have to weigh down his novel with conventional pieties. He can use any style of writing. He can be truthful about the bigot and the pretender as well as the truly spiritual character. He can analyze the religious aspirations of some apparently worldly character. *The Razor's Edge* by Somerset Maugham is that kind of story. Alec Waugh in *Brideshead Revisited* spares no detail that will reveal the decadent charm of Sebastian Flyte or the passions of his sister Julia. He shows the variety of the family's religious struggles tenderly and mercilessly, and his conclusion that in the end they are obedient and dependent on religion is all the better proved.

But because the field for the novel involving religious forces is plowed and not yet overcrowded, because the novelist is given the right to sow what he chooses, does not mean that the task is easy. Anyone who sets himself to it must be sure that he is fit to approach religious themes in fiction, adequate to treat them with dignity, and thereafter be continually on guard lest he forget that he is a novelist and not a propagandist.

The Writer's Fitness

In considering his own fitness a writer must be sure that he is unbigoted, tender, and sympathetic. He cannot allow himself the ardor of a missionary or the dogmatism of the preacher. He must have no axe to grind. He must set out only to tell a story. If the story saves souls, that is incidental to his purposes. His novel may inform millions of readers about the hierarchy of the Roman Catholic clergy, as did *The Cardinal*, by Henry Morton Robinson, but the aim was to tell the story of one man. For this reason a good novelist should neither be, nor want to be, labeled as a Catholic novelist or a Jewish novelist or a Methodist novelist. He is a novelist, who is a Catholic, a Jew, or a Methodist. The differentiation may seem slight, but it is extremely important, both to mood and performance.

Nor is a writer fit to attempt a novel with religious content because he can describe brilliantly some religious background or setting, or is familiar with the daily routine of minister or monk. The convent, the synagogue, or the Negro revival meeting can never make a novel. The novel must concern itself with human character, with its struggles, desires, development or degradation. To try to write a novel because one has a picturesque setting or a spiritual humming in one's ears is as useless as ringing up the curtain on a stage setting without actors. As with every other novel, a story involving religion begins and ends with what happens to the people about whom it is told.

However, there is that matter of adequacy. No one can write any novel which uses a faith as force or motive without fully understanding the religion with which his character is struggling, or which he may be defending. It is probably very doubtful whether a novel dealing with Catholics would ring true unless the writer had experienced faith in the Catholic religion. Unless he had accepted certain mysteries for himself, he could not write with full sympathy and understanding of those who had accepted them. The same would probably be true of a Quaker or a Baptist. I would be utterly incompetent to write a novel which had for a hero one of Jehovah's Witnesses, because I do not understand the motivations or persuasions of that sect. I can describe them as they look from the outside, but I do not understand them spiritually.

One of the most remarkable examples of an exception to this rule, which is not quite a rule, is shown in a novel written recently by Sheila Kaye-Smith, called *A View from the Parsonage*. Told in the first person, the narrator is a Protestant clergyman in rural England. The story involves the passions, the apostacies, and the marital confusions of some of his closest friends, who are Catholics, a faith which he understands as well as a Protestant minister possibly could. The author, a convert to Roman Catholicism, understands the Catholic faith, how it looks to the Protestant minister, and the limitations of understanding between her characters. Not so important or tender a book as *Brideshead Revisited*, it illustrates the possibility of an almost perfect vision.

Much Research Is Necessary

In preparation for the writing of novels like these, a great deal of research is usually necessary. If a novel incorporates religious customs or if the characters practice religion, the writer must make no slightest blunder in accuracy. He must write from a full and well-informed mind, steep himself in material which surrounds his subject even if he never uses any of it, and be the careful student who is always the servant of the good novelist. During all of my life I had been instructed about the Catholic religion. But when it came to the time that I presumed to write a novel which involved certain phases of its doctrine, it was essential to keep within reach a considerable number of the most authoritative volumes available on the history and doctrines of the Catholic Church.

There is nothing so intellectual as religion. There is nothing that can be more emotional than the struggles of human beings who seek religion, are pursued by a need for it, or deprived by its tenets of human satisfaction. Devotion and love of God often demand the greatest sacrifices, not only of self but of others. In these problems lie the novelist's material. He will find himself dealing with deep and cruel rivalries. And always with love. Love has always been the primary subject of the novel, and when the love of God conflicts with love of man or woman and this story is truly told, there can be no more profound one. There is no more realistic story, for up and down every street, in every income bracket, and at all levels past childhood, these conflicts occur every day. Few of them have been adequately treated by American novelists. English novelists on the whole have so far done better.

A young Protestant in an American college wrote to his astounded parents, "I am going to become a monk." His family urged delay and finally persuaded him to go to Europe for a year. What forces had been at work? What sexual disappointment? What happened next? There is material for a novel there.

There is material for a novel in the story of a young and successful businessman who had a frivolous wife and several children and decided in his early thirties that he must give up business and study for the Protestant ministry. What happens to his wife? What is the true story back of the fact that a beautiful young girl whose family have avoided formal religion for two generations, and rather laughed at those who practiced it, suddenly becomes a practicing Lutheran?

Novelists Must Not Proselytize

Now the novelist may not argue about the right or wrong of such decisions. He may not proselytize. He can only expose human situations with the most delicate skill, and if he shows the healing of a torn situation he must not overlook the scar. Normally he must deal with religion only in the lay world, for unless he has experienced Holy Orders he cannot understand such dedication, and his treatment of it would be ignorant. But religion in the lay world has never had more impact than today. There is plenty to write about.

Each novelist must stick to his last. He must choose the sector of the world which he thoroughly understands, and know the ways religion affects people in that environment, whether it be middle-class, aristocratic, poverty-ridden, ignorant, academic. It makes no difference what the milieu is if it is familiar to the writer and he can make it actual to the reader. This often necessitates a certain identification of writer and character, which can be painful.

Recently a period of confused unhappiness in my own mind was analyzed for me by a wise person in the literary world who wrote to me, "You are building up the mood for the new book and I am afraid you will feel very much worse before you have finished, because you will have to establish a very deep longing and a very real dissatisfaction with all life has been for you (and it can look very good on the surface) before you can even start leading the lost soul on his lonely search."

There is no more difficult task for any novelist to attempt than to go along with his characters as they face struggles of faith and conscience. His reward will come not from the interested public but from his sense that he is getting to the roots of life, of human conduct and emotions.

The Business of Writing

There remains the business of writing. To do justice to such subjects and characters one can use no trickery and no contrivances. But a story with religion in it has the right to use beautiful scenes and magnificent settings. If one were competent to write the story of one of the black-shawled Indian women in the gold church (and it is gold!) in Quito, the story would be dramatic from the start. Once I saw a woman in Seville standing by a column in a church, weeping without hiding her face, which was almost miraculously like one carved in stone above her head. A novel began or ended there, but it was beyond my knowledge.

A story that tells of the reach of any human being or beings toward God also needs great care in the telling because it can easily become long and monotonous. As any parson or priest knows, effort and failure closely follow each other. So the novelist, working with this material as with any other, must select the most significant beginning, and end his story before it repeats itself. There is no rule. In one of my own novels which dealt with a religious struggle, I found it necessary to explain at the very beginning something of the history of the family of my heroine. Otherwise the reader could not have understood her docility or firmness. In a second novel, which also confronted problems of faith and morals, I began with a revolt against church discipline because that was what the story was about.

In now contemplating a third, I find that the beginning still eludes me, but the character who will be this novel's strength must at the start somehow resist and condemn what eventually may conquer him.

I have said that there is a large and interested public ready for the novel that deals with religious forces. But it must not be forgotten that it is a public which includes the intolerant, the bigoted, and the prejudiced. The novelist who attempts to enter this sensitive field must be willing to face a cruel reaction to his book and he must not allow it to surprise or defeat him. He will be attacked, misunderstood, and maligned. But none of that matters very much to a novelist who can tell truly a story of men and women moved by deep and eternal spiritual needs.

Margaret Culkin Banning's ancestry on both sides is Irish and English, and most of her family were Roman Catholics. Educated at the Sacred Heart Convent, Vassar College, and the Chicago School of Civics and Philanthropy, her interest in human affairs, particularly in social problems, has been reflected in many of her articles and novels. Mrs. Banning has published twenty-eight books of fiction and non-fiction, among them two novels dealing with the problems of the Catholic layman. *Mixed Marriage* (1930) dealt with people who had to meet the problems of birth control in such a marriage, and was published in the United States, England, and France. *Fallen Away* (1952) was a novel portraying the struggle of a woman between human and divine love. It was published both in England and America and reprinted in the *Reader's Digest* Condensed Books. She has written hundreds of short stories and many essays, contributing to all leading magazines; some of the articles have been reprinted in textbooks. Mrs. Banning reads constantly. This prolific author says that she does not believe anyone who says he has no time for reading.

CHAPTER Four

Giving the Short Story Meaning

ROBERT ROOT

THE FIRST STEP in writing short stories for church magazines is easy: Read the fiction being published in those publications. Read a lot of it. If you study those stories—really become expert on them—you'll know more about what religious editors are buying than this or any other book can tell you.

Ask yourself the questions you would put to the editor. What are the typical plots? What subjects are treated? How long are the stories? Then write the kind of story being used. You may find that copying off some paragraphs will help. On your own paper, the published stories will show you the kinds of sentences, the type of dialogue, and so on, being used, and you'll see that this is English such as you can write. Then write your own story; rewrite; and write some more. No one plays the piano—or writes good stories—without a lot of practice.

At little cost you can get a stack of these magazines a foot high. Obtain addresses from Appendix I of this book or from the writers' magazines or yearbooks, which are at many newsstands and libraries, and send a few stamps with your request. Editors will gladly mail samples. The Presbyterian Publication Division in Philadelphia, for example, offers all four of its story papers for a three-cent stamp. Even if copies are not requested, the Methodists at Nashville send them free to writers showing promise. Church editors are glad to help because they complain that too many who submit stories to them don't find out what the publication wants. So one editor writes me succinctly, "My main advice: Study the market you want to make. See what they buy; go thou and do likewise."

Defining the Story

What is a short story? We all know; but the countless definitions cannot agree. So we are not going to give another academic definition, but a working one—a practical description. *In a short story, a character is put into a situation where he has to solve a problem or make a choice, and he does.* It's as simple as that.

This "formula" doesn't cover all stories, but I submit that it covers most of the good ones being printed in church publications. If you have a "literary" background, you may have to prove that statement to yourself by reading them, since certain classics and many contemporary "quality stories"—in *The New Yorker* or the "little magazines," for example—are more anecdotes than they are stories of struggle or decision. Some of the most promising students in my university short story classes also, I find, are in the habit of writing mood sketches or "slices of life" or bits of sheer self-expression, and calling them stories. All right—but few editors pay money for these. They want stories in which something significant happens to a human being.

Recognizing this truth, other neophyte writers go from formlessness to the other extreme and search for a recipe, the perfect formula. They figure that all they have to do is dress up a master plot dug out of some book. But writing religious stories is not merely that, either.

We do not, therefore, offer our practical definition as a sure-fire formula. Rather, this chapter will suggest guides which offer the beginner more promise of being published than would the advice to soar unguided into the stratosphere of undisciplined "self-expression."

So, to repeat: you create a good character and you give him a problem; then you make him struggle to solve it or to choose correctly.

If he doesn't struggle, we lose interest in him. This is the essence of "conflict" in a story. Even in religious stories there has to be this conflict if the reader is to be gripped—*especially* in religious stories, we might say; for it has been pointed out that usually the conflict of a short story is between good forces and evil forces, and religion has a great deal to say about the conflict of good and evil. The hero represents the good force with which we sympathize, and he is pitted against the evil force, which may be a villain (the "bad guys" of the Western), or evil in society or nature, or weakness in himself.

We know that in most stories right will win. The trick is to make it look as if the evil is going to win. So the evil force must be great and real. If it almost overcomes the good, suspense is high. Perhaps that is so because that is the way life is. With namby-pamby heroes and insignificant "sins" for them to battle, we cannot develop much interest or excitement. We have to have real-life characters who face and conquer some real-life problems if a story is to hold interest or be genuinely "religious."

Short stories of course have minor characters, and sometimes several major characters too; but our greatest problem is with our main character, the protagonist. He must be real, and we must select and create him with care. Memorable stories, I have observed, generally center around a distinctive, memorable character.

Sometimes I ask my students to analyze and write up "the most interesting character" they ever knew, and from these essays some have created fictional characters of considerable power. Probably this was because the writers' minds centered on unique, individualizing characteristics. But I am not suggesting that characters be lifted right out of life; student stories which claim to be factual reports generally do not come off as fiction. We should draw from life, however, combining two or three real individuals in one make-believe, or perhaps taking a gesture here and an attitude there.

Building Character

Striking speech, individualizing mannerisms, type of dress, and physical traits help build the character, as does the very name we give him. But as we might guess, it is *character-istics* which are most important. When we try to describe an acquaintance, we are likely to say that he is "a hard worker who gets up to study at 4:00 A.M. and earns A's" or is "an easy-going guy with a good personality, likes people, and is well liked." We can picture persons described in that way better than by reading about "horn-rimmed glasses" or a "tic in the left eye," and certainly better than by hearing of the perennial "blue eyes and blonde hair."

Each character should have a major characteristic or dominant trait. In the chief character, of course, the trait should ideally be related to his problem: Can he overcome his laziness well enough to reach his goal? Can he use his courage effectively enough to beat the villain? And so on. We may even find it useful to think of our characters as Mr. Honesty, or Joe Coward, or Priscilla Vanity. Certainly this is true of minor figures, who have to be characterized swiftly as personified traits.

But critics usually want main characters to be "well rounded." In the length of a short story, it is hard to portray several characteristics realistically, though, and attempting to make a character complex may only make him confusing. William Byron Mowery, in *Professional Short-Story Writing*, summarizes a study of classic fictional figures by saying that "the creators of memorable characters used the principle of one dominant trait; . . . that they dwelt on this dominant trait and it alone throughout their novel or story; that they achieved the *illusion* of completeness and this was all that counted." Published religious stories which I have read lately appear to follow this rule, whether they are about a dictatorial teen-age girl, an insecure, uncertain bride, or an enthusiastic cheerleader. So if your main character has several traits, be sure that one stands out clearly in your mind and in your story.

The ways of portraying character are readily mastered. One of the most obvious, which has been much used in the past, is simply to devote a few paragraphs to telling all about him. But this is considered rather old-fashioned now, and the more acceptable method today is to characterize subtly, by indirection. Bring out the traits through the action of the story.

There are only three things a character can do, and he reveals himself in each: (1) think, (2) speak, and (3) act. Similarly, other characters can think about him, speak about him, or act in relation to him; as they do, they help characterize him, and incidentally characterize themselves. Are the thoughts of your character kind or mean? Does he say "you ain't gonna" or "it seems hardly thinkable that this could transpire"? Does he shake hands weakly, drive a car carelessly, or amble along aimlessly? As you answer such questions in the action of the story, the character miraculously comes alive.

The character should be stable through the story—in a novel he may change, but not in the few thousand words of a short story. We feel cheated if the hero "changes on us." How would you feel, for example, if an author roused suspense by giving the care of a temptingly large sum of money to the hero, a weak, unreliable, and probably dishonest fellow, and then in the "twist," at the end, you read that the hero is brave and strong and honest enough, after all, to turn it over to the orphans' home? You would say that people didn't change that way—and you'd be right.

But don't characters sometimes change in published stories? In some weak ones, yes. But the stories are better where the character does not so much change as he does *come to the realization* that there is a better way. We have to have the feeling that there has been this right, good element in him all along. To be sure that we will feel that, the author should take care to drop hints at the start, to foreshadow subtly. In several current stories in church papers, the hero appears to be characterized primarily by an undesirable trait. He is not very sympathetic at the start, and his "conversion" at the end is unconvincing. Would it not be better to have him do some little decent thing at the start to make us friendly and ready to accept the "change"?

One of the major complaints of church editors answering questions put by me is that characters in submitted stories are often poor—"unrealistic," "not sharp enough," "just stock figures moving through the plot." They want characters with real-life characteristics. They want good but not goody-good people.

"I look for characters who are real, live young people acting normally in the situation the story provides for them," writes Bruce Hilton, editor of the Evangelical United Brethren *Friends*. "Though the purpose of our fiction is to create a desire for higher actions and ideals in the mind of the reader, we don't want hanky-panky heroes, spouting noble thoughts all the time without ever making a mistake."

Telling the Story

When the character we have created is plunged into the situation of our story, we begin to have plot. This is made up of the steps he takes as he tries to solve his problem or wrestle with his decision. For a fast beginning, we should get him into his "fix" at once. Interest lags until we see the character in meaningful action about his situation.

After a fast start, we should tell the story so that the reader can see it. It is tempting to summarize action, like those "story-thus-far" blurbs at the beginning of serials; more than one of my students has summarized action enough for a heavy novel in the space of five thousand words. But nothing will bore us more quickly than that. Instead of summarizing, *dramatize!* Put the characters on stage, and let them speak and act. Let us see them as they struggle, let us hear them as the problem is solved, the decision reached.

We should also be sure that the hero solves the problem himself. We must see him actually overcoming each obstacle, meeting greater obstacles, but finally overcoming the greatest and reaching his goal. We will feel cheated if some good fairy lifts him over the last hurdle, or if "Fate" intervenes. Some neophytes feel that they can create "a good trick ending" by having another character solve everything for the hero in a "surprise." Others give a "twist" by sneering at the end: "See, it wasn't really a problem after all—we were just kidding!" The one who feels tricked by such trick endings is the unhappy reader. So have the main character do his own work; and if there must be a trick, let it be in the ingenuity or cleverness of his solution.

Especially in religious stories, theme is important. This

term refers to the meaning or significance of a story. Theme is the basic idea you put across. It is the moral or message, if those words are not understood as implying that the point of the story is underlined.

In mass magazines, story theme is typically a popular stereotype, such as "true love always wins," and the religious writer who would publish in them must find such widely accepted ideas. In quality magazines, perversely, theme is apt to negate such a mass moral; it becomes, perhaps, "true love is hokum," though here the idealistic writer may find a way to explore religious complexities. The challenge of the writer for the church-related publication is to discover and write about themes which are neither the clichés of the slicks nor the too-often jaundiced and cynical negations of the literary periodicals.

In the introduction to *Stories to Grow By*, J. Edward Lantz, the editor, gives a hint of how this can be done by pointing out that in the stories chosen, the heroes live with the temptations and struggles of everyday life. "They discover the best course to follow, make decisions nearest right under the circumstances, lose their bitterness and hatred, finally get straightened out, and learn that they have grown through the experience. These stories . . . can help us to mature." [1] That is successful treatment of theme.

Such treatment need not, of course, be confined to church-related publications. Especially now that interest in religion is high, big commercial magazines publish some "religious" fiction; *Stories to Grow By*, for example, includes seven stories from four "slicks"—*American Magazine*, *Family Circle*, *The Saturday Evening Post*, and *Woman's Home Companion*. Such magazines will publish idealistic stories if the theme is not sectarian or too controversial. Because he can pay enough to get what he wants, the secular editor has

[1] J. Edward Lantz, Editor, *Stories to Grow By* (New York: Association Press, 1953), p. viii.

an even finer net than the church paper editor to strain out
the pious or preachy or namby-pamby story, however.

Herman C. Ahrens, Jr., editor of *Youth*, draws a useful
distinction between the "slick" and the religious paper
story: "I feel the difference in the two types of stories
comes in the basic attitudes developed in the characters and
the way in which the characters face life and solve their
problems. In romance, for example, a religious short story
should have real people, real-life problems, and genuine
settings similar to the secular stories; but in the religious
story there should develop a wholesome attitude and atmosphere toward love itself, so that even a secular reader is held
by the real-life problem, but more than this, he is caught
in the beauty of the environment of and reflection of Christ-
like love illustrated by the story. And this can be done without a sermon in every line."

Ahrens reminds us that Jesus' parables did not use religious terms, yet told religious truths. He believes editors
might use stories on such subjects as "narcotics, drink, excessive petting, cheating on exams, reckless driving, gang
warfare, little lies in gossip, dancing, temptations to armed
forces personnel, etc." He says, "Doesn't Christianity have
anything to say to teens in these situations?"

The Question of Theme

This question of theme stirs some of the sharpest comment from church editors. They want their stories to hold
up high ideals and build character, but by and large they
do not want them to moralize or sermonize. "We like fiction that says something, but want no fictionalized sermons,"
said Robert Elfers, while editor of *Young People*. "My
concept of a good short story is built around the idea that a
story should say something important."

"I feel stories for us should differ from those in secular
magazines only in having a plus value for character building

—an inspirational message so woven in that it is not obvious," says Aurelia Reigner, editor of the Presbyterians' *Venture*.

Similarly, Bruce Hilton of *Friends*, who considers "preachiness" one of the major shortcomings of manuscripts he receives, writes, "Our stories should differ from standard magazine stories in the type of motivation they produce in the reader. We can use stories producing sympathy, inspiration, devotion, admiration. . . . This does *not* mean, of course, that we want preachy stories with an obvious moral tacked on the end.

The position of the Light and Life Press was effectively put this way:

A story, message-wise, is—

NOT a flimsy attempt to simulate a religious position you neither hold for yourself nor can boast exposure to—

NOT a sermon thinly disguised as pious mouthings of characters as lifeless as sagging fenceposts—

BUT an assumption of our stated religious position inherent in the story structure. A message is not to be wriggled in or superimposed, but is to be an inextricable part of the story, worked out in the characterization of at least one strong Christian, who is not necessarily the main character, however. Then no matter what struggle or rebellion is otherwise present, our religious position is never out of focus.

Rowena Ferguson, associate editor of Methodist youth publications, also points out that stories "must not be moralistic." But, she writes, there are subtler problems in relation to theme. Stories must not lie. "One of the main ways stories lie about life is to imply that virtue is rewarded materially, quickly, and in line with your heart's desire," she says. "Another way in which they lack integrity is the support of dubious motivation on the part of the characters."

Miss Ferguson also points out that sometimes stories which seem Christian really are not. Recently, for example, a distinguished writer submitted a story about Midwestern farmers who faced death and drouth and other afflictions, and triumphed. "But how? By simply setting their teeth in dour and somber fashion and toughing it out. Nowhere was there any indication that . . . that is not all there is in life." She concludes with this pointed advice to writers: "Be sure you have something to say (it does not have to be world shaking). Say it the best way *you* know how. Say it honestly. That usually adds up to a good story."

Making the Religious Point

The religious free lancer, in brief, must see that his whole story is built so as to say the religious thing he wants to say. Perhaps this is where he should start his planning. We can start to create with a character, or a clever twist, or an incident, or a setting. But Professor Kempton is right, I believe, when he says in his excellent little book, *The Short Story*, "The area to brood in is not plot, the events, but idea or theme, the meaning."

Let me illustrate with a story of my own which was anthologized in *Stories to Grow By*. Without implying that this is a good plot, I cite it to show how I developed a story-line by thinking about what I wanted to say. I had noticed how many teen-agers are putting a lot of their enthusiasm into trivialities, and had been struck in Asia by the shocking contrast between that frivolity and the need for help which I saw. I got the idea for a suitable character—a missionary daughter in India who yearned for all the comfort of America. But how to show her that there is more to life than that? I tried to do it by involving her in the severe sickness of an Indian friend's baby, having her help save him from death, and making her decide that she should study medicine and help other Indians. Adding a moral was unnecessary. For understatement, I think, is the key to successful presentation of theme. If emotions are lengthily described, as in the old days of fiction, they seem corny or funny; emotional impact is best conveyed if carefully understated. Similarly, preachiness can be avoided by soft-pedaling the moral, by letting the reader figure out the meaning himself.

There are many important aspects of story writing beside character and theme, but I have emphasized these two because they seem the most important in religious stories. If you can make a meaningful point through the action of an interesting character, you will have gone a long way toward writing a good story for any age group. We have referred especially to stories for young adults and teenagers. As you write for younger groups, plots and themes may of course be lighter, but real characters are still wanted. The more mature the reader, on the other hand, the more important it is that your treatment of character and theme be professional and your action convincing.

Reading books on story writing and studying stories will help a lot in learning the ways to portray that action which makes the story live. One of the suggestions that has been most useful to me is the idea of planning by scenes. Beginners' stories tend to ramble. By thinking of the story as a play and working out the scenes with which you are going to show it to the reader, you can give tight unity, and you can also force yourself to dramatize the happenings.

Ask yourself, for example: What should be the setting for the start of the story? Who should be in the first scene? What should they do? What can they say? What logically should be the next scene? What do I want to accomplish with this scene—with every other scene? Such questions will help you outline your story in a dramatic way, give it movement, and keep your writing in the category of story rather than sermon.

In brief, study the magazines to see what they are using. Then create characters with clear, individual traits, and let them illustrate a meaningful truth about life as they struggle with their problems. Don't *tell* the reader how they solved the problems, or how he should solve his; but *show* your characters solving them, in their actions and talk and thoughts. If you can do that, and practice and practice, and write and write, editors will be interested in the stories you send them.

Robert Root is an associate professor and head of the religious journalism program at the School of Journalism, Syracuse University, where he teaches commercial short story writing. He became interested in short story writing as a boy, won an honorable mention during high school in the *Scholastic* short story competition, at about the same time he sold his first one to a Sunday school paper. At Iowa State College he became first editor of a literary magazine, *Sketch;* went on to get his master's degree at the Columbia School of Journalism, and traveled a year in Europe on a Pulitzer scholarship. Back in his native Iowa, he worked seven-plus years on the Des Moines *Register* and *Tribune*. From 1945 to 1947 he was correspondent in the relief program of the World Council of Churches at Geneva, and then free lanced for a year in Asia. Later, while executive editor of Worldover Press, he also studied short story writing under Herschel Brickell, long-time editor of the O. Henry Memorial Award anthologies. His story, "Decision Under the Stars," published in *Young People*, was included in the anthology, *Stories to Grow By*. He is author of *How to Make Friends Abroad*. As this chapter was being written, he had begun a new book on Christ, the church, and race.

CHAPTER Five

The Religious Drama

HAROLD A. EHRENSPERGER

"WHEN THE WORLD was so new and all," to use Kipling's delightfully descriptive phrase, primitive man apparently tried to act out his awe and wonder at the mysterious powers that controlled his universe. When these were kind to him, he attempted to act his thanks. When they suddenly struck him down, caused his enemies to triumph, or brought him hunger and want, he sought ways to appease them and to placate what he supposed was their anger toward him. His action always came at a moment of crisis or climax, and he brought into it, we conjecture, the other persons who might be involved, either as friends or as enemies. This was man's first drama, spontaneous and natural. It was, interestingly enough, religious drama, because it dealt with man's relation to ultimates, to the creative force of the universe, and to the crisis moments in struggle when man achieved his noblest stature.

From that prehistoric time to the present, man has attempted to act out his intensest and deepest feeling. While this action has often been related to ultimate causes, it has also been concerned with man's struggle with himself, with his fellow human beings, and with the earthly forces that he thought controlled his destiny. It has given rise to some of the greatest drama in the world, to the tragic drama of Greece, to some of the most delightful plays of the medieval period, to many of the classics of the Renaissance, to some of the best of Shakespeare and Goethe, and to several of the plays that seem destined to be remembered in the contemporary theater. It has also been the expression of some of the most pathetic, puerile, and stupid things that have ever been done in the name of drama and religion. It is what has been popularly called "religious drama."

Writing down this action into dialogue through characters at a crucial moment in their experience is actually the art of playwriting. As a transcribed, salable form of writing its popularity is fairly recent. In the past fifty years the printing of plays and their wide use for amateur performance has made a market for manuscripts. The use of plays in churches for other than Christmas or Easter celebration is also a phenomenon of the twentieth century, and has given rise to the contemporary name applied to this type of play: religious drama.

The Changing Attitude

When religious drama is remembered as the nightgown nightmare that characterizes some church plays, it is rightly shunned and scorned by the writer who has integrity. When, however, religious drama is used to designate plays that bring to an audience a depth experience of legitimate conflict, not artificial, not fantastic, not burlesque, but rather a story that is accepted because its characters and plot come out of genuine life situations and call forth emotional responses that are constructive and elevating, then the form has the characteristics that win it the respect of the best writers.

This change is precisely what has happened in the past twenty-five years. Many of the plays of Ibsen, Shaw, and other Continental dramatists are religious dramas. The beautifully written plays of T. S. Eliot and some of those of Christopher Fry have given new dimensions to the name of religious drama and have redeemed this form of play in the eyes of the contemporary world. The fact, too, that from the time of the Drama League of America (founded in 1911) to the present time, amateur drama has improved in standards through trained leadership has also helped to make church productions more respectable. The quality of plays as well as productions has been gradually improving. There are still too few good plays available for church production, even though there are some excellently trained persons willing to help in producing them.

All good plays, that is, all plays that have serious importance, have religious values. There is no essential difference, then, in the technique of writing the religious play and in writing any other type. A difference does come in the intended use of the play and the place where it is to be performed. A play designed for the chancel of the church will naturally have a different set of technical requirements from the play designed to be performed in a large theater or before television cameras. The need now is for plays that can be performed in the chancel of the church. Such plays can be performed anywhere, to be sure, and with the proper setting in the television studio, can be used to excellent advantage in this medium to help lift the so-called religious broadcast to a level of greater interest and significance.

Characteristics of the Play

To be worthy of performance in the chancel of a church means that a play must have serious intentions, that it must actually be worship in the broader sense of the term—the experience of being lifted out of oneself to be related to something higher than oneself. Its other primary characteristic is that its subject matter must always be elevating rather than degrading. Its uniqueness is that it attempts to establish the climate of great living, living toward ultimates, the experience of which is inspiring and elevating. Religious drama depends on conviction achieved through attraction toward the highest reaches of man's experience.

Religious drama, like any other art form, is first of all a form, which means that it has the structure of a play, a beginning which must be understood so that the participating audience accepts it, a consistent movement toward a climax which resolves the struggle, and an end which gives the whole thing a unity. Lewis Carroll's famous advice is delightfully pertinent: "Begin at the beginning and go on till you come to the end. Then stop!" Another writer has suggested an opposite procedure: "Begin at the end and go back till you come to the beginning. Then start!" [1]

Religious plays cannot be created merely because a writer has a desire to convert the world to his ideas, nor merely because he has a worthy desire to write worthwhile plays. To write good plays, plays that are likely to have religious values, the sincere craftsman must learn first of all to write, and, in this instance, to write in the technique of the dramatic form. There is no short cut to this accomplishment. It is a matter of thorough knowledge of the techniques of the drama, even the techniques of the theater which can be gained through the reading and seeing

[1] See Percival Wilde, *The Craftsmanship of the One-act Play*, p. 103.

of plays. *To write religious plays one must know how to write plays.*

To write plays for the chancel of the church requires something more than this. Plays written for the parish house, for the enjoyment of an audience in a community theater, may have definite religious values. But plays written to be brought to life in the chancel require a technique as old as the *Quem Quaretus,* which has often been described as the first play of modern drama. It was a medieval attempt to give dramatic interest to the Easter story and it was performed before the altar of a church.

To write any play one must have a feeling for the place where it is to be given. That is, to write for the theater one must have a sense of the theater. To get this, the writer lives in the theater. He is sure that the method of communication by which a character speaks in action before an audience is more compelling, more nearly right for him than any other means. The dramatic structure is a constantly intriguing one for him. He reads plays, not merely plays that he has seen, but any plays. He cannot keep away from them. He visualizes as he reads, so that he sees the characters creating the action in which they move. He lives with the characters of a play, imagining what they do when they are not in the scenes of a play.

He reads dramatic criticism, evaluating the critic's analysis, comparing it with his own conclusions. He goes to see a play when he knows it is a failure because he wants to understand why the play has failed. He is interested first, last, and all the time in people, how and why they do the things they do, their motives and their interactions. All life is raw material for his imagination as he takes what he sees and thinks about it and finally transforms it into the action and dialogue of a play. He observes, he thinks, and *then* he writes.

He must discipline himself to write, and specifically, to

write in the form of a play. He must work to make himself
feel completely at home in dramatic technique. He must
know the leading books on the technique of the drama, to
get the perspective of famous teachers and practitioners and
to weigh these against his own experience and observation.
Most of all, he recognizes that a play is written to be performed, and that it will not be born until it comes alive before an audience. A play exists, says Professor George P.
Baker, "to create emotional response in an audience." [2] In
this way it is different from any other form of writing.

A play designed to be used in the chancel of a church
does not mean that it is *ipso facto* a religious play. But it
does mean that it is conditioned in its theme, in its manner
of presentation, in its purpose, and in its anticipated response. To write plays for the chancel, the dramatist must
have a sense of the chancel and its significance in the
church. He must have a sense of worship. He must have a
sense of the church as a structure in the same way that a
dramatist writing for the theater must have a sense of the
theater as a structure. He must have a sense of religion,
which means that he sympathizes with man's yearnings to
understand the meaning and purpose of life, and that he is
alert to the most effective revelations of divine purpose as
he sees them in man's experience. He must have a sense of
worship so that he can be sensitive to the capacity and the
need for man to be lifted out of himself by relationship to
something higher than himself.

The theme of a play is central for its specific use in a
chancel. Too much of the time a so-called religious play has
been thought of in terms of the dramatization of the Bible.
This view has meant that some plays have had historical
values, but unfortunately these have often been unrelated
to present-day life. Or it has meant that pompous language
has been identified with religious dialogue, and audiences

[2] *Dramatic Technique*, p. 43.

have been unimpressed if not disgusted. The time of the action of a play, ancient or modern, is not of primary importance. The only necessary condition is that a play have a story, a situation, and characters that can be understood, that come within the experience of an average group of people today. The dramatist must be sure that the time of the play, the setting, and the circumstances of the action are capable of being understood with the minimum of explanation. A biblical story can be as relevant as a story that happens this week if the story is about a universal experience and is couched in language that is intelligible to the audience for whom the play is intended.

The Language of the Play

High-flown literary language is extremely difficult as dialogue. Biblical characters in their day did not speak in the artificial "thee" and "thou" language of the King James Version of the Bible. More likely, they spoke in language equivalent to that used in the Goodspeed translation. For this reason biblical plays in stilted language are often meaningless to a contemporary audience. Kings should speak like kings, and common men like common men. Because a play happens to be set in biblical times does not mean that it must be unintelligible.

Poetic dialogue is excellent when the subject matter calls for poetry.[3] The style of a play conditions the kind of writing that should be used. Several of the best contemporary religious plays use poetry because the subject matter and the dramatic heightening call for poetry. When emotions and feelings are too deep for prose, poetry fulfills its accustomed role in trying to express the inexpressible. When depth of feeling reaches religious proportions or when feeling reaches the point of inspiration, poetry may be the normal and the only method of communication.

[3] T. S. Eliot, *Poetry and Drama.*

The religious play has often been guilty of playing up a "moral" theme. A play does need a theme but the theme must be interpreted by a story. The story may be "stiffened into a plot." "Ought a theme, in its abstract form, be the first germ of a play?" William Archer asks. Ought the dramatist to say, "I will write a play on temperance, or on woman's suffrage, or on capital and labor," and then cast about for a story to illustrate his theme? This is possible, Archer proposes, but it is not a promising method of procedure. A story made to the order, he goes on to say, of a moral concept is always apt to be obvious as to its origin, to the detriment of its characteristic illusive quality. If a play is to be "a moral apologue" at all, it is well to say so frankly—probably in the title—and "aim not at versimilitude, but at neatness and appositiveness in the working out of the fable." [4]

The dramatist must always bury the theme in the play. The business of the dramatic writer is to bring the theme to life. Sometimes themes may have little or no dramatic value. And a dramatist must always remember that a theme which may interest him may not be good at all for drama.

Many religious dramas seem false because they suggest sudden changes in the character of a person—changes that are untrue and unreal. The play seems manipulated, the characters are strikingly opposite types, all good and all bad, and the playwright causes the all bad characters suddenly to become good. Characters in a well-constructed play must be differentiated so that they take on individuality and yet not seem to be contrived or to be mere puppets. They will act as if they are motivated by their character in the situations in which they find themselves.

A character acts in a play because that is the way he must act, being the person he is in the situation in which he finds himself or causes himself to be. Characters must have in-

[4] *Play-Making, A Manual of Craftsmanship,* p. 17.

tegrity, therefore, to act so that they will be true to their natures. This means that a bad man, a man who is weak and who causes evil, does not suddenly become good. He may be brought to see goodness, and he may suggest that he hopes to change. In this sense there is no actual character development. It is hinted at and may be hoped for. A character merely exposes his inherent characteristics, his goodness and his badness, but in the course of a short play he does not change. His action may indicate a moment of decision, and if the playwright were to raise his curtain a year or two hence in the life of his villain, he might show some development of character. Playwrights need to remind themselves that character changes slowly, that to root out negative tendencies in most men takes a good deal of probing and a long therapeutic process.

The Limits of the Chancel

The chancel does limit the kind of play that is to be produced there. Farce and burlesque, possibly, do not belong there, yet some excellent performances of *The Second Shepherd's Play* have been done in chancel settings. This merely means that the spirit of a play, its intentions and the attitude and purpose of the producers and actors, is all-important. The word *reverent* might be used to describe the attitude of the producing group if by *reverent* is meant something that is not stuffy and artificial. Under no circumstances should anything cheap, tawdry, trite, or banal be allowed in the chancel, or, for that matter, any place else. Too much religious drama has been guilty of being some or all of these.

"Truth of theme makes a play valid," suggests Percival Wilde, one of the most expert craftsmen of one-act plays and the author of the best book on how to write them.[5] He

[5] *The Craftsmanship of the One-act Play*, p. 78.

goes on to say that truth of character makes a play persuasive, truth of situation makes a play entertaining, and truth of atmosphere, mood, and point of view makes a play real. The important word here is *truth*. Truth of theme, character, situation, mood, atmosphere, and point of view is the common denominator of any play worthy of being called religious.

The play with religious values has often been thought of as lacking in interest. One of the primary rules of playwriting is to be interesting. A play is always a story that must be interesting to an audience. The adage of the playwright was "to make them laugh, make them cry, and make them wait." Suspense is a genuine means of interest. This does not mean the suspense of a mystery show. It means "a straining forward of interest, a compelling desire to know what will happen next," to quote George Pierce Baker. He insists that whether a hearer is totally at a loss to know what will happen, but at the same time eager to ascertain; or whether he partly guesses what will take place, but deeply desires to make sure; or almost holds back so greatly does he dread an anticipated situation, "he is in a state of suspense, for be it willingly or unwillingly on his part, on sweeps his interest." [6]

Someone has said that when a play is a success it produces the effect intended by the author. To write religious drama a playwright must be sensitive to religion. He must respect and, in a way, love the place where religious drama is to be produced. He must have a sense of the place and the need of the people who come to the place. He must be interested and absorbed not only in life but also in the meanings and purposes that men have found for life and for the motivations that have led them to do both the heroic and the tragically bad things they have done. He must be fascinated by the theories they have about their ultimate

[6] *Dramatic Technique*, p. 207.

destinies, particularly as these relate to their concepts of the meaning and relationship to the God they worship.

The writer of religious drama not only must have a concern for man's religious nature; he also must think of man in terms of drama—of action, character, and dialogue knit into a conflict situation at a critical moment. No play can rise above its level of characterization. Human character, Percival Wilde reminds us, is but the concretion of larger factors which become vocal as man searches for the underlying truth that is likely to determine the human combat.

When the scope of the canvas on which drama is written is too large for the average stage, when effects demand sufficient size to employ crowds, processions, and movements of masses, when the action is so expansive that large movement is alone satisfactory, then the writer employs the techniques of the pageant. There is less chance for minute character analysis or detailed action. The development of the outdoor pageant and its recent popularity offer incentives to the author who sees in this form an excellent medium for religious subject matter.

The work of Paul Green in *The Lost Colony* and *Wilderness Road* and of Kermit Hunter in *Unto These Hills* and *Horn in the West* points the way for the writer in the field of religious drama. The history of religion as well as the history of the church is full of exciting and meaningful episodes that are waiting for the writer to give them dramatic significance in the same way that Green and Hunter have made American history come alive so convincingly in their plays.

Religious drama deals with human characters, with situations, and with themes which are best understood by means of religion, by man's relationship with his God, and by his relationship to himself and his fellow men because of the nature and meaning of his relationship to God. A religious play should have high seriousness of purpose. It must have

meaning related to man's struggle to fulfill his destiny to
the best of his ability.

A religious play, finally, ought always to be a good play
technically to embody subject matter which concerns the
great affairs of man. It may touch the sublime so long as it
does not lose the common touch. It may touch eternity—
hell or heaven—so long as eternity is a locale that can be
understood in man's terms and be peopled by figures who
have the common characteristics of human beings.

George P. Baker's definition of a play comes back to us
again: "A play exists to create emotional response in an audience." If this is the legitimate purpose of drama, then a
play with genuine religious values produced in a chancel
of a church will, in turn, create an emotional response in a
congregation. This is the purpose of drama. To be responded
to, religious values have to do with man's attempt to live in
terms of his divine destiny and to fulfill his purpose in life
as a son of God. Response to this ideal is the purpose of
religious drama.

———————————

Harold A. Ehrensperger studied under Professor George
P. Baker in the famous school of playwrights, the "47 Workshop" of Harvard. He taught in the School of Speech at
Northwestern University and introduced the first courses
in drama at Garrett Biblical Institute. He organized the Department of Plays and Pageants of the Methodist Church
and wrote and produced several pageants having to do with
Methodist celebrations, including *The Spreading Flame*, for
the one hundred and fiftieth anniversary of the Methodist
Church in America. Professor Ehrensperger also has taught
at the Breadloaf School of English, was on the editorial staff
of *Drama*, editor of *Little Theatre Monthly*, and founder
as well as editor for ten years of *motive*. He has studied the

theater in Austria, England, and Russia. His book, *Conscience on Stage*, is the authoritative text on church drama. From 1950 to 1953 he was in India, where he experimented with drama at Leonard Theological College and taught at Nagpur University. He now is associate professor of religion and the creative arts, Boston University School of Theology.

CHAPTER Six

Religious Poetry

GEORGIA HARKNESS

THERE ARE three main types of religious poetry, with subtypes and graduations within which the types merge: first, the long dramatic or epic or narrative poem; second, the short lyric or bit of meditative verse; and third, the hymn. In this chapter we shall deal with the second and third types, with only passing mention of the first.

The Long Dramatic Poem

The first type is illustrated in classical literature by such poems as Dante's *Divine Comedy*, Milton's *Paradise Lost* and *Samson Agonistes*, Browning's *Saul*. In contemporary writing, W. H. Auden, T. S. Eliot, and Christopher Fry are among its most successful exponents. Such poems are, for the most part, full-length books written in rhythmic but unrhymed verse, often in dramatic form. Some deal directly with religious themes, as Auden's *A Christmas Oratorio*, Eliot's *Murder in the Cathedral*, or Fry's *A Sleep of Prisoners*; in others, as in Eliot's *Four Quartets*, the total meaning of existence is under consideration but with religious overtones subtly implied. In such modern writings the understanding of the reader—or of the spectator in dramatic presentation—is often heavily taxed by the obscurity of the symbolism in which the meaning is clothed.

We shall pass by this type of poetry writing, first because the present writer has had no experience in writing it and could give no helpful suggestions. For further interpretation of its religious significance the reader is referred to Amos N. Wilder's *Spiritual Aspects of the New Poetry*. There is, however, a further reason for not including it here; namely, that its writing is not for the novice. Great literature though such poetry may be, it takes a great poet to write it! A poet of insight and tested accomplishment who chooses to write in this manner needs no instruction; one who is learning to write had better choose a simpler medium. Fortunately this is available in both the second and third types we have mentioned.

Religious Lyrics

Webster's dictionary defines lyric poetry as "songs and short poems having reference to the poet's own thoughts and feelings." Though a lyric poem was originally intended to be sung to the accompaniment of the lyre, a religious lyric is not usually a hymn. Some such poems, notably those of Whittier, have become hymns, but the purpose and some of the techniques are different. Religious lyrics—which we had perhaps better call simply "religious verse"—are brief expressions in poetic form of something that the author feels he wants to say about his faith and experience.

There is a popular notion that only a few highly gifted people can write religious poetry. Of *great* poetry this is true, for as there are relatively few great musicians or great artists, poetic genius is a rare gift of God. But anybody who makes the effort can be a careful craftsman! The chief requirement for writing good religious verse is not some unique genius, but a mood or thought one desires to express, a sense of fitness in the choice of words, and disciplined care in their selection. These requirements are quite within the capacity of many more people than are now writing religious poetry. This chapter is not addressed to one who either is or aspires to be a great poet, but to the person who wants to write authentic and fitting religious verse in order to communicate what is in his mind and heart.

Poetry, like any other style of writing, must have both form and content. Said the philosopher Immanuel Kant, "Form without content is empty; content without form is blind." Verses may be correct enough in rhyme and meter and still be doggerel. Who has not written such "poems," facetious or sentimental, to accompany a gift, or as whimsey for entertainment at a party? Or verses may express sentiment that is deep and true, and turn out to be only prose arranged in separate lines. Both doggerel and lined prose have their place, if they are kept in their place and recognized for what they are. Most of the published sermons of Peter Marshall are written in the latter form, and with great effectiveness. But they are not poetry, with all their vividness of language, and it is unlikely that he ever thought they were. There is clever doggerel, and there is striking lined prose, but without an appropriate union of form and content, we do not have religious poetry.

The greatest religious poetry ever written is in the Hebrew psalms. Here, too, there is both content and form, though not the forms currently used in the poetry of today.

In Hebrew poetry the various types of parallelism—synonymous, synthetic, antithetic, or stairlike—take the place of rhyme and meter as we have them and the rhythm is mainly a rhythm of thought, which fortunately can be preserved in the translation.[1] Yet the unknown authors of these psalms gave us great poetry, not alone because they had exalted thoughts to express but because they wrote within definite structures.

This point must be emphasized as a caution against any random fitting of words together. Yet it must also be said that of the two, the content is more essential than the form. There are poets like Walt Whitman and Carl Sandburg whose work appears to be nearly formless, yet their lines pulsate and stir deep feeling in us. They have something to communicate, and their mood bursts through the unconventional forms. Lesser poets, we must insist, had better not attempt such liberties! Yet whether one is a great poet or simply, like most of us, a humble aspirant caught with the fascination of writing verse, the first necessity is to have a feeling to express, a truth to state, an event to describe, a picture to portray—in short, to have something to say.

The Unlimited Resource for Themes

For the writer of religious verse, the result can be as varied as the total range of our faith. A mood of adoration and joyous thankfulness to God, a sense of sin, individual or corporate, sorrow before the mystery of pain, calm assurance as we trust the goodness of the Most High, petition for the things we seem most to need as we look within, commitment to God of all that we have for the doing of his will, confidence in God's gift of eternal life—these are

[1] See Elmer W. K. Mould, *Essentials of Bible History*, Revised Edition (New York: Ronald Press Co., 1951), pp. 75, 112 f., 169, or any other good treatment of Old Testament literature, for an explanation of these types of parallelism.

among the most prevalent notes of religious verse. Treated abstractly, they are likely to run into prose; made concrete with imagery and potent with feeling, they can yield authentic poetry. Such concreteness often becomes the easier to achieve as faith comes into focus about some arresting human incident, some magnificent or moving scene in nature, some stirring event, whether intimate and personal or of world-shaking significance.

For Christians there is an unlimited resource for themes in the birth, ministry, teachings, the person-to-person contacts, death, resurrection, and living presence of Jesus Christ. It is amazing that so many poems—all with a common center, yet all different—could be written about what is contained within the slender compass of the Four Gospels! Yet this, of course, is not surprising in view of the fact that the luminous personality of Jesus captures men in every generation and evokes wonder, devotion, and discipleship.

Opinions differ as to whether religious poetry ought ever to preach or to theologize. "You may walk to the edge of the pulpit," one is counseled, "but never mount it." In the present writer's judgment, whether one ought to mount it depends on what is done there. Poetry ought never to be dull, or plodding, or so abstract that it severely taxes the mind to get sense out of it. But neither ought preaching or theology to be! The difference lies not so much in the nature of the themes or even in the effects intended as in the fact that poetry uses fewer and more imaginative words, consciously aims to clothe thought in beauty, and paradoxically, by channeling words into explicit forms it emancipates meaning by constricting the compass of its expression.

What, then, of these structures to which poetry must conform? Their elements are simple, and assuming that the reader may wish to "start from scratch," we shall outline them.

All English poetry has meter—rhythmic beats in the accent of syllables; much of it has both rhyme and meter. Each metrical unit consisting of one accented and one or more unaccented syllables is called a "foot," and lines of poetry are designated by the number and type of feet they contain. The principal metrical feet are (1) iambic, consisting of one unaccented and one accented syllable (˘ ‒); (2) trochaic, with the accented syllable coming before the unaccented (‒ ˘); (3) anapestic, with two unaccented syllables followed by one accented (˘ ˘ ‒); and (4) dactylic, three such syllables with the accented one coming first (‒ ˘ ˘). A line of poetry may contain from one to seven or eight such feet. For example, the characteristic verse form of a sonnet is iambic pentameter, in which each of the fourteen lines of the sonnet has five feet and each foot consists of an unaccented followed by an accented syllable. In the hymnbooks where many tunes are designated as C.M. (Common Meter), the verse form consists of four lines in which the first and third are iambic tetrameter (four feet), the second and fourth lines iambic trimeter (three feet).

If one is not already familiar with such metrical arrangement, the simplest way to understand it is to take a book of poetry and "scan" the lines by marking the accents as indicated above and drawing vertical lines between the feet. An occasional interpolation of a different type of foot is permissible, and lends variety, but most poetry will be found to have a prevailing type and a uniform number of feet in each corresponding line. Accordingly, one who attempts to write poetry should school himself to stay within these limits.

There is more variation, but still a structure, as to rhyme. In a couplet two successive lines have their last syllables rhyming (or in a double rhyme the last two syllables); in a quatrain the alternate lines are usually rhymed. An Elizabethan sonnet consists of three quatrains of iambic pentameter with a concluding couplet. Designated by letters, the rhyme scheme is a b a b c d c d e f e f g g. With seven quickly changing rhymes, this permits considerable freedom to the author, and is much easier to write than the Petrarchan sonnet, which uses only two rhymes in the first eight lines (the octet) and three in the last six (the sestet). Here the rhyme scheme is a b b a a b b a c d e c d e. Though difficult, it gives excellent practice in writing within forms.

Mastering Verse Forms

Verse forms must be mastered, like scales on a piano, if the product is not to sprawl incongruously. For self-discipline in this area there is no better practice for the amateur than the writing of sonnets, first the simpler and then the more complicated form. It is a long step forward—and a great sense of achievement—when one is able to construct fourteen lines that say something and have the rhyme and meter right! There are simple couplets and quatrains in which practice may be gained; sonnets are at the same time the most exacting and the most rewarding. If one is unwilling to accept their rigid discipline, he is not likely to get far in writing poetry.

The chief requirement, then, for writing religious verse and occasional poems is, first, to feel moved to say something that is worth saying and then to be willing to try, experimentally, any number of ways of saying it, until one is found that will bring the rhyme and meter as it should be and express the thought in smooth, unforced, grammatical English. The constant temptation of immature poets is to try to write free verse, which usually ends up in being prose arranged in lines of uneven length. There is free verse that by its beauty and moving quality is really poetry, as there are improvisations at the piano, but such writing and playing can most safely be left to the artist of skilled experience.

A few further cautions may be in order, though I mention them reluctantly lest fear of error may stifle the attempt. Certainly, perfection is not to be expected, though if one is on guard, fewer flaws may appear. (1) One has to watch the grammatical structure of sentences. Nothing that would be incorrect English in prose is permissible in poetry. This is often inconvenient when one is wrestling with rhyme or meter, but a necessity! (2) Though an occasional inversion of word sequence is allowable (as in "a kingly crown to gain" instead of "to gain a crown"), such inversions should be kept to a minimum, and not used if the meaning is made unclear. (3) Archaic words, such as *fain, ken, wot*, had better not be used. We are no longer living in Shakespeare's time. (4) Abbreviations like *'tis, ne'er, o'er*, though they are found in some of our great hymns, should be used sparingly if at all. They interrupt the smooth naturalness which the lines should have. (5) One had better avoid long words, most of which are more prosy than poetic.

In the way of affirmative suggestions, in addition to the general procedures already stated, the following may be proffered. (1) Use a rhyming dictionary, or in the absence of that, run through in your mind all the words that rhyme with the last syllable of your previous line. Some you will discard immediately as incongruous. If the word is "God," you might use "trod"; you cannot use "cod"! If none of the rhymes will fit with propriety, you may need to back up and rewrite your first line. (2) Beat out the meter as you proceed, and if your line is supposed to have five feet, do not be satisfied with four or six. (When I write iambic pentameter in a sonnet, I thump it out on my cranium, and the ten fingers are just enough!) (3) Use as many figures of speech, pictorial images, fresh phrasings, as you can, but do not let the unusual run into the bizarre. The meaning need not be perfectly obvious; there is often more artistry where it is adroitly suggested. Yet it ought never to be fantastic, or so obscure as to be muddy. (4) Finish with a strong ending. This may be a powerful crescendo, a delicate suggestion, an unexpected turn of thought, an intriguing query—but the poem must not run down and dwindle out at the end.

It may be noted that in these suggestions I have not said much about "inspiration." There are poems that seem almost to write themselves and may well be called inspired. But that is not the way one usually does it. If one waits for an inspiration he may never start, and in this field as in any other, "God helps those who help themselves."

The Writing of Hymns

There is remaining space only to say a few words about a type of religious verse which many more people should be writing. This is the hymn, by which religious aspirations are both expressed and stirred, and our adoration becomes "comely praise." The Christians of the first century were enjoined to "be filled with the Spirit, addressing one another in psalms and hymns and spiritual songs, singing and making melody to the Lord with all your heart" (Eph. 5:18, 19). We need to do this as much as they, and need new hymns along with the old by which to do it.

In some respects a hymn is like any other religious lyric. It must have a sound content; it must conform to a definite pattern; it must avoid stylistic errors; it must be a unit of thought with a strong ending. All that has been said previously applies to it. Yet it has some characteristics of its own.

A hymn aims to express corporately the mood and feeling of a body of worshipers as they sing praises to their God, or address their deity in prayer, or affirm their assurance, devotion, and commitment. Hence, in a hymn the reference to God or Christ or the Holy Spirit must be explicit, not indirectly suggested as it may be in other forms of religious verse. Furthermore, though a few hymns are written in the first person singular, the corporate "we," "our," "us" form is almost always used.

Whatever complexity may exist in other forms of religious verse, a hymn must be simple. It must contain no unusual words—no subtle, fancy, slangy, or colloquial terms. It should contain few long words, preferably not over three syllables. While it may have figures of speech, the symbolism must be clear enough to make the meaning evident at first reading. It will be sung, if it is a good hymn, by the educated and the uneducated, by people of different cultures and social groups, by people of all stages of maturity except possibly the very young. It must say what all can grasp without undue effort and what, as they sing it, the people will feel to be their own affirmation.

Any poem should express both true feeling and true thought. This is the case with the hymn, but with a particular necessity. It must induce and affirm faith; it must express praise and prayer; it must stir the Christian who sings it to Christian action and give him comfort and assurance in his sorrow. Often its purpose is to celebrate an event of transcendent importance to the Christian, as in the Christmas, Good Friday, and Easter hymns. If the note of authentic feeling is not present, it falls dead, and is sung no more. Yet feeling is not everything. Though it is difficult to draw a sharp line between "gospel songs" and great hymns, one criterion is in the fact that the former appeal almost entirely to feeling, while a great hymn is also the expression of some basic theological conviction. The difference between "Brighten the Corner Where You Are" and "Rise Up, O Men of God" does not lie in the truth of one and falsity of the other, or entirely in the tune, but in the groundwork on which the challenge is made.

Finally, a hymn must fit the tune. This is of great importance, for both words and music convey moods; and if the

moods do not correspond, the result is a hodgepodge. While
in ordinary poetry an iambic foot may occasionally be sub-
stituted for a trochaic or even for a three-syllable foot, this
will not work well in a hymn. The meter is of great importance, for in a stanza arrangement the regularity of beats
must be preserved. Any variation confuses the congregation
and detracts from the mood of worship.

In view of these differences, it need not surprise us to discover that in general the great hymn writers, such as Charles
Wesley and Isaac Watts, have not been great poets, and the
great poets have not contributed extensively to our hym-
nody. Only a few, among whom Whittier, Tennyson, and
Cowper take the lead, have excelled in both fields.[2]

While the writing of religious poetry, whether occasional verse or hymns, is an exacting discipline, it is a most
rewarding experience. One writes first for his own soul-
satisfaction. Yet the *Christian Century* and most of the denominational journals publish religious verse, and welcome
fresh voices. The Hymn Society of America promotes frequent contests for new hymns on specific themes, and these
opportunities should be heeded. One who writes with true
feeling and thought and with due attention to form will not
lack a publisher. Yet whether one becomes a first-rate poet
in the world's eyes is not what matters. What does matter
is that one should yield to God whatever one has to give,
and leave the fruits with him.

[2] Dr. Albert E. Bailey in *The Gospel in Hymns* (New York: Charles
Scribner's Sons, 1950) uses as his basis for including a historical treatment of 313 hymns their presence in at least six out of ten standard
hymnals. I have examined his selection to discover the frequency of
hymns written by outstanding poets and find six by Whittier, three
each by Tennyson and Cowper, two each by Milton, Addison, Kipling,
and Henry van Dyke. However, the collection contains fourteen hymns
by Wesley; ten by Watts.

Georgia Harkness, professor of applied theology at the Pacific School of Religion in Berkeley, California, is the author of numerous books in the field of religion, of which three are religious verse. These are *Holy Flame, The Glory of God,* and *Be Still and Know,* the last two being devotional manuals consisting of poems and prayers. In 1954 her hymn, "Hope of the World," was the first choice of the Hymn Society of America in a contest for a hymn in recognition of the Evanston Assembly of the World Council of Churches. Dr. Harkness has taught at Elmira College, Mt. Holyoke College, and Garrett Biblical Institute. An ordained Methodist minister, she was for many years the only woman member of the American Theological Society.

Writing Religious Non-Fiction
for Print

CHAPTER *Seven*

Religion Is News

PART I—REPORTING RELIGION

GEORGE DUGAN

To WRITE EFFECTIVELY about religion in America's news media, whether it be for the daily press or for weekly news magazines, requires the professional approach of the competent reporter. Everything else is secondary—including theology.

In other words, religion makes the same demands on its chroniclers as do science, education, politics, and labor. Specialists in these fields are first of all good reporters.

This is also to say that religion no longer occupies the bottom rung on the journalistic ladder.

Time was, and still is on some newspapers, when "church

Editor's Note: Readers will find it helpful to read this chapter in conjunction with Miss Smith's on "Publicizing Religion," which follows it.

news" got short shrift. The weekly chore of preparing a church page was bucked down to the lowliest staff member. He, or more often she, grudgingly added it to an already over-stuffed portfolio including the day's news from the bridge club circuit.

Several years ago, the late James O. Supple, religion editor of the Chicago *Sun-Times,* made this pointed remark:

> Until recently the treatment of church news in the secular press bumped along at a deplorable low, paralleling the death notice, the betrothal announcement, and the garden party to raise funds for the Junior League's pet philanthropy. Church news consisted of an occasional sentence about mission collections or a report on the ladies' aid. The church made the front page only when death with due apology swooped down on a bishop of any denomination whatsoever (the press has always been morbidly fascinated by bishops) or on the pastor of the most fashionable local suburban congregation.[1]

Mr. Supple, who was killed while en route to Korea as a war correspondent, probably did more than any single religious news reporter to rectify this situation.

The picture is changing—and rapidly. "Church editors" are now being called "religious news editors." Church pages are becoming "religion" pages. Somebody has discovered, albeit belatedly, that there are synagogues as well as cathedrals.

Religion—a Prime News Source

Most of this country's major dailies and news weeklies are now convinced that religion is a prime source of news—not something to be killed because it had "controversial" angles, or ignored because there were no trained reporters to handle it.

[1] James O. Supple, "Church and Press—Enemies or Allies?" *Christian Century,* August 17, 1949, p. 960. Used by permission.

Along with this discovery came the realization that people are intensely interested in what religion is doing in the world today. Proof of this is in the tremendous press coverage of the second Assembly of the World Council of Churches in Evanston in 1954 and in the front-page treatment of evangelist Billy Graham.

Now that religious news has found its place in the sun, church and synagogue must raise their sights as well. This they have not done, primarily on the local level. It is at this point that the competent religion reporter finds himself stymied.

But before we examine the local problem, praise must be heaped on the religionists of the national and international levels. They, for the most part, have kept pace with the trend toward effective religion reporting.

In Protestantism, the National Council of the Churches of Christ in the U.S.A. has established a public relations department that provides incalculable help to religious news reporters. Its information department is unexcelled. The staff leaves no stone unturned to help a reporter prepare a story. The Council represents thirty Protestant and Eastern Orthodox bodies in the United States.

Similar accolades must be directed to the press departments of a number of denominations, particularly the Presbyterian, the Lutheran, the Methodist, the Protestant Episcopal, the Baptist, and the Seventh-day Adventist. These groups have caught the significance of the trend toward professional religion reporting at the national level. Incidentally, most of the personnel on these press staffs have had news experience.

Judaism, on a country-wide level, also has caught this spirit. The Roman Catholic Church, with its National Catholic Welfare Conference News Service, offers an important source to its own weekly papers, but largely neglects the secular press so far as assistance to reporters is concerned.

The Reporter's Cross

But the cross the religion reporter is forced to bear these days—if he wishes to do a professional job—comes almost solely at the local level.

With a wealth of material in his community, all untapped, his desk is loaded with trivia and his telephone clogged with inquirers whose typical plaint goes like this: "Did you get our release on the church's twelfth birthday? We are expecting a lot of space, you know."

It is difficult and sometimes impossible to explain that the twelfth birthday of a church does not constitute news. The rejoinder often is, "Oh, but we never get mentioned in your paper."

It is astonishing to discover that many clergymen are convinced that a paid advertisement on Saturday will assure mention in the news columns of that day's paper or the next. Nor is it unusual for a respected cleric to observe sagely during a telephone conversation, "I've placed an ad this week, but of course I know that's none of your business."

At this point it might be well to clarify the difference between religious promotion and religious news. It is at this juncture that the local churches and synagogues often lose their heads. Newspapers are not promoters in their news columns. One of the most unrewarding tasks of a religion reporter is to try to get this point across to the local clergy. It is not the function of a daily to plug a forthcoming meeting in order to assure a good turnout.

It is the function of the press to report what happens at that meeting, provided it is newsworthy. To be sure, if a meeting shows news possibilities in advance, then an advance story is perfectly valid.

Mr. Supple once addressed an American Press Institute seminar at Columbia University. This is what he discovered, as he explained it:

> What was most discouraging was the contention by some of the editors that they were bored to distraction by their paper's church coverage, that they greatly wanted something better, but that when they went to the local clergy to suggest changes they were told that the monotonous listing of sermon topics, with the frequent insertion of photographs of ministers, was eminently satisfactory. Some of these ministers had actually turned thumbs down on the proposal to print news of an active Christianity in the space which their unvarying calendars were preempting. These pastors had tragically failed to understand that the church belongs in a newspaper not as a list of Sunday school and preaching announcements but as the record of one of the most dynamic forces at work in the making of today's and tomorrow's history. . . .
>
> This is not to say that the local pastor is to withdraw his own church completely from the local newspaper picture and leave the field open exclusively to national or international religious news. But it is to point out that in the public prints he should try to relate his own church to the genuinely important movements that are taking place within religion, so that the local church suddenly assumes an importance to the unchurched it has not had before.[2]

An admirable case in point was the country-wide response to President Eisenhower's plea for prayers on the eve of the Geneva Big Four Conference in 1955. Literally millions of churchgoers bowed their heads in solemn prayer. The World Council of Churches and the National Council both issued in advance well-publicized supplications. Yet, when the stories of this vast outpouring of prayers were written, only a handful of clergymen made any effort by telephone or letter to relate their churches to the event.

[2] *Ibid.*, p. 961.

I am among those who strongly urge the abolition of the old-time Saturday church page, with its dreary lists of sermon topics and dull and drab little notices of teas set up by the women's groups. I strongly advocate, however, the development of the Saturday religious news column. Here, the significant events in local church or synagogue affairs may be noted, new clerical appointments recorded, anniversaries announced (not the twelfth or the sixteenth, but the fiftieth, one hundredth, or two hundredth), and important conferences accorded advance billing.

The Nature of Religious News

Probably this is the spot to make a check list of what constitutes religious news:

1. *National and international meetings of religious bodies.* Here is where the churches and the synagogues show their medals. These constitute the formal report of what they have done in the past and what they plan for the future. A competent reporter with a background knowledge of religious organizations can mine many major news stories in these sessions.

2. *Religious feature stories.* This source is untapped; it requires all the capabilities of an experienced reporter. With time and effort many top-flight stories are just waiting to be pounced upon. (See Chapter 9.)

3. *Interdenominational and interfaith developments.* These are normally prime grist for the religion reporter's mill. Projects accomplished by joint effort always interest more people and get more space. In this area, the press departments of the National Council of Churches and the World Council are always prepared to help.

4. *Trend stories.* These entail considerable research, but the end results are worth all the digging. Like features, the harvest is ripe and ready for the plucking. Possible subjects:

the current religious revival, the church and delinquency, the church and segregation.

5. *Religious unity*. Protestantism is constantly making forays and sending up trial balloons in this field. Often this is technical and ticklish—but, as usual, a competent reporter need have no qualms about delving into the church union problem.

On the local level, the substitutes for church teas are legion. Frequently a minister sits on top of a good story for years without realizing it. A casual remark from him may be all that is necessary for the reporter to start his pencil scratching. Later, the clergyman very likely remarks: "Why, I didn't have the slightest idea that there was a story there for you."

News that even most churchmen can recognize (some do not, believe it or not) falls into the area of major anniversaries, new buildings, new pastors, topical seminars, and visiting V.I.P.s of the religious world.

One of my favorite anecdotes wraps much of the general theme of this part of the chapter into a neat package.

Early in 1955 an eager, young general assignment reporter for the *New York Times* was sent to the Poconos to cover a major Protestant gathering. The principal speaker was a churchman who at that time filled a top advisory post in the government's information service. The press department of the group prepared an advance copy of this gentleman's alleged address, apparently in the greatest good faith.

Our young reporter was both able and conscientious. He listened attentively, realized that the copy had no bearing on the address, and so prepared to take notes. The speaker made a brief reference to a proposed religious census under consideration in Washington. This was news. Reporter X headed for the dais at the end of the speech and politely asked for more information on the census angle.

Our churchman then made a major mistake. He became angry, demanded the reporter's credentials, and threatened to telephone the paper if the scribe so much as dared call his story in. Eventually, both the churchman and the reporter called the *Times*. A cool head on the desk managed it all very well. A query was sent to the Washington bureau and two days later the religious census story broke exclusively in the *Times*.

The Moral of the Story

This anecdote is full of morals. Some are: churchmen in high position should not threaten reporters; news writers must never take advance texts on their face value (hearing is always better than seeing); a reporter usually gets his story.

This occasion is also one of many where a possibly overly efficient public relations department got caught with its hand-outs down. Hand-outs can be of the utmost value, particularly when early deadlines require a reporter to file early copy. They also are of great help when a writer needs the exact text of statements or announcements. Sometimes, however, good stories are missed when too much trust is put in the advance text of a speech, for instance. Churchmen have been known to depart from their prepared addresses.

Religion reporters, either by study or sheer osmosis, pick up an astounding fund of knowledge concerning their field. This knowledge is not confined to one group. In effect it may be compared to a huge panorama of contemporary religious thought. From this vantage point a reporter sees his field in the broadest possible scope.

Most clergymen—there always are exceptions—make no

effort to gain even a rudimentary picture of the operation of a daily newspaper, wire service, or news magazine. They seem content with the stereotyped newsman—gay, cynical, and always looking for an angle.

Deadlines, to many ministers, is a catch-phrase that reporters use in order to get home earlier.

It seems to this writer that a little reciprocity is in order. Let this be Lesson Number One.

Most religion reporters today are engaged in their life's vocation. They like their work, they are serious, the only angles they are looking for are legitimate news stories. Some years ago this reporter was accused by a top leader of the ecumenical movement of attempting to sabotage Christianity. The charge was made unthinkingly, of course, when some particularly ticklish questions were brought up in a press conference. The churchman in question, it must be added, has come a long way since those days. His understanding of what the press is trying to do is admirable.

The Problem of Objectivity

This brings us to that much-maligned word, *objectivity*. Theodore M. Bernstein, assistant managing editor of the *New York Times*, once said, most succinctly, that newspaper readers demand objectivity until "their own oxen happen to be gored." He said that the essence of objectivity is a "neutral attitude" and added that a newspaper or newspaperman "will never consciously or deliberately favor one side or the other."

This is Lesson Number Two. Most churchmen find objectivity in a news story when it tells their side of the issue only. Anything else is unobjective. The moment a reporter adds, "while on the other hand," he is immediately going over to the side of the opposition.

But being fair is part of the reporter's job. Only when

this is understood by the clergy can there be complete rap-
prochement between the two. A classic example of the
"gored oxen" occurred in this reporter's field some months
before this was written. A widely known fundamentalist
clergyman teed off one day about alleged "modernism" and
"leftish" tendencies within the World Council and the National Council. In the news story, the conservative brother
was identified as the leader of an aggressive minority group.

His right to make the charge was unassailable—as unassailable as the right of the two bodies to deny those charges.
At this point a prominent denominational executive heat-
edly demanded that newspapers cease printing stories concerning the fundamentalist leader. Yet, some months earlier,
when the ultraconservative brother was publicly censured
for "disruptive" tactics, our denominational leader was the
first to cheer when the story hit the news columns.

Since one of the main objectives of religion is to spread
its gospel to the so-called "unchurched," through the pulpit, yes, but through all modern means of communication as
well, it would seem derelict on the part of seminaries to
neglect the teaching of press practices and procedures.

Sometimes it is done, in the nature of an afterthought,
with instructors who themselves need a course of sprouts in
the subject. Some seminaries provide courses in "interpreting the news." These often end up as "gripe" sessions on
the poor handling of religion in the daily press.

What is sorely needed in the seminaries of America is
down-to-earth, practical courses in Journalism I: what constitutes news, how it is gathered, how it is written, and how
it is edited. This course should not be taught by a theolo-
gian. It should be given by a practical newspaperman with
many years of experience in journalism.

More and more able reporters are entering the field of
religious news writing. They find it a fascinatingly new
area with tremendous potentialities. It is up to the churches

and the synagogues to raise their sights to meet this challenge.

George Dugan was too modest to say much about himself when he sent in his portion of this chapter, so the editor reprints part of what the *New York Times*, which he serves as religious news editor, said about him in 1954. Calling him "Reporter in the Pew," it recorded:

"It's inevitable that around the shop George Dugan is sometimes called Bishop . . . [his] father was a Presbyterian minister. . . . Not long after his graduation from the University of Michigan, in 1931, he was working as a reporter for the *Presbyterian Tribune*.

"Having started in religious journalism, George Dugan was content to stay with it. . . . For eight years before he joined the *Times* in 1947 he worked for Religious News Service. . . . He has covered religious assemblies in Europe, South America, and Canada. His 'outstanding service' to religion won him the National Religious Publicity Council's award of merit."

Mr. Dugan also won a special award from the Associated Church Press. He has been president of the Religious Newswriters Association.

PART II—WRITING THE STORY

ROLAND E. WOLSELEY

How does one write all those stories that Mr. Dugan lists as newsworthy? Entire books have been published for people who ask this question. By learning a few fundamental principles a writer can equip himself to produce readable news accounts acceptable to most news media.

News writers dealing with any subject arrange the facts into patterns determined largely by the need for speedy production of the material and the speed at which readers desire to learn what has taken place or is to occur.

By putting down his information in a particular order, say in a descending sequence according to importance, the experienced journalist can prepare a page of copy in a few minutes, a printer can set it in type almost as fast, and the reader can scan it easily, not having even to read more than the opening paragraph or two to get its essence.

Religious news fits into these patterns as readily as any other type. Because such news rarely is sensational or flamboyant, however, the patterns it follows are among the more simple and regular. These are the commoner patterns for news:

1. *The inverted triangle.* This pattern is for spot news. The climax of the event is put first; chronology is violated purposely. In the opening paragraph or two appear the most interesting and vital facts; the details follow as they grow less important or pertinent, with the least-needed at the end, where they may be deleted without essentially damaging the news account. The triangle of news stands on its tip in this pattern, with the broad end at the top.

2. *The triangle in normal position.* This plan should be used for telling feature news, that is, news that is not especially timely; it may be odd rather than important. A typical example is the familiar story of an old Bible found in a corner of a church building during renovation and the names of the old members inscribed therein. The minor details are related first, usually in chronological order, working to the climax at or near the end, much as in a conventional short story.

3. *The rectangle.* In this type the news is more or less of equal importance throughout, as with an interpretative article about religion for a newspaper or magazine. The upper end of the rectangle, assuming it to be standing on one of its narrow ends, may be slightly wider than the body, to represent the greater importance of the opening section, known as the *lead* in journalistic parlance.

Patterns like these are followed in building news stories about religion whether the accounts be for print in newspaper or magazine or to be read over radio or television. There are differences in the distribution of the facts (in the way the building blocks are laid) among these media but not in the general, over-all arrangement or sequence. Thus a triangular pattern can be used for any medium, if speed of publication or dissemination calls for it.

Writing a Specific Story

Religious news can be international in scope or of concern to persons merely within the limits of a specific congregation. Most professional news writers, such as staffers of news agencies, newspapers, magazines, radio and television stations, and persons in publicity and public relations offices assigned to news writing, handle a wide range of religious information. Typical are sermons, speeches, dedications, installations, building program plans, finance campaigns, acceptances into membership, weddings, christenings, and scores of other events.

Church organizations, ranging from national bodies to local parishes, wishing to assist the news media in their coverage of religion and to make sure stories of their own activities are not overlooked, often entrust the news writing to persons on their own staffs, with more or less adequate preparation for the job, often too little, as Mr. Dugan points out.

Let us suppose that one of these or a reporter on a local daily is asked to write a news story about a given event coming up in the news, a story known as an *advance*. It concerns the celebration of a centennial. Here are the main facts possessed by the news writer:

> The church is the Central City Presbyterian.
> Its building is at Warren and Water Streets, Central City.
> The minister is the Rev. Royal Price.
> The celebration has been planned over the past two months.

It marks the founding of the church one hundred
years ago.

The anniversary date is October 15, now three weeks
away.

A special week-long program has been planned; its
major details are in the writer's possession.

The story under preparation is to be the first detailed
general one to be printed or broadcast or telecast. The beginning step is to select the lead and decide on the general
pattern to be used. The first version is for use in print,
chiefly in a daily or weekly newspaper. The inverted triangle pattern (No. 1) is most suitable for this particular
story, for the reporter should communicate the main information promptly. There would be no point in featurizing
this story except in a metropolis like New York or Chicago,
where many churches have such celebrations. In small towns
and cities, celebrations of the sort are exceptional news and
should at first announcement be treated in straightforward
manner.

After remembering that the copy is to be typed double-
space, on one side of the paper only, with paragraphs running between four and six lines, and lines of ten to twelve
words each, the writer decides on the lead material. There
are several dozen ways in which news media phrase leads;
they bear such names as *summary*, *quotation*, *question*, and
explosive. The summary lead lends itself best to most
straight-news stories, and particularly the dignified material that comprises most church news.

The summary lead literally *sums up* the news. It puts first
what is most newsworthy, most important, most significant.
Reporters remind themselves of what they are to find out
and to include by answering as many as they can of these
six questions: Who, What, When, Why, Where, and How:
the five W's and the H, as they usually are called, and cred-

ited to Rudyard Kipling, who called them his six honest
serving men.

What is most important in our batch of news facts about
Central City Church? It is that there is to be an observation
of the centennial. What are the answers to the Kipling
questions?

> *What:* Centennial.
>
> *When:* October 15 next and October 15 of a cen-
> tury ago.
>
> *Where:* Central City Presbyterian Church, Warren
> and Water Streets.
>
> *Who:* The members of the church and the minister,
> the Rev. Royal Price.
>
> *Why:* To mark church progress; to develop still
> more interest in the church; to stimulate the
> loyalty of the present members.
>
> *How:* The details of the program that constitute the
> celebration.

Let us say that the news writer starts the story this way:

Central City Presbyterian Church was founded
on Oct. 15, 1857, at its present location at Warren and Water Streets.

*(And so on through its history, at the end announcing
the celebration plans.)*

Such an opening and over-all structure are dull, for they
follow strict chronological order and do not highlight the
timely. This pattern (No. 2) is the wrong one.

Another try:

The Rev. Royal Price, minister of Central City
Presbyterian Church, which was founded on Oct.
15, 1857, has called a meeting of a special com-

mittee to make final plans for the celebration of the 100th anniversary of the church, which is at Warren and Water Streets. The meeting will be held next Tuesday night at 8 p.m. at the church house, 1143 Warren St.

Although this opening is better, the emphasis is on a comparatively unimportant (from the public's viewpoint) committee meeting, instead of on the celebration itself, which is news of wider interest. The opening sentence is far too long, such sentences being most effective when restricted to between ten and twenty words. Note also the redundancy of *Tuesday night* and *8 p.m.*

The writer composes a new story:

The 100th anniversary of the founding of Central City Presbyterian Church will be observed next month with a week-long celebration.

The church was founded Oct. 15, 1857. Its first building was erected on the northeast corner of Warren and Water Streets, a site it still occupies.

A special committee, headed by the Rev. Royal Price, the minister, has planned a program that begins with the worship services of Sunday, Oct. 16.

(And so on, through a general story, minor details being put last.)

A variation on this might be:

A week-long celebration next month will mark the centennial of the founding of Central City Presbyterian Church, according to the Rev. Royal Price, minister.

(Then pick up at the second paragraph, as above; omit the minister's first name and identification, saying simply, "by the Rev. Mr. Price, has, etc.")

So far this story has been prepared for print, for readers. The writer next tries one for the ear, for listeners. For radio and television, copy must be much shorter than for the newspaper or the magazine, for there is less time (space) for news on the air than in print. A story for print about this event might be five hundred words long; for radio-TV the same story should not ordinarily go over one hundred words. The story for the ear is informal and friendly in tone; it is somewhat loose-jointed writing. This is to make it sound natural, more like conversation. The facts must be related more slowly than for the eye. The main facts cannot be confined to one short opening paragraph, unless the news event itself is slight. The mind cannot retain facts that are too closely put together unless the person to whom they are directed can stop to study them, which is impossible with material coming over the air.

Here is the radio form of the same centennial story:

One of Central City's oldest churches will celebrate its 100th anniversary next month.

The Central City Presbyterian Church is getting ready to observe its founding on Oct. 15, 1857. The church was established a century ago on that date. It still occupies the site where its first building was constructed, which is at Warren and Water Streets.

There will be a special worship service on Sunday morning, Oct. 16, which will begin a celebration lasting a week. The planning committee is headed by the minister, the Rev. Royal Price.

(If time is available, one or two more paragraphs might follow, containing other committee names and major details of the celebration.)

News Writing Principles

A few simple principles of news writing appear from this analysis:

1. Put the most important facts first in a straight news story.
2. Delay them in a feature news story, where novelty, oddity, human interest, or some other element outweighs the importance of the news being announced.
3. Convey the facts more slowly when writing for the ear than for the eye.
4. Make sure the major facts are there by checking against the five W's and the H.
5. Put the secondarily most important facts in the central section of the story.
6. Put the least important facts at the end.
7. Do not use connectives (*therefore, but, and*) to unite paragraphs or relate sentences. This practice makes it difficult to cut down or expand news accounts to fit the time or space requirements of the publication or station.

CHAPTER *Eight*

Publicizing Religion

HELEN F. SMITH

Most of the forms of writing treated in this volume are used by the publicist to carry his story to the public. A full-fledged publicity campaign makes use of radio, television, magazines, trade journals, advertising, letters, direct mail pieces, church bulletins, parish papers, and many other media. Writing for daily and weekly newspapers, however, is the indispensable core of the publicist's job and therefore is given the major emphasis in this chapter.

Unlike other types of writing about religion, publicity writing cannot be done on a free lance basis in the sense that a novelist or magazine feature writer works with only the publisher or the reader in mind. The publicist must be hired, or at least assigned on a volunteer basis, to write for a particular organization or group. His is a dual responsibility to serve the best interests of the church he represents

100

and to meet the requirements of the newspaper, magazine, or other media with which he works.

The publicist must also accept the limitation of having the subjects he writes about determined largely by other people, since it is his task to interpret the church to the public by means of its personalities, activities, and pronouncements. His creative skill, however, often increases the news-making potential of the facts he has to work with.

Publicity vs. News

The word *publicity* has acquired an unhappy connotation because of its association with press agents and stunts deliberately concocted to get newspaper space.

The publicist, however, has a legitimate function in supplying editors with information on newsworthy events that their staffs are not large enough to cover.

"Indeed," as the columnist Meyer Levin points out after tracing to publicity sources a large share of a typical day's news, "it is quite possible that without public relations men, news gathering would be a prohibitively expensive operation for many a small paper. Publicity is legit."

The religious publicist need make no apologies if he has learned to distinguish between news and propaganda. By evaluating the news potential of church events in terms of what the editor wants rather than what the members would like to see in print, he will best serve not only the editor but also the organization he represents.

Margaret Donaldson, Methodist public relations director for the New York area, draws this sharp distinction between news and publicity: "When a person says, 'How can we get more publicity for the church?' the answer is, 'By publishing leaflets and brochures, distributing posters, circulating letters, buying advertising space.' We should recognize that a newspaper is not a publicity organ. A newspaper is just what it says it is—a NEWS paper, and when there is a NEWS story, the paper prints it. The publicity the church gets from the story is a by-product."

News Values

The antagonism editors sometimes express toward publicists and their "hand-outs" is an understandable reaction to the hundreds of unusable releases which pile up on their desks day after day. It need not concern the publicist who learns to think like an editor and makes sure that the copy he turns in conforms to city desk standards. The following check list is useful in sizing up the news-making possibilities of an event:

1. *People.* Is it related to the physical, emotional, spiritual, or intellectual needs or interests of people?

Does it concern social or group interests? (Church action toward desegregation, for instance, or organization of a new club for young married people.)

Is it related to family interests? (Family Altar Day or a project to curb juvenile delinquency.)

Does it affect the individual physically? (A blood donor drive.) Or psychologically? (Sympathy for others: church members build house for needy family; humor: benefit sale so successful the rug is sold from floor of rented building; identification with others: awards for achievement, unusual hobbies or experiences.)

2. *Size.* How "big" is it, either physically or psychologically?

Are many people involved? (Large attendance at a special meeting; large number volunteered for community service project.)

Do many people have some previous knowledge of it? (Annual observance, such as World Day of Prayer well publicized in previous years.)

Will many people be affected by it in some way? (A community-wide survey or fund-raising campaign.)

Does it touch some point of interest or experience common to many people? (Sermon on "Ten Commandments of Happy Marriage.")

Is it big physically—does it involve large amounts of property or money? (New church building.)

If it is not "big" in itself, is it related to something or someone that is? (Church co-operation in March of Dimes; address by mayor at dinner for church members aiding a civic project.)

3. *Time.* Is it news *now?*

Any of the items mentioned above might refer to some major event of history, but the news columns of the paper are devoted to current information about contemporary ideas, people, and events. What happened two centuries or sometimes even two days ago is not news unless some new development of significance is revealed today. (Ladies' Guild announces clothing collection drive to replenish supplies distributed to fire victims the previous week—the fire is no longer news but the drive is.)

4. *Place.* Is it news *here?*

The local angle is important. (A large convention in a distant city is not as important as the fact that someone from *here* is going to attend or that it affects local people in some way.)

To sum it all up in a definition, the most newsworthy events or ideas are those of greatest interest *today* to the *greatest number of people* living *here.*

Such a definition or check list will be useful only if the publicist remembers that the editor's judgment of what will interest the largest number of people will be influenced by many factors, such as geographic location, educational level of his readers, political affiliation. The publicist learns to measure news values in terms of the preferences and requirements of the particular editors he works with.

A survey of the front-page stories in the seven New York City dailies on a single day points up how wide the difference in editorial choice may be. (The study included pages 2 and 3 of the tabloids.)

Out of the fifty stories tabulated, not one appeared on all seven front pages. Only one appeared in six papers; one in five papers; and one in four papers. Three stories appeared in as many as three papers, and nine stories ran on two front pages. Thirty-five stories—the great majority—turned up on only one front page.

Publicity Planning

The mechanics of writing a news story are the same for a publicist as for a staff reporter. (For a summary of news-writing principles, see the books listed in the bibliographies of this and the preceding chapters.) But there is an important part of the publicist's job that does not concern the reporter who usually handles only the assignments he receives from his city editor.

Before he is ready to write a news story, the publicist must be able to organize and plan. He must be able to size up its interest for the various media available. He must make such decisions as the time to break a story in order to get the best space. He wouldn't, for instance, release a story for use on Election Day if it could be avoided. A story cannot be held up after the event has occurred but it may even be possible to persuade the people involved to choose a better date. Or the choice between an advance announcement or a report after the event may provide the needed time differential.

In spite of his careful planning, every publicist has had the disappointment of having stories that were scheduled to appear pushed out by a last-minute break of major news, such as trying to announce the opening of a church conference in Missouri the day assassins made an attempt on the life of President Truman.

Announcing a fellowship dinner or a new pastor is a simple news assignment that would be handled much the same by the publicist as by a staff reporter. Organization and planning become an increasingly important part of the publicist's work, however, in handling larger and more complex events. Coverage of anniversary, open house, or dedication observances, for instance, should be planned well ahead to get maximum results.

Once the date on which the story should appear is determined, the publicity writer must work backwards, setting up a schedule of news releases, publicity photos, memos to the editor, and other materials, taking into account the deadlines of the newspapers involved. Material for the church page is due in most newspaper offices the preceding Wednesday. Some request it even earlier. Deadlines for weekly papers usually fall on Monday or Tuesday. Copy for morning dailies should be on the editor's desk by 5 P.M.; for afternoon papers by 9 A.M. Stories get better space if they reach the editor even earlier than these deadlines, since church stories rarely fall in the category of spot news and may be pushed aside in the last rush of going to press.

If the story merits coverage by a staff reporter or photographer, the editor should receive information in writing about the event two or three days ahead so that he can include it in his news schedule. Spot news is telephoned to the city desk as it breaks.

An intimate knowledge of the media he must work with is an essential part of the publicist's equipment that can be acquired only by experience, careful study, and hard work. He learns editorial preferences by personal contact with the newspaper staff, and even more important, by studying the content of the paper itself day after day.

What is front-page news in one paper may rate a paragraph on page 27 in another. Some papers limit religious news almost entirely to the Saturday church page. Increasingly, however, religion is competing successfully for space in the regular news columns of the American press.

There are no hard and fast rules by which the publicity writer can be sure whether he should (a) send releases to all papers, (b) notify editors of a coming event and request staff coverage, (c) give an exclusive to one paper, or (d) call a press conference. The importance of the event, accepted procedure in a particular city, the time of day a story breaks, and other factors influence the decision. There are, however, a few basic principles that serve as a starting point for the beginner while he is learning to "play it by ear" as a veteran publicist:

1. Never give a straight news story to one paper exclusively.

2. Feature stories may be given on an exclusive basis, but be careful not to play favorites. When offering an editor an idea for a feature, ask if he wants an exclusive. If not, offer it to all papers in the area, but be sure they know it is not exclusive.

3. Do not call a press conference unless you have news of unusual significance or a prominent or unusual personality to offer. Ordinary news is best handled in a written release.

The facts from which news stories are made seldom drop in the publicist's lap without effort on his part. Like the staff reporter, he must cover a beat. For the religious publicist, that means making friends of all the key people in the church organization and winning their co-operation in providing the facts for news stories as they occur, posing for photos when necessary, and at times even adjusting plans to fit the exigencies of news coverage.

Dramatizing the Story

The publicist's initiative in producing a news story must often go beyond digging up the facts. His trained eye will spot possibilities for dramatizing the life and work of the church that will not only increase the newsworthiness of its activities but will make those activities more interesting for the participants.

And here the church publicist must make a sharp distinction between trying to make a pure publicity puff or piece of propaganda look like news, in contrast to increasing the value of an event which has a legitimate place in the news columns.

The standard elements by which the editor evaluates any event are sometimes listed in journalism texts as timeliness, proximity, prominence, consequence, human interest.

Creative thinking by the publicist plus co-operation from the program planners often strengthen one or more of these elements enough to affect materially the prominence editors give to an event.

A few examples out of hundreds of news-making events being produced by alert church publicity people may clarify the point:

At the constituting convention of the National Council of the Churches of Christ held in Cleveland, the colorful processional of church dignitaries which opened the assembly and the solemn affixing of signatures to the constituting document added measurably to the impressiveness of the occasion.

Both of these dramatic moments were originally conceived at the suggestion of Donald C. Bolles, director of public relations for the National Council, to add visual interest for news, television, and newsreel cameramen.

* * *

A Methodist congregation had already received the usual coverage of its plans for a new church building in announcements of the quota, the building plans, the campaign leaders. How could the progress of the fund-raising campaign be reported without duplicating previous stories? Here is how they did it: Boy Scouts were enlisted to help with a big mailing to be sent to the congregation. When the letters were ready they were piled in a small wagon and three youngsters pulled it to the post office. The result was a picture that pleased both the editor and the church.

* * *

A widely known hymn writer was scheduled to appear at a Seventh-day Adventist conference on the occasion of his seventy-fifth birthday. The man handling press relations for the conference prepared a huge blow-up of the writer's best-known hymn. A photo of the hymn writer against the unusual background made newspapers across the country via Associated Press.

* * *

It isn't news that a church deplores gambling, horror comics, juvenile delinquency, or drinking. But if a minister or church official makes a pronouncement, a convention passes a resolution, or a mass meeting is held to map plans for fighting a community problem, a news story is in the making. The letters-to-the-editor column is also a good place to express the attitude of the church on such questions.

An Added Ingredient

Hardest of the news elements to inject into publicity copy is human interest. Anyone can learn to report the "Five W's" of routine church events, but it takes a high degree of creative ability to see in those events the often minor sidelights that will touch the reader's sympathies or his sense of humor.

The editor of the Redding, California, *Record Searchlight*, who found this item among a day's grist of publicity releases, must have had a moment of unexpected pleasure —and incidentally a moment of gratitude to the publicist who turned it in:

> The proud papa of a 3-day-old baby pulled a switcheroo on the old cigar act this week when he gave away toothbrushes to announce the happy event.
>
> There were two reasons for his actions:
>
> 1. He's a dentist.
> 2. He belongs to the Seventh-day Adventist Church whose members do not smoke.
>
> Dr. John A. Billington became a father Sunday morning. On Wednesday, Dr. Billington attended mid-week prayer services at the church and handed out toothbrushes to other members.

The church publicist's job is more than reporting facts and figures, names and places. In its highest sense it is a Christian witness of singular effectiveness. Most religious publicists feel the need of escaping occasionally from deadlines and typewriters long enough to remind themselves that they are working for more than column inches. For one of them the touchstone is a yellowed clipping datelined Dayton, Ohio (U.P.):

> This is a story about two small boys who quietly entered Christ Episcopal Church and left offerings of candy at the altar.
>
> The Rev. Phil Porter said the "mystery of Christ Church" began two months ago when the sexton found

small pieces of candy on the high altar beneath a picture of Jesus.

"The offerings were discovered there again and again and no one knew who had left them. It became the mystery of our church," he said.

"We set up a watch, but no one saw anything left there. Still the offerings appeared again and again.

"Sometimes they were pieces of hard candy, sometimes fruit, or chocolate bars."

Several days ago Dr. and Mrs. Porter found two small boys looking about the church.

One, a fourth-grader, readily admitted he and his friend, a first-grade student, had been leaving offerings for some time.

"We come here to the church and kneel before the chancel to say our prayers," the boy said. "Then we give our offerings.

"My offerings are to Jesus. I want to share what I have with him."

Mrs. Porter said that before the boys left, she explained that offerings are used to teach other people about Christ. She mentioned that candy is perishable.

The next day a nickel was found on the altar.

Writing the Story

Although, as stated previously, the mechanics of news writing are the same for the publicist as for the reporter, an editor would be quick to point out that there is a vast difference between staff-written copy and the releases that flood his desk.

Most of those differences would be eliminated if publicists observed sound news-writing practice. Over-long releases filled with too many unimportant details are probably the most common offenders. Just as bad are releases that omit necessary information.

Aside from the avoidable differences of incompetent

writing, certain characteristics of publicity writing are intrinsic. The release, reprinted below, was prepared by Charles Hushaw, director of the United Lutheran Church News Bureau. It is nearly twice the length of the *New York Times* story, which follows it, yet very little could have been omitted without making the rewrite man's job harder. He would undoubtedly want to know, for example, when and where the announcement was made, even though the fact does not appear in the published story.

Plans for the erection of a new $250,000 building adjoining the Evangelical Lutheran Church of the Holy Trinity at 65th and Central Park West were announced at a "loyalty dinner" of the congregation last night (Thursday night).

More than 300 members of the congregation attended the dinner, held at the Broadway Congregational Church, 56th and Broadway, and heard plans for the building program, which involves demolition of the present parish house on 65th Street and the erection of a modern office building which will house the church administrative offices, a chapel and apartments for the pastor, Dr. Robert Hershey, and the assistant pastor, the Rev. Franklin S. Lambert.

(Two paragraphs of church history follow.)

As printed in the *New York Times*:

The Evangelical Lutheran Church of the Holy Trinity has announced plans to construct a $250,000 building adjoining the church property at Central Park West and 65th St.

The present parish house on 65th St. will be demolished to make way for the modern office building that will house the church administrative offices, a chapel and apartments for the pastor, the Rev. Dr. Robert Hershey, and the assistant pastor, the Rev. Franklin S. Lambert.

Holy Trinity Church was founded Jan. 27, 1868, at a site on West 21st St. It moved to its present location in 1904.

In trimming away the verbiage and trivia that often clutter releases, the publicist must be careful not to omit dates, names, clear identification, addresses, and other specific facts which speed the editing process, even though they may not all appear in print.

Former newspaper men who have moved over into the field of publicity agree that there is a more basic difference in their writing which grows out of a changed point of view. Their objectives may not change but they at least take a different order of importance. The publicist is still interested in writing what people are interested in, but he now has the primary responsibility of writing about those events and ideas which will win friends for his organization. If he conforms to the ethics of his profession, he will not try to suppress legitimate news even when unfavorable. Neither can he be expected eagerly to take the initiative in digging up facts that do not further the purposes of the church.

In the nature of things, the publicist will probably continue to feature the final unanimous vote on a resolution, while the news reporter plays up the heated arguments of a dissenting delegate. The difference grows steadily less, however, as churches achieve greater objectivity by hiring professional public relations people and newspapers demonstrate a growing understanding of the importance of the church in modern life.

Other Media

Radio and television are second in importance only to the public press as media through which the churches may tell their story. By providing time for spot news, interviews of interesting personalities, public service announcements, sermons, and dramatic programs, these channels of communication are helping tremendously to spread the "good news."

In the past few years editors of secular magazines have "discovered" religion as a rich source of feature material. The publicist with a really good story of religion in action will find the magazines receptive. It is more common for the publicist to turn such material over to a free lance writer than to do the writing himself.

Even more than the daily newspaper, these media demand a mastery of their particular writing techniques (discussed in other chapters of this book) and a close study of the material presently used by them. In these more complex media it becomes increasingly true that success is the result of learning to write what the editor or program director wants, with the resultant publicity to the church becoming a small but valuable by-product.

Qualifications and Opportunities

From even so brief a survey of the field of religious publicity it is obvious that the qualifications are high. Job opportunities are still very limited, although the number of professional publicity or public relations people employed by the Protestant denominations has approximately doubled in the past ten years. Since most of the public relations offices now operated by the churches and by interdenominational organizations are not much older than that, the doubling of personnel still does not represent a very large number.

At present these jobs exist at denominational headquarters, on mission boards, and in interdenominational or nondenominational boards and agencies. There are some parttime publicity jobs in local churches, particularly for those who also qualify as secretaries. Free lancing is almost non-existent in this field.

The job applicant must, of course, be a competent journalist with a well-developed news sense and ability to work under the pressure of deadlines. A pleasant personality and the ability to work with people are indispensable. Church public relations directors agree, for the most part, that when vacancies occur on their staffs they look for young people with not only journalistic training but actual newspaper experience.

Over and above these qualifications which would apply to any publicity job, leaders in the field are unanimous in emphasizing that the work demands loyalty to the church, a desire to serve it, and willingness to represent it properly in personal conduct. Most of them prefer people from their own memberships because they feel it gives a helpful background for interpreting the church.

To work successfully and happily in this field, the writer must be looking for more than a job or a chance for personal advancement; he must come to it with a sense of Christian vocation and must find his highest satisfaction in helping to tell the greatest story in the world.

Helen F. Smith, director of the New York public relations office of the Seventh-day Adventist Church, was for ten years assistant director of her denomination's Bureau of Public Relations in Washington, D.C. Her previous experience was in denominational and government editorial offices. She has had wide experience in handling publicity for major news events of her church in all parts of the United States and Canada and in conducting publicity workshops for laymen and pastors. Miss Smith, an active member of the National Religious Publicity Council, was vice-president in 1955.

CHAPTER *Nine*

The Religious Feature Article

GLENN D. EVERETT

A FEATURE ARTICLE, to give a simple definition, is a story about some person, place, or event that is newsworthy, but which, if it fails to make today's edition, can just as well be used in tomorrow's or even next week or next month.

The news story must necessarily deal with current happenings. There is little space in the news story for background or sidelights. The feature story fills this gap. Newspapers and magazines would be exceedingly shallow if they dealt only with today's events today and did not give a considerable portion of space to feature articles.

In structure, the feature story (which is not a story in the fictional sense, for it is true) is the reverse of the news account. A news story usually concentrates the essence of the news in the opening paragraph or two. But a feature is in no rush to tell us what has happened or will happen, for its news is subordinate to the human interest, history, or other main content that makes it publishable. There are features, for instance, like the O. Henry short story, with the surprise at the end. Features have many varieties of beginnings, middles, and endings. A little time spent with one of the books in the bibliography for this chapter will provide many guides to building attractive feature stories.

Feature stories are particularly important in the field of religion because religious news only occasionally rates the front page. Only when some great conclave of religious leaders occurs, such as a meeting of the World Council of Churches or a Roman Catholic Eucharistic Congress, does religion really make front-page news. For the most part, if religion is to get into secular newspapers and magazines, it is through the medium of the feature article.

At the same time, the religious press itself depends largely on feature material. Church-sponsored periodicals come out weekly, semimonthly, or monthly. The amount of news being generated within the publication's denomination, diocese, or parish is relatively limited, and suffers from the delay that necessarily occurs in reporting it. If a religious publication is to be sprightly and readable, it must give a substantial portion of its space to feature articles.

Thus, in both the secular and the religious press, the religious feature article has an unusually important place.

Daily Newspapers

In writing feature articles on religious subjects for the daily press, the writer must be guided by what the typical editor wants, and restrained by those things which the secular editor, because of his position, must avoid.

Easily the most popular feature article with the daily newspaper editor is the anniversary story. A religious anniversary is always considered a suitable occasion for a story by a daily paper. In part this is because the editor has probably given space in time past to some previous anniversary, say the one hundredth observance of the founding of a large downtown church; once having done that, he cannot with good grace tell any other religious group that its anniversary isn't news.

Editors, on the whole, are eager to please their readers, and a good anniversary story being one to which no one could reasonably object, it always finds a welcome. The story may concern the anniversary of the founding of a church, the anniversary of its present edifice, the anniversary of the ordination of the pastor or of his service to the local congregation. It can also be the anniversary of the service of some member of the church, such as an organist who has played for twenty-five years, a man who has taught in Sunday school for thirty, or a member who has faithfully attended every Sunday for fifty years.

The author recently saw an interesting feature story in the Philadelphia *Inquirer* about a woman who has attended the same Sunday school since 1870.

Religious writers who are alert to the possibilities inherent in anniversaries will find many of their feature articles in print. Hidden clues to stories must be pursued: the author found a feature in a church pictured on a postage stamp; by following up its background, a timely story was produced.

Next in the preference of the daily newspaper editor is the "unusual service" story that tells of the unusual activity of some individual or a unique service being rendered by some religious group. Does the mayor teach a Sunday school class? It is unusual to find a busy man with time to devote to such church activity and it's newsworthy. Is there a woman who has made two hundred quilts for missionaries? A church with a special class in Braille for the

blind? A religious group with a summer camp for under-
privileged children?

Any unusual community service being performed by a
church can be an acceptable subject for a feature story.

The religious writer should always try to give his story
a legitimate "news peg" for the editor to hang it on. It is
not enough to point out that a story was carried about the
Lutheran Church and its Saturday evening chicken dinners,
and that the Reformed Church would like to have a story
about its Saturday bake sales. The editor may yield to such
pressure, but not graciously, and the newspaper reader
probably will detect a somewhat unchristian spirit of rivalry
in such stories. If the Reformed Church has a woman who
bakes fifteen pies or a dozen cakes at one time for its bake
sale, however, a visit to her busy kitchen might be genuinely interesting to the reader.

Newspaper editors always have to keep in mind that their
readership includes members of all religious groups, many
of whom have strong doctrinal feelings, and that any reference to denominational rivalry or theological controversy
usually evokes a sensitive response. Any editor who has
been visited by an irate delegation that claims its denomination has been treated unfairly in a news or feature story is
not likely to forget the experience.

In coping with the strictly enforced rule against engen-
dering controversy, therefore, the religious writer does well
to avoid any invidious comparison of one religious group
with another, directly or indirectly.

A feature story which tells about a remarkable record of
giving attained by members of a local church should not as-
sert that the church has set a new record for benevolences,
unless that record is within the church's own denomination
and is substantiated by an official report or citation. It is
better to say that the "First Community Church has found
a new way to increase its benevolences" or to say that it has

"attained a very high goal," even if this is an understatement. This avoids making a direct comparison with other churches and thereby allays jealous antagonism.

Similarly, a story which tells about twenty-five years of service by a local pastor may relate the fact that he received several hundred persons into membership, and conducted many baptisms, but should never state that he has made "conversions." This would suggest that he has been proselyting from other faiths. Even if this is true, it would be best to avoid mention because it would arouse animosity from followers of other creeds and thereby undo the good public relations which the article might create.

These inhibitions against invidious reflections on other churches and creeds should be scrupulously observed by the writer of religious features, lest editors become hostile to religious stories on the ground that they breed community controversy, and lest the feature story itself lose its effectiveness in promoting the cause of religion.

Secular Magazines

The religious feature writer is finding an increasing market for his stories in the nation's secular magazines. This is a reflection of the increased interest in religion that has been evident throughout the United States in the past few years.

The magazine feature is more adaptable than the newspaper story. It can be longer, because a magazine has more space. An article of two to three thousand words does not look so formidable to the reader when spread over the width of the magazine page as when confined to the long, narrow columns of the newspaper. The horizon is also wider from the standpoint of subject matter. A daily newspaper must be concerned principally with the events and developments that occur in its immediate local circulation area. Most magazines are national in scope, and while each caters to a particular level of readership, the subjects they are prepared to cover are of broader range. The time factor is not so important, since most magazines operate with deadlines from six weeks to three months ahead of the date of publication, made necessary by their long press runs and distribution problems. Finally, the magazine feature may be more flexible as to the structure of the lead and the story outline.

Magazine editors are attracted by the unusual and the colorful. Unfortunately, the article that might be most useful to religion or the most important from the serious theological viewpoint is not that which will necessarily attract the typical magazine editor.

The writer has to adapt himself to the requirements of the popular magazine field. A serious piece about the progress of the ecumenical movement among Protestant churches would ordinarily be rejected by a popular magazine, with the suggestion that it be offered to a scholarly journal read by Ph.D.'s or Th.D.'s. But a clever writer can make the ecumenical movement interesting to the average layman.

Dr. Caspar Nannes, church editor of the Washington, D.C., *Evening Star*, showed that it could when he sold *Collier's* a story under the title "Will All Protestants Unite in One Church Some Day?" His conclusion was in the negative, of course, but in the process of answering the question, he detailed the progress being made toward federation within Protestantism and quoted many religious leaders as to the objectives of the ecumenical movement.

By giving his article such a catchy lead, Dr. Nannes interested all readers. The title shocked people. It encouraged those who thought Protestantism should unite and appalled those who held special devotion to their own creeds. It attracted Roman Catholics and Jews who were curious to get a glimpse of what was going on among Protestants. In short, the article was given that wide reader appeal which a national magazine considers essential for publication of an article on any subject.

In the religious field, magazine editors are most attracted by the "unusual person" type of feature story. Dr. Billy Graham, the noted evangelist, has been the subject of feature stories in several national magazines because he is such an unusual and dynamic personality. Dr. Norman Vincent Peale, Bishop Fulton J. Sheen, and Dr. Albert Schweitzer, the great missionary, have also been the subject of features in popular magazines because they have become "celebrities" in the sense that millions know of their work and are interested in their messages.

Unfortunately, magazines are only rarely interested in stories about persons who are not "celebrities." The popular magazines are engaged in a grim battle for newsstand sales. Even the largest magazines feel this pressure. Unless subscription renewals come in on schedule from mail subscribers and unless the newsstand buyer sees something on the cover so commanding that he decides to spend twenty-five cents to read it, the magazine will soon fail.

The clever writer tries to take advantage of this. If this is the way to get a story about religion into a secular medium that would otherwise avoid the subject, he will search for such an angle. For example, if he wants to write about a minister who has an unusual parish along the rugged, remote, rockbound coast of Maine, perhaps he can put the lead on the fact that the pastor, in between other duties, has aided in saving several score of shipwrecked mariners. That would give it the necessary color.

A careful search must be made for a novel lead or a sensational angle which will catch the eye of the editor and his readers, but still stays within the bounds of ethical honesty. This is hard to accomplish, but with magazines becoming more interested in religion, the opportunity for serious feature stories is becoming broader. Magazines are developing more maturity in this field, as witness *Life* magazine's penetrating series in 1955 on "Religions of the World."

Inhibitions against Controversy

The same inhibitions against religious controversy that apply to the newspaper story are encountered in the magazine field. A story has to have general appeal to readers from all groups, and the less said about denomination or creed the better. For instance, recent articles about Dr. Graham and Dr. Peale have ignored their denominational affiliation, not even mentioning it. While Bishop Sheen's affiliation is obvious, most of the popular articles about him avoid mentioning his work with the Society for Propagation of the Faith or glide over it. He is not presented as a Roman Catholic figure, but as a universally beloved Christian preacher and counselor.

Magazine editors are extremely sensitive to any aspect of denominationalism and seek to avoid it lest they offend substantial groups of readers. The religious writer needs to be tactful in writing for mass-circulation magazines.

Another word of caution might be sounded. A number of magazines of the rather lurid variety, emphasizing sex and crime, have lately been going in for religious feature stories. The purpose of these stories seems to be to give the magazine a veneer of respectability it might otherwise lack. Here the religious writer faces the moral question of whether he should take the opportunity to get a few good moral topics across in a medium which reaches an audience that needs them most, or whether he should refuse to give any aid or assistance to publications whose over-all influence is certainly not uplifting.

A similar problem is encountered with certain extreme right-wing publications whose major purpose is propaganda, and which like to use religious articles that tend to support their views. "Use" is probably the word to apply to the basic attitude of these magazines toward religion.

This author once faced such a problem when a magazine devoted to the hysterical school of anti-Communism wanted to reprint a feature story he had written in collaboration with an ex-prisoner of war, entitled "How We Worshipped in the Korean Prison Camps." Although the story was an epic of the courage with which some young Americans faced their Communist captors, this writer finally decided that to contribute anything to the magazine in question would be a disservice to the over-all cause of advancing Christianity and combatting Communism, and the manuscript was not sent. Such decisions must be faced when writing religious articles for popular magazines. To some extent, the writer can go along with the desire of the magazine editors for sensational treatment of the subject, but at some point a moral line has to be drawn, even if it means losing a sale.

Religious Magazines

The largest market for religious feature articles will be found among the periodicals produced by church groups themselves. Virtually every denomination in America has a national denominational magazine. Many denominations also maintain special publications for young people of various age groups, for lay persons, and for missionary workers.

Several religious groups, notably the Methodists and the Salvation Army, publish regional editions of their denominational publications. The Protestant Episcopal Church has magazines for both "high" churchmen and "low," and there are theological divisions discernible among the various Presbyterian publications of the United States.

The Roman Catholic Church, in addition to its two "national" papers, the Denver *Catholic Register* and *Our Sunday Visitor* published at Fort Wayne, Indiana, maintains more than a hundred diocesan weeklies, some of which, like the Brooklyn *Tablet* and the Boston *Pilot*, have circulations that rival those of metropolitan dailies. In addition, various religious orders of the Catholic Church maintain publications, such as the Jesuits' *America*.

There are really a larger number and greater variety of religious publications in America than a writer might at first expect to encounter. Individually, these publications do not represent a lucrative market because their budgets are sorely limited. Church publications do not have much advertising revenue. Some have no advertising at all. They are reluctant to increase their subscription rates because their goal is maximum circulation rather than a financial profit. Many denominational publications are subsidized, some rather heavily. This means that the editor is under budgetary pressure at all times and has only a small fund available for "honorariums" to writers who contribute feature articles. To some extent, editors are realizing that they ought to increase the compensation of their employees and contributors in order to produce a better product, and that a larger editorial budget is an investment rather than an expense. Returns to the religious writer are still meager, however, in comparison with other media.

On the other hand, the growth of the ecumenical spirit among Protestant churches is being seen in the journalistic field by an increasing willingness of one denomination to publish articles written by a member of another. This means that a single article can often find an outlet in three or four different denominations, since the circulation of the respective magazines runs along denominational lines with little overlap. It also means that if an article is turned down for any reason by one editor, there is a chance that another religious organ may be interested in it.

Certain fundamentalist denominational magazines are getting away from the idea that all their feature stories have to be "home grown." If a denomination of only 200,000 or 300,000 members restricts itself solely to publishing what its own clergymen or lay members happen to write, it is restricting itself to a rather narrow field of talent in a population of 165,000,000.

In addition to the growing market among the denominational publications, the religious writer will find a market for his feature articles among the nondenominational publications, such as *Christian Century*, *Church Management*, and the various publications of the National Council of Churches and its agencies. These nondenominational publications are pleased to draw upon writers from all denominations. So do such publications as the *Christian Herald* (Christian Endeavor Society), the *Upper Room* (Methodist), and the quarterlies *Religion in Life* (Methodist) and *Theology Today* (Presbyterian), which have readers in all Protestant denominations. Thus, no religious writer need feel that he has to confine his work to his own denomination. The field is open on a broader basis.

The writer finds that there is an increasing awareness among religious groups of the vital role that a good church magazine can play in the life and spiritual ministry of its sponsoring denomination. For many years some Protestant churches have regarded their national organs as a sort of necessary adjunct to the denominational management, but have overlooked the vital role that the printed word can play in educating lay members and making them loyal and eager workers for the church.

In the writer's own denomination, the Congregational-Christian, the church magazine *Advance* has had a circulation of only 29,000 among 2,000,000 members. In the smaller Evangelical and Reformed Church, with which the Congregational-Christian Church is now merging, an alert, well-edited biweekly paper, the *Messenger*, has built up 67,000 circulation among 750,000 members. Not until *Presbyterian Life* passed the 750,000 circulation mark recently did Protestant groups really wake up to the fact that a well-edited, church-sponsored periodical could rival popular magazines in mass circulation and readership.

The increased emphasis upon journalism in the Protestant churches has been paralleled by a corresponding development in the Roman Catholic Church. Some of the ablest Catholic journalists have been recruited to staff the growing number of Catholic diocesan weeklies and national magazines. They are obtaining good results.

We should also point out the increased number of youth publications being produced by church agencies. Concerned by the lurid sex-and-crime "pocket" magazines flooding newsstands, church leaders have been increasingly eager to put good literature in the hands of their young people. These modern magazines for Christian youth are a far cry from the sanctimonious and dull Sunday school papers that used to be dutifully handed out at the church school door. Such teen-age and college-age publications as *One*, sponsored by four Lutheran synods, *Conquest* of the Nazarene Young People's League, and *Youth* of the Evangelical and Reformed Church have formats that closely resemble those of popular magazines on the newsstands.

These new-style youth publications are a market for the religious feature writer. The editors, always eager for good material, are gradually getting better budgets with which to pay for free lance work. In addition, the writer has the satisfaction of feeling that he has contributed something to the campaign against vulgar, cheap literature that is debasing the values of too many young people today.

What types of articles appeal most to editors of religious publications? An old stand-by that is always reliable is an article about a prominent member of the publication's own denomination who has performed outstanding service in some field and at the same time has remained active in church work. Editors of all denominations like this kind of story. If the article is really to serve a useful purpose, however, it should not be a simple "success" story in the materialistic sense, but should go into the question of how that individual has applied his religious convictions to practical everyday problems.

Thus, in a recent article for the *Christian Advocate,* national organ of the Methodist Church, entitled "A Christian Approach to Labor Relations," this writer not only told about the successful career of a veteran Methodist churchman and federal labor conciliator, Fred C. Croxton, but also devoted considerable space to his views as to what the Methodist Church needed to do to minister more effectively to industrial workers.

To cite another instance. In an article for *The Lutheran* about a United Lutheran layman, Winfield J. Hain, who had been elected president of the Collectors of Religion on Stamps Society (COROS), not only was his successful career as a stamp collector described but the usefulness of his hobby as an adjunct to Sunday school instruction also was stressed.

Feature stories about individual church workers offer a wide and varied field for the religious writer, and are almost certain to be published by the editor to whom they are submitted.

Religious editors also like stories which show the church playing an effective role in a new area of work. This might be a story about religious counseling among the mentally ill, or of social work among residents of a low-rent public housing project, or help to refugees being resettled in new homes. Wherever a church or religious organization is to be found pioneering some new service, the writer can find

a topic for an article. He may even be able to find an outlet both in the secular press and in the religious press for
the same article if it is sufficiently unusual.

In the Roman Catholic field wherever a priest or a nun
is to be found performing some unusual service, a sure-fire
feature article for the Catholic press (and quite likely the
secular as well) can be written. It may be a priest who plays
the saxophone for crippled war veterans in a Veterans Ad-
ministration hospital or a nun with a special class for handicapped children, or even a devoted layman who runs a hos-
pice for homeless men, but wherever it is a new or unusual
service, the Catholic press is interested.

The religious press also is responsive to stories of a general inspirational nature. Typical topics on which this writer
has written in his time include the new Prayer Room in the
United States Capitol building, the story of how the motto
"In God We Trust" came to be on United States coins, and
now on stamps and currency, and how Protestant churches
successfully fended off an attempt by certain zealots to
brand the Protestant clergy as sympathetic to Communism.
These topics did not have any special denominational angle,
but were of general interest to persons active in church
work. A multitude of such topics can be found by the alert
religious writer; there is a good market awaiting them among
periodicals of all denominations.

Observe Style

In writing for religious publications of different denominations, the writer would do well to observe certain elements of style that are peculiar to the various groups. If he
is sending a manuscript to a Quaker or Mennonite publication, for instance, he does well to remember not to address
the editor as "Reverend" or to use that term in his manuscript, since among the plain people such titles of address

are frowned upon. A Lutheran minister is always called Pastor, a Roman Catholic priest Father, and a Church of Christ minister is called an evangelist, never a clergyman. An article submitted to the denominational organ of a conservative, fundamentalist church would do well to quote appropriate verses of Scripture at every turn.

In short, the writer should inform himself as to the doctrines and beliefs of the various denominations in order to avoid giving unintentional offense.

In marketing his manuscripts, the religious writer should not be discouraged if editors of church publications are slow in replying. Most of them have more correspondence than they can handle and often give the appearance of being rude because they are pressed for time. While an author finds that the material reward is small, unless he sells the same article (or versions of it) to two or three denominational editors, he will have the satisfaction of seeing his material in print, a most real satisfaction to the writer who has received several rejection slips in a row from secular publications. The young writer, especially, finds religious publications a useful field for practice.

The religious feature writer, like all other writers about religion, has a greater goal than material reward and such small measure of fame as may come to him by contributing religious articles to various publications. He is using his talents in furthering the cause of God's kingdom. He recognizes that all church groups are seeking to further the moral order of society at a time when there are many disintegrating forces present in the world. He is trying to bring people who read his work a sense of inspiration and faith. The intangible rewards are perhaps greater than in any other type of writing.

Glenn D. Everett has been writing feature stories and articles for religious publications for more than a decade. He has contributed them to the *Christian Century*, *Christian Advocate*, *The Messenger*, *The Lutheran*, *Advance*, *Presbyterian Record*, and many others. His work also has appeared in the *Saturday Evening Post*, *Look*, *Pageant*, and other secular magazines. In addition, as Washington correspondent for Religious News Service, he frequently writes features on Catholic subjects that are carried widely in the Roman Catholic press, and other features that appear in Protestant publications generally and in numerous daily papers. His work also has been picked up by the Jewish Telegraph Agency. Mr. Everett writes the monthly feature story column, "Religion in Stamps," which appears in fifteen different denominational publications. Except for his RNS work, all his religious writing is a spare-time avocation. He earns most of his living by serving as political correspondent for a string of Ohio newspapers. He has been a member of the Congressional press galleries and White House Correspondents Association since 1945.

CHAPTER *Ten*

Editorial Writing about Religion

SAUL BERNSTEIN

The title of this chapter can be employed to cover a wide and diverse range of journalistic interests. The occasion to editorialize about so pivotal a force in human life as religion can and does arise in literary and journalistic media of every kind.

Practically all periodicals are committed to social, political, or ideological premises of one kind or another; the editorials which appear in them, however objective in treatment, are bound to be consistent with these premises. Making due allowance for this common qualification, one must recognize a radical distinction between the general periodical and the religious organ. The former is, so to speak, an end in itself; all of its contents must, as a first and last condition, serve the interests of the publication from a purely literary or journalistic point of view. With the religious organ the case is reversed. Here the primary need to be served is that of the creed, denomination, movement, or institution for which the publication speaks; literary or journalistic values are secondary. This factor applies to all contents of such publications, but with especial force to their editorials.

Primary Function

We can see in the above premise the first function of the editorial in religious media—that of applying to given topics and issues the teachings or viewpoint of the sponsoring agency, and that of appraising given developments in terms of the interests and values of the cause for which the publication speaks.

This premise, of course, does not signify that the canons of good editorial writing which apply in general do not apply also in the religious field. For the most part they do —but always subordinate to those special criteria which apply to religious media. Indeed, the measure of success achieved by the editorial pages of religious publications can be seen in the extent to which the principles of good editorial writing are made to serve the cause of the publication.

Qualifications of the Editorialist

From the foregoing it will be apparent that those who undertake editorial writing about religion must themselves possess corresponding qualifications, without which they cannot successfully function. To speak, editorially, for a religious cause, one must identify himself completely with that cause. Mere "acceptance" or appreciation of the cause is not enough. The editorialist must have comprehensive knowledge and deep understanding of his creed, but more than that, because religion is rooted in the spiritual rather than the intellectual realm, he must be moved by profound conviction. It goes without saying that he must have—or must be able to develop—the technical literary skills called for by his job. He must have a fund of broad human knowledge and experience, for the religious editorialist is engaged in the broadest area of human concern. And beyond all these, he must be endowed with such insight and judgment as will enable him to navigate the internal currents and crosscurrents of his movement while retaining, and transmitting, his higher perspective and sense of ultimate direction.

Editorial Responsibility

In this last statement we find the broader function of the religious editorial. It must bring to its cause *perspective, direction,* and above all, *leadership.* It must think through the problems which face the movement; it must defend the cause and advance its collective thinking.

Yet we must remember that in most cases the editorship of the religious periodical is not invested with independent authority. In varying degrees, the editorial in a religious publication is the voice of a formally constituted denominational leadership. Shall the editorial writer then simply form a literary echo for the ideas, utterances, definitions, and judgments formulated by others? Is he to consider himself minus the responsibility of exercising individual judgment? There can be no categorical answer to these questions. The situation varies with each denomination or movement, with each publication, and with each editorial staff. But in viewing these points, we must now take cognizance of the third function of the religious editorial: to effect the maximum of influence over the mind of the reader.

Here we enter into the field of creative writing and journalistic skill. Whatever may be the structure, doctrines, and purposes of the group sponsoring the publication, and whatever types of personalities may be responsible for the publication, it must be assumed that they do want their periodical, and specifically its editorials, to bear the greatest possible impact. In pursuing this aim it must sooner or later be realized that editorial writing characterized by individuality of approach is far more apt to achieve the desired purpose than is a mechanical technique, however expertly done. The religious editorial, no less than that in the general periodical, must bear the flavor of personality, of a distinctive individuality functioning vitally within its orbit. The editorial pages of a religious publication should not be and cannot be a free forum; yet, to function successfully, its editorial writers must be granted wide latitude for the formulation and expression, within a defined sphere, of their assignments.

It is in the nature of things that few religious editorial writers can expect to achieve the degree of editorial independence under which they believe they can achieve their best work. The religious editorial bears a heavy responsibility—to its creedal cause, to all those of the past, the present, and the future who belong to that cause, to the ecclesiastical authorities and governing board of the movement or institution, to their own publication, and to the community at large. Few are the individuals who are equipped to bear alone so great a trust, even were there governing or editorial boards willing to freely delegate an unencumbered responsibility. More realistically, the editorial writer must attune himself to his harness and strive to earn for himself a pretty free rein.

Granted, then, a fair modicum of independence, the writer of religious editorials is in a good position to capitalize upon his opportunities. He has at least partial choice of topic, a voice, at least, in its ideological or theological interpretation; the literary approach is likely to be left to his discretion—in short, he enjoys pretty free rein in *writing* his editorials, even if, as is likely to be the case, final decision as to publication lies with others! Let the editorialist ever be prepared to see some of his best efforts—as he in his human vanity judges them—land in the wastebasket. He will find ample compensations, among which may be, from time to time, plaudits for editorials as to whose merits he himself had had qualms of doubt.

"*What*" and "*How*"

We have spoken of the primary functions of the editorial and of the equipment and working conditions, as it were, of the editorial writer. Now we must consider the "what" and the "how" of the religious editorial. Here we find ourselves in areas in which few general statements can apply. No two religious bodies are alike; no two religious publications are alike; no two editorial pages can (or should) be alike. Charting our path with such broad principles as are applicable, we must lean heavily on common sense and journalistic instinct to instruct us.

One dictionary which lies before the writer defines "editorial" as "an article written by an editor." One finds that definition helpful, insofar as it states one of the things which an editorial must not appear to be! While the importance of individuality in the field of the religious editorial has been stressed, the personality to be conveyed is that of the publication, not of a given man or woman. Let all other contents of the publication speak for their authors. An editorial is a publication speaking; a religious editorial is a religious force speaking.

What Is an Editorial?

A more acceptable definition of the editorial than that quoted above reads:

> An editorial is a journalistic essay which comments on the news. It has the three common purposes of other types of journalistic material: to inform, influence, and even to entertain. In form it ranges through the types of composition: narrative, descriptive, expository, and argumentative, with emphasis on the latter two. The pattern for the editorial is essentially simple: it has a title, an introduction, a discussion, and a conclusion, although not all these parts are distinct.

We would amend the foregoing to the extent of applying the editorial not only to "the news"—that is, to developments which have occurred—but also to developments which, in the view of the publication or organization, *ought* to occur. The religious editorial, particularly, will often have occasion to call for action in one or another aspect of the current scene which may not necessarily have been in the public eye at the time. But in any event, the religious editorial must often be directed to the advocacy of, or the opposition to—as the case may be—some specific course of action in one or another area of interest of the group for which the publication speaks. This type of editorial is the one most likely to arouse interest and discussion, both within and beyond the immediate circle of readership.

Outstanding examples of such editorials are frequently to be found in the *Christian Century*. Editorials of this publication bear a wide impact upon public opinion and are followed closely by the daily press and leading national magazines. *Liberty*, publication of the Seventh-day Adventists, while addressed to a more restricted range of concern, also offers helpful illustrations of the "action" editorial, as does also *Congress Weekly*, published by the American Jewish Congress.

The Audience

We know *for* whom the editorialist is speaking; the question to be considered now is *to* whom is he speaking? In the first instance, obviously enough, he is addressing his known readership—the subscribers, the people on the periodical's mailing list. For the most part these are sure to be the ones who identify themselves with the publication and its cause. This does not necessarily signify that they constitute a homogeneous group. In the case of many religious publications and the denominations for which they speak, the following comprises a diversity of social interests, economic classes, educational and cultural backgrounds, and personal viewpoints. Their common bond is their religious creed—a bond which may be the most compelling force in their lives, or may be merely an incidental influence, or some degree in between, depending upon the nature of their religion or their response to it. But even in the circumstance that their faith is the all-dominant influence in their lives, they nevertheless constitute a broad diversity of mentalities.

It is likely to be the case with most religious periodicals, too, that the readership includes a number whose association is but tentative, people whose identification with the periodical's cause is new-found and hesitant. Others among its readers are merely sympathizers, others again are simply interested to be informed as to the viewpoint of the publication, while still others are actually antagonistic, scrutinizing the publication for critical purposes.

All these constitute the more or less regular readership of the publication. Yet even these diverse elements do not constitute the total potential audience. There are those, both within and beyond the known memberships of the movement, whose interest and association is desired. More often than not, this element outnumbers the subscriber group, and any religious publication must ever hold as a primary aim constant recruitment amongst them. And finally, there is the public at large, to whom the message of the periodical must effectively be made known. First and last, the religious publication is an organ of public relations and its editorials must be the spearhead of its public relations objective.

Since the readership and broader audience of the religious publication is apt to be characterized by diversity rather than by homogeneity, it must be assumed that its editorials must be written in such language, style, and construction as will compel the interest of, and bear conviction to, almost any type of reader.

Addressing the Readership

In this difficult sphere, the editorialist is quite on his own. He can learn this technique, but he cannot be taught it. It derives from within himself—from his intellectual equipment, his knowledge of the subject, his familiarity with the subject of his writing, his ability to communicate basic ideas. He must dig deep into the substructure of events and human developments and derive therefrom some primary motif, link it, with sure, telling strokes of his pen, to its manifestations in outward life, and disclose its ultimate significance in terms of the values and principles of his creed. All of these elements must be present in the editorial, yet none must be apparent. Apparent only must be the thought— complete, logical, lucid.

Let "lucid" indeed be the watchword. Write, if you will, in a thousand words, or in ten, but let your thought come forth plain and clear, and, by all means, direct. Be forever on your guard against the pitfalls of words. Into what untold blind alleys is the editorial writer lured by the sheer magic of the words and phrases that issue, almost unbidden, from his pen! Think through, again and again and once again, the message of the editorial, aim directly at the target, use most sparingly of your verbal ammunition, never a cannonade where a single bullet may serve, and with each shot, with each sentence and paragraph, check and recheck: is this directly serving the purpose?

With economy of expression, never using two words where one may do, never using abstruse terminology where an everyday phrase may serve as well, with the aim of directness and lucidity ever in mind, the editorial will take shape for the maximum audience. But remember, this does not mean writing "down" to your audience any more than writing "up." The job is to elucidate the message—not to dilute it. The need to be intelligible to a mixed audience does not signify that the readership is to be addressed on a comic-book level.

It is to be expected of the religious editorial that it will exercise balanced judgment and employ temperate expression. While such usage is, fortunately, characteristic of most religious publications, others focusing intensively on the arousing of public opinion tend to take an extreme position and to utilize sensationalistic expression. The *Tablet*, publication of the Roman Catholic diocese of Brooklyn, can be thought of in this connection.

In the religious sphere, one deals with the basic elements of life. Sometimes the problems with which the editorialist deals lend themselves to the utmost simplicity of expression, and in that case should certainly be so treated. But although the basic elements of life are—being basic—profoundly simple, their manifestation in society is apt to appear much less simple. Too often do we find religious editorialists resorting to mere superficiality in the attempt to reduce a complex issue to familiar terms. The present writer holds that in so doing, such editors are not fulfilling their responsibilities.

Certainly, an editorial is not a scholarly thesis, but it is nevertheless an educational medium. While employing the most accessible literary technique, it must enable the reader to come to grips with the fundamentals of its subject. On occasion, this process must make intellectual demands of the reader. In the opinion of this writer, no religious publication of any worth need hesitate to do so.

True, grumbles may be heard from a few discontented readers—but no periodical can expect to please everybody all the time! A far greater number of readers, most likely, will signify their affirmative reaction to such editorials, and the ultimate result is bound to be heightened prestige for the publication and increased interest in, and respect for, its editorial pages.

For examples of this approach to editorializing, the reader may refer to the *Christian Science Monitor* and the Roman Catholic weekly *Commonweal*, and, with modesty be it said, to *Jewish Life* (Orthodox) published by the Union of Orthodox Jewish Congregations of America.

Length

How long ought religious editorials to be? This is a question which exercises most editorial boards and it can be answered only in the spirit of Abraham Lincoln's classic rejoinder to the wisecracker who asked of him how long ought a man's legs to be: "Long enough to reach the ground!" An editorial must be long enough to make its point. No less, no more. Yet, withal, the size, format, and character of the publication must have a definite bearing on the size and number of editorials. It is a pretty well, and wisely, accepted view that editorials should complement, rather than outweigh, the contributed articles or news features which must form the primary bill-of-fare of any worth-while publication. Good sense dictates that editorials in religious publications be few and relatively short, as well, of course, as being more succinct and pungent in style than the general run of the article appearing in the publication.

Topic and Treatment

Always a difficult matter to decide, needless to say, is the choice and treatment of topic. The problem, as this writer sees it, is one of superabundance rather than limit of choice, for in his opinion the purview of the religious editorialist is that of society as a whole. From this point of view, there are presented the following general classes of topics, whose relative importance is not necessarily in the order given:

> Outstanding developments within the group sponsoring the publication.
> External issues directly affecting the interests of the sponsoring group.
> Local, national, or world events immediately affecting religious interests as a whole.
> Local, national, or international developments of general interest, as seen through the eyes of the movement.
> Seasonal topics, in the light of the current scene.
> Social problems.
> Cultural issues.

It is to be recommended that in the course of the periodical year the topics chosen range as widely as possible over the above and other categories. Diversity in the editorial pages is an aim always to be pursued, for the good alike of the reader, the publication, and the editorial writer himself. We realize that this may appear but a truism, yet it is all too true also that the editorial pages of religious publications bear often an aura of monotony. Limited range of editorial interest appears to be the major cause of this unfortunate circumstance, which vitiates to a considerable degree the prestige, following, and influence of the editorial pages. It is a matter, however, not merely of topic but of attitude. The process of editorializing issue after issue over an extended period of time, under the confines of a restricted outlook, involves a degree of attrition which increasingly penalizes the editorial pages. The remedy for this ailment is surely not in attempts to transcend the bounds of denominational concern, but rather to constantly explore them and to freshen one's thinking again and again from the innermost depths of creedal lore and belief. Projecting reinvigorated understanding onto a universal canvas, the editorials will be marked by freshness and vigor of viewpoint, pertinence of interest, and timeliness of application.

Saul Bernstein was born in Salford, England, of Polish-born parents who had left their native country in their youth. He went to public elementary and Hebrew schools in Stockport, England. In 1922 he migrated with his family to America, settling in Chicago. He has worked in a variety of occupations ever since arrival in the United States and now resides in Kew Gardens, New York, and has an office in lower Manhattan. Mr. Bernstein's primary interest always having been Judaism and the Jewish people, he has pursued lifelong studies in Judaica and Jewish affairs. He has participated extensively, for the past fifteen years, in Jewish organizational life and in congregational activities. In that time he also has contributed articles to Jewish periodicals and to the *Universal Jewish Encyclopedia*. In 1947, Mr. Bernstein became assistant editor of the then newly established magazine *Jewish Life* (Orthodox), published by the

Union of Orthodox Jewish Congregations of America. Shortly thereafter, he took on also the position of associate executive director of the Union. He was appointed editor of *Jewish Life* in 1948 and administrator of UOJCA the next year. He has been serving in both capacities since.

CHAPTER *Eleven*

Reviews and Criticism

WINFRED E. GARRISON

CRITICISM AS A BRANCH of writing about religion normally takes the form of reviewing religious books.
Before discussing that topic, which is the main theme of
this chapter, recognition must be given to another type of
criticism, more ambitious but less distinctive.

A book or a group of books may be taken as the hook
on which to hang a critical essay about the point of view or
system of thought represented by the book or books under
consideration. Such an essay deals primarily with a body of
subject matter, only incidentally with the particular books
from which it takes off. It may take the direction of appro-
bation and defense, or of confutation and correction, or
may combine elements of both.

An extended piece of writing which thus deals critically
with a body of doctrine, or with a religious or theological

position, generally will, and ought to, develop into a constructive statement. Thus criticism of this kind merges with other forms of writing. This type of criticism does not need to be separately treated further than to say that whenever writing about religion or any other subject has this polemical or argumentative character, the first essential is to give a fair and unbiased statement of the position which is to be criticized. This attitude is a fundamental matter of intellectual honesty, but it is not easy in practice. Many otherwise honorable persons cannot resist the temptation to state a position which they propose to bring under criticism in such terms as to make it seem obviously untenable. No amount of cleverness can atone for the unethical character of this strategy. Indeed, the more cleverly it is carried out, the more inexcusably vicious is the practice. The commandment, "Thou shalt not bear false witness against thy neighbor," has an important field of application when one is bearing witness concerning a body of teaching, religious or other, with which one does not agree.

From this point we will proceed on the assumption that the second noun in our title is limited by the first—that the "criticism" with which we have to do is the kind that finds expression in "reviews" of books or other instruments of mass communication.

A Rarely Gainful Occupation

It should be said at the outset that reviewing religious books is seldom a gainful occupation. If the reader is considering how he may earn money in significant amounts, as well as how he may serve the Lord and enlighten his generation, he had better skip this chapter and turn at once to the next. Whatever it is, it can scarcely deal with a less remunerative form of literary endeavor than the writing of reviews. Reviews in religious papers are seldom paid for, and other papers do not publish enough reviews of religious books to make writing them more than a precarious and infrequent source of financial return.

The only chance would be to become literary editor of some religious paper which takes its department of book reviews seriously enough to employ a literary editor, and that is a slender chance. Being lucky, I held that post with the *Christian Century* for thirty-two years, but I do not know of any similar position. My successor is a young man whose expectancy, both actuarial and professional, is too long to make it worth while for anyone to wait for a vacancy there. The book editors of the better religious publishers, like the directors of the religious departments of those general publishing houses that have such departments, are constantly engaged in the criticism and evaluation of manuscripts, though not in writing reviews. Some of these men are among the most competent and conscientious critics. This is a profession of dignity and importance and, I suppose, of adequate emolument, but such positions are not numerous.

Let us assume then that the reader of this chapter, if it still has a reader, has a disinterested desire to engage in the reviewing of religious books and realizes that this otherwise rewarding activity is not likely to bring him financial returns of any appreciable amount. How shall he go about making connection with media and outlets for his work? And what are the essentials of good critical writing—that is, of a good review? These questions will be considered in that order, which is the inverse order of their importance.

What Not to Do

1. Do not write to a publisher requesting a review copy of a certain book, a review of which you intend to submit to such-and-such a periodical. If you have been commis-

sioned to write a review, the editor will send you the book. If you have not, you have no right to use the name of the paper in order to get it. If you do ask the publisher, he may possibly send you the book, especially if you have some special relation with him which would make it embarrassing for him to refuse. However, the editor of the paper to which you send the review will always resent your action if he learns all the facts, as he generally does. He does not want Tom, Dick, and Harry—or even Dr. Thomas, Dr. Richard, and Dr. Henry—cutting in between him and the publishers. He wants to receive the books so that he can examine them and assign such as he selects for review to reviewers of his own choice. Always and as a matter of principle I have blacklisted reviewers who have tried to short-circuit the editorial office by using the name of the paper to induce publishers to send them review copies of books.

The prospective reviewer has, however, a perfect right to ask the publisher for a book on the strength of his own reputation and prestige if he has a status or a connection that gives him reason to believe he can place a review somewhere—subject to the conditions hereinafter to be mentioned. He and the publisher will both have to take their chances in regard to the placing of the review. Persons who have independent radio or television programs devoted to reviewing books, or who conduct review columns, are in effect their own editors. Their relations with the publishers will naturally be direct.

2. Do not, except for special reasons, send volunteered reviews. Editors seldom use them. A review of an unknown book by an unknown reviewer cannot possibly be accepted by a careful editor. It may be a well-written article, but the editor has no way of knowing whether it is a good review of the book. Competent editing permits the acceptance of a volunteered review only when one of the two following conditions is fulfilled: either the reviewer is known as a

competent authority in the particular field covered by the book; or the book is already on the editor's desk but has not yet been assigned to a reviewer, so that the volunteered review can be checked by the book itself and some judgment can be formed as to its fairness and competence as a review.

3. Do not ask the editor to let you review a certain book because the author is a friend of yours. If he is a conscientious editor with the interests of his readers at heart, he probably spends a good deal of his time in preventing the publication of "friendly" reviews—and that includes uncritical laudatory reviews of books by his own friends. One is always glad if the author and the publisher are pleased with a review, but that happy result, when and if it occurs, is purely incidental. The sole purpose of a review is to serve the interests of the readers.

What to Do

To get started, write to the literary editor of a periodical in which you would like to have your work appear. Tell him you are interested in reviewing books of a certain kind and give him some indication of your qualifications. For example, if you want to review books on the philosophy of religion, you may say (if it is true) that you have a Ph.D. degree in that subject from X University and have taught it for fourteen years at Y College or Z Seminary. Less academic qualifications are often ample.

Do not say that you can review any kind of book or that you want to review "general" books. If you are not a writer with an established reputation, it will do no harm to enclose clippings or carbons of two or three things (preferably but not necessarily reviews) that you have written, so that the editor can get some idea as to how you write. If he is favorably impressed, the chances are that he will soon send you a book to review. He *wants* to get competent new reviewers. He will welcome your letter and if later you give him some acceptable reviews he will feel that you are doing him a favor—as indeed you are, for all you are likely to get out of it will be copies of the books you review, a few copies of the issues of the paper in which they appear, a certain amount of publicity, and the real pleasure of carefully studying a book that is worth the effort and writing a good review of it.

The What and How of Reviewing

1. *Two essential elements.* A review consists of information and evaluation.

First, a review announces that a certain book exists. The top-matter—title, author, publisher, and price—gives this basic information. Note and follow exactly the "style" of the periodical in which you expect publication in regard to the order of these items, punctuation, and the inclusion or omission of other items such as number of pages, date and place of publication. Do *not* single-space this top-matter. It is the editor's business, not the writer's, to give typographical instructions to the printer. Similarly, do not single-space quoted paragraphs in the body of the review; giving them a wider margin will sufficiently indicate that they are to be "set off," and the printer will appreciate the double-spacing.

The body of the review should give factual information about the scope and coverage of the book, its main "thesis" if it has one, and its general line of argument or the structure of its presentation. Principal divisions may be indicated, but it is seldom advisable to list the chapter headings. If the topic is one about which there are various schools of thought, the author's approach and position should be indicated. In many cases it is helpful to give some background material concerning the author. Do not quote excessively, and be careful not to quote out of context in such a way as to misrepresent the author's thought or distort his emphasis. In all this there is often opportunity for the exercise of one of the finest of the intellectual virtues, which is that of grasping clearly and stating without prejudice ideas with which you disagree radically.

Finally, the review should give an evaluation of the book's strength and weakness. This is what makes a review "criticism." That term applies as correctly to a critical appreciation as to an unfavorable verdict. A good judge does not find every defendant guilty, and a good critic is not a professional fault-finder. Criticism is passing judgment, not just "criticizing." The reviewer should modestly remember that his temporary role as arbiter tends to create an illusion of superior wisdom and to exaggerate the importance of his opinions. The author probably knows a good deal about the subject too, since he has spent some months or years in writing a book about it. There are few books that do not deserve to be treated respectfully if they are reviewed at all. The critic may deal drastically with some, but flippantly with none. He must not be too eager to exhibit his own cleverness or rhetorical ingenuity at the expense of the author. However bright it may be in style, the review must be a sincere expression of a considered judgment. The reviewer's sense of responsibility and his devotion to fairness may well be enhanced by the realization that a review in a periodical of large circulation reaches a great many more people than the book itself is likely to reach. Reviewing must not on that account be timid, but it must be responsible and fair.

One who writes many reviews will soon learn to avoid superlatives, whether laudatory or derogatory, and certain words that are inherently superlative. Few books are "monumental," fewer still are "definitive," and no book "should be in every preacher's library." There may be a few "must" books for students in their particular fields, but there are not as many as one might infer from the frequency with which that cliché is used.

Information and evaluation are the two elements of a review, but they do not necessarily constitute rigidly separate divisions of the text.

2. *How to start.* Start by reading the book. It is advantageous to make careful notes during the reading. Marginal marks are only supplementary to full notes. I have found it effective (though not exactly comfortable) to sit at the typewriter while reading a book that is to be reviewed. One makes fuller and more legible notes on the typewriter, and the necessary posture discourages merely passive reading. The notes should include page references. When the book has been read and the notes have been made, study the notes. Generally one will then want to reread many of the pages to which the notes refer. Pick out salient points and number them in the order in which you want to treat them. Then write.

3. *How to end.* The most important thing is to end when you have filled the space allotted by the editor. If he has been so reckless or trusting as to set no specific limit, stop when you have reached the average length of reviews in the paper in which you expect publication. Surprisingly few writers of occasional reviews know that an ordinary typewritten page with normal margins has about 300 words. Some who may know this elementary fact have never carried their arithmetical research to the point of discovering that two such pages would amount to 600 words. The "limitation of our space," to which editors often refer in their rejection slips, is no merely evasive excuse. It is one of the sternest facts of editorial life.

The predetermined length of any composition affects its whole structure and the scale of treatment. This must be considered from the start so that it will be finished when it reaches the place where it must end. The writer of a sonnet does not simply saw off his poem at the fourteenth line; he plans from the beginning to make it end there. The portrait painter considers in advance the placing of the figure within the fixed dimensions of his canvas. So the reviewer must think well ahead and adopt a scale of treatment that will not force him to omit important material at the end because he has used up his space in unnecessary elaborations at the beginning.

There is no standard method of closing a review. It is not necessary to end with a "punch line." A final sentence summing up the estimate of the book is appropriate and common but not imperative. Neither this nor any other pattern should be followed with monotonous regularity. The important thing in closing is that the complete review and the allotted space shall come out even.

Winfred E. Garrison has been president of three colleges and for many years a distinguished author and reviewer of religious books. Dr. Garrison was president of Butler College, New Mexico Normal University, and New Mexico State College, as well as headmaster of Claremont School for Boys in California. He holds degrees from Eureka, Yale, and the University of Chicago; at the University of Chicago he was professor of church history for twenty-two years and has been professor emeritus since 1943. Now he is professor of philosophy and religion at the University of Houston. Early in his career he was a staff writer and assistant editor of the *Christian-Evangelist*, Disciples of Christ weekly. From 1923 to 1954 he was literary editor of the *Christian Century*, where he produced some of the most incisive and penetrating critical writing available in American religious journalism. He is still contributing editor of the magazine. Dr. Garrison's books include *Alexander Campbell's Theology, Religion Follows the Frontier, Catholicism and the American Mind, Affirmative Religion, Intolerance, The March of Faith, An American Religious Movement, Disciples of Christ; A History, Protestant Manifesto,* and *Christian Unity and Disciples of Christ.*

CHAPTER *Twelve*

Curriculum Materials

RAYMOND M. RIGDON

TEACHING LIES near the heart of the true function of a church. Usually we think of two persons, a teacher
and a learner, participating in an effective learning situation.
But behind virtually all formal teaching situations a third
person works silently with tremendous influence. He is the
writer of curriculum materials.

Although usually unidentified in classrooms in which his
materials are used, this writer's thoughts help to guide the
growth of persons in open country churches, thriving sub-
urban churches, and great metropolitan churches all over
our land. Even as Jesus fed five thousand people with five
loaves and two fishes, our Lord uses the dedicated efforts of
curriculum writers in nurturing the spiritual growth of un-

numbered multitudes. Few writers of religious materials reach and influence as many people as does the writer of curriculum materials.

What are the requirements for preparing such materials? Few, if any, of the denominational boards have set up a list of rigid requirements for writers. Almost all of them agree, however, upon several highly important qualifications.

Essential to effective curriculum writing is a genuine Christian experience. Writing lesson materials, in a real sense, is helping another person to understand and to experience something which already has happened to the writer. To paraphrase words of Horatius Bonar, "the heart must overflow to give the pen full reach."

Effective curriculum writers, like those whom they serve, need to be growing persons. They need to continue to grow in at least four areas if they are to produce materials which can help to guide the growth of readers. Virtually all denominations require of their writers outstanding proficiency in one or more of these areas and a working knowledge of all of them. Exact requirements, if such could be given, would depend upon the norm of lesson writers for the particular denomination for which one writes. These four areas are as follows:

1. *Familiarity with the Christian revelation and tradition.* A growing knowledge of biblical truths and their relevance for life is virtually essential. An understanding of the sweeping movements of church history, especially the history, beliefs, and polity of the denomination for which one writes, is also highly important.

2. *Experience with the age group for which one writes.* Writers need an increasing understanding of the characteristics, interests, and problems of persons for whom they write.

3. *Knowledge of educational principles and methods.*

Curriculum materials are educational instruments. If they are to be used successfully in real learning situations, the writer must be able to understand changes that are needed in the lives of his readers and ways by which these changes might take place. He must understand clearly the exact nature of curriculum materials and the role they play in the learning process.

4. *Mastery of literary skills.* Writers need to possess a thorough grasp of the literary skills. In a sense, these are the transmission belt which helps the writer to project himself into the reader's learning situations. Without these skills the writer's outstanding mastery of the other areas might never be brought to bear upon the lives of those for whom he writes.

Successful curriculum writers are not necessarily authorities in each of these areas. Most such writers are persons who have been willing to pay in "blood, sweat, and tears" the high cost of continuous growth. This is not to discount outstanding ability in all of these areas. It is to say, however, that the beginner who is willing to pay the price has good prospects for becoming a successful writer of curriculum materials.

What Are Curriculum Materials?

Prerequisite to developing skills in curriculum writing is a thorough understanding of the exact nature of the materials. A writer who uses his lesson-writing assignment merely to deliver a moral lecture or to report on his biblical research is building his reputation as a curriculum writer on an insecure foundation.

Vieth defines religious curriculum as "all those materials, activities and experiences which are initiated or utilized by the church for the achievement of the aims of Christian education." [1] Thus by curriculum materials we mean printed materials which a church uses in achieving its goals in Christian education. By common usage, the term refers to Sunday school lessons and leadership helps and lesson or program materials for use in the other educational organizations of the church. A classification of these materials appears later in this section.

The church's objectives of religious education have not always called for printed materials other than the Bible itself. Early in the nineteenth century, when the Sunday school became an organization of the church, memorization of Scripture verses was virtually the only curriculum of the school. With the belief that undirected, indiscriminate memorization of the Holy Scriptures shapes conduct, children were urged, through an intricate system of penalties, rewards, and recognitions, to memorize long passages of Scripture. The *Fourth Annual Report of the New York Sunday School Union* reported, in 1820, that a seven-year-old boy recited 1,003 verses of Scripture in eight weeks.

Growing dissatisfaction with memorization was accompanied by an increased interest in the "selected Scripture plan." In this plan, a committee, appointed by the American Sunday School Union, specified special Scripture passages for study in the churches.

The next logical step in the historical development of religious curriculum was the preparation of lesson helps to explain and to apply to life the teachings of these "selected Scriptures." With the establishment of the International Uniform Lesson System in 1872, the plan for providing printed lesson helps was assured a definite, important place in the scheme of religious education in this country.

The inability of most of the churches to prepare their own printed materials led the various denominations to

[1] Paul H. Vieth, "The Content of the Curriculum," *Religious Education*, XLVII, No. 5, September–October, 1952, p. 308.

undertake the task of preparing curriculum materials for use in their churches. Today, in this highly important function, more than thirty denominations co-operate, through approximately seventy representatives on the Committee on the Uniform Series, in selecting Scripture references and topics for use in Uniform Lessons. Approximately twenty denominations, most of whom are represented on the Committee on the Uniform Series, co-operate, through their representatives on the Committee on the Graded Series, in preparing outlines for graded materials.

In each lesson system, Scripture materials are selected by the lesson committee; the actual lesson materials are prepared by the various co-operating denominations. Each denomination is free to make any changes it desires in the references and topics selected by the lesson committees. For a more nearly complete discussion of the work of the Committee on the Uniform Series and the Committee on the Graded Series, see Chapter 8 of *A Guide for Curriculum in Christian Education.*[2]

Today there are many types of religious curriculum materials used in the churches of America. Some of the most familiar are:

1. *Uniform lessons.* Probably the most popular plan for Bible study in America, this system provides separate age-group lessons built around a central theme and Scripture passage. The lessons are organized into a six-year course of study of the major teachings of the entire Bible. Although critics accuse it of violating the "life-centered" principle, exponents point to the values in having each member of the family study the same passage.

2. *Group graded lessons.* Sometimes called "department

[2] Published in 1955 by the Division of Christian Education, National Council of the Churches of Christ in the U.S.A., 79 E. Adams St., Chicago 3, Ill.

graded" and "cycle graded," this system provides for a single, separate lesson for each of the age groups. No attempt is made to correlate the passages and topics studied by the various groups.

3. *Closely graded lessons.* In this system of Sunday school lessons, separate units of study are provided for each age level within a department. The organizing principle for the graded courses of study is found in the specific interests and needs of the respective age groups. Selected biblical materials have direct bearing upon these interests and needs.

4. *Elective courses.* Several of the denominations prepare a series of elective units of study. These units and the accompanying materials are designed to guide specific age groups in a study of special areas of interest and importance. The lesson materials are prepared in pamphlet or book form. They cover a wide variety of subjects, ranging from biblical archeology to Christian home building.

5. *Vacation Bible school texts.* Usually these are in the form of leadership helps for workers in the vacation Bible school.

6. *Weekday school texts.* The diversity of materials available in this field reflects the variety of plans for weekday religious education. Despite controversial issues in this area, weekday materials are playing an increasingly important role in the educational programs of the churches of America.

7. *Other organizational materials.* No cursory investigation of religious curriculum materials could include all of the many types published in America today. In addition to the ones mentioned, there are others containing program materials for use in Christian Endeavor organizations, Baptist Training Unions, youth fellowships, camping movements, women's organizations, brotherhoods, and other organizational groups in the churches. Failure to discuss all of these by no means reflects upon their importance. Whereas the similarity of Sunday school materials used in the various

denominations makes possible a general treatment, the diversity of materials used in other organizations defies general classifications and brief descriptions.

All of these curriculum materials grow out of certain theological assumptions and educational theories. Limitations of space make it impossible to compare and contrast the theological assumptions and educational theories of all of the denominational boards which publish curriculum materials. It is obvious, however, that a writer can do his best work with a publishing agency whose theological beliefs and educational theories are closely akin to his own.

One of the most controversial issues in educational theory is the "organizational principle" for the curriculum. If a writer is to prepare acceptable materials, he needs to understand the theory represented by the specific periodical for which he is to write. This is not always easy, for there are many variations of a few basic theories. Frequently, the difference is more in approach and emphasis than in basic viewpoint.

If a writer keeps in mind three basic theories, however, with careful study he can discover the position of a periodical in relation to one or more of them. These theories are:

1. That the "organizing principle" lies in acquainting the learner with and adjusting him to certain aspects of the Christian faith and heritage. Courses of study (and curriculum materials) growing out of this theory usually take the form of a logical organization of important areas of content. Applications to human life come only as they grow out of a study of the prescribed content.

2. That the "organizing principle" is in the needs of the individual and his immediate life-experiences. Curriculum materials representing this viewpoint usually are developed

around normal needs and experiences of average individuals in a given age group. References to the Bible and other aspects of the Christian heritage and faith come only as they bear directly upon immediate, felt needs and problems under study.

3. That the "organizing principle" is in the changing needs and experiences of the individual as these include his relationship to God, Jesus Christ, the Bible, the church, others, moral law, and the universe. Curriculum materials growing out of this theory are likely to use a familiar problem or interest of a given age group to introduce that group to a guided study of an important aspect of the Christian faith or tradition which bears directly upon the individual's relationship in one or more of these areas. In a sense, therefore, this view is both "person centered" and "content centered." This third theory is more than an attempted reconciliation of the first two.

How to Obtain an Assignment

Many persons who read these lines are experienced writers of curriculum materials. Periodically they are invited to accept writing assignments. They may choose, therefore, to skip the following lines and turn directly to the next section, which deals with the actual process of preparing curriculum materials.

A big question in the minds of other readers may be: How do I "break into print" my efforts at curriculum writing? The answer to this question may seem at first to be discouraging, but actually the opportunities are virtually unlimited—if the writer possesses patience, persistence, and the basic preparation.

In the research for this chapter, a survey of fifteen leading denominations revealed that almost all of their curriculum materials are prepared on an assignment basis. This means that opportunities for free lance work are unpromising. The reason for this will be understood quickly if one considers some basic differences between a short story and curriculum materials. Whereas a short story may be suitable for use in many types of periodicals, virtually all curriculum materials must fit into carefully organized courses of study. Some types of curriculum materials, such as a character story for use in vacation Bible school, might be written without consideration for the total course of study, but this is the exception and not the rule.

By no means does this mean that persons interested in writing curriculum materials are unable to do anything about securing an assignment. Most editors are constantly on the alert for qualified writers. If approached in the right way, editors welcome prospective authors' making known their interest in curriculum writing.

Four steps can place a would-be writer in an excellent position to receive an invitation to accept an assignment:

1. Discover the periodical (or periodicals) for which you are best qualified to write. It is obvious that no person can write with equal effectiveness all types of curriculum materials. Answers to these three questions will guide in this discovery: For which denominational board am I best qualified to write? For which age group am I best qualified to write? For which periodical, published by that board and for that age group decided upon in response to the first two questions, am I best qualified to write? (Watch the third question! There may be important differences between the form of Sunday school lessons and Sunday evening study topics for the same age group.) A careful survey of several lesson periodicals will help you answer some of these questions.

2. Write a letter to the editor of the periodical (or peri-

odicals) selected. Inquire about his plan for selecting writers, and ask him to send you available materials explaining the policies of his publications. Advise him of your interest in writing, and explain with modest frankness your qualifications. Ask if he would be willing to receive and criticize a sample of your work.

3. If the editor expresses an interest in receiving a sample of your writing, submit material prepared especially for his periodical. Unless he suggests a special topic, select one from his current issue and write your own program or lesson on this topic. Study carefully the theme, form, and length of the printed program or lesson, and seek to conform to each of these specifications.

4. Utilize advantageously your period of waiting for an assignment. Do not expect to receive an assignment by return mail, for many editors make assignments only once a year. While you are waiting to hear from him again, demonstrate your interest in writing curriculum materials by working in your own church with a group who would use the materials you would write. (You might even try out on this group some of your attempts at curriculum writing. Be certain, however, to write materials which fit into the regular course of study.) Use this time also for sharpening your literary skills.

It may appear that obtaining an assignment is a complicated process. Two things can be said in this regard. First, unless a person is willing to work in a face-to-face relationship with a particular age group, it is unlikely that he can prepare effective curriculum materials for that group. Moreover, most editors seek curriculum writers whom they can use with some degree of regularity over a period of years. It may require three years to get the first assignment, but assignments then may be offered each year for a decade or more. Therefore, the successful writer of curriculum materials has a regular market unavailable to most free lance writers.

How Materials Are Written

Imagine yourself attempting to write a chapter on "How to Operate a Locomotive." Although there are basic principles which apply generally to the operation of all kinds of locomotives, you would find it difficult to apply these principles, in one chapter, to all vehicles.

There are also several basic principles which apply to the writing of all kinds of curriculum materials. The very moment we begin to apply these principles to one special type, however, our suggestions become less appropriate for other equally important curriculum-writing assignments.

Thus it is not the purpose in this section to give complete instructions for preparing all kinds of curriculum materials. Although some of the principles that follow may apply to the writing of leadership helps and children's materials, space limitations forbid a discussion of these important areas.

As an example of how certain types of curriculum materials are prepared, however, let us consider some principles that apply generally to the writing of lesson and program materials for adolescents, youth, and adults.

Most curriculum materials are prepared for use in specific ways by special groups of persons. Thus an assignment must conform to definite specifications if it is to fulfill its proper function. You may save yourself—and your editor—time and heartaches later if you acquire a thorough understanding of exactly what is expected of you before you begin work. Several questions may help you to define the boundaries of your assignment: (1) *In which department in the church will my lessons or programs be used? What are the basic objectives of that department? What is* the age range of its members? (2) *What is the function of the materials I am to prepare?* Are they to be studied at home by individual members? Are they to be used as resource material for group discussions? Are they to offer guidance to leaders? (3) *What is the relationship of my assignment to the total course of study?* Are there established objectives for the course of study or broader unit of which my assignment is a part? If so, how is my assignment to fit into the total scheme? (4) *What are the topics, themes, Scripture passages, aims, which have been assigned to me?* (5) *What is the form to be followed in preparing a lesson or program?* (A current issue of the publication may be a convenient guide in answering this question.) (6) *What is the prescribed length and the deadline for my manuscript?*

These may appear to be obvious matters which every thoughtful writer will know. Yet most editors can cite tragic examples of misspent hours and hurt feelings that resulted from a writer's failure to understand these important specifications for his assignment.

Painstaking research is essential to effective curriculum writing. No successful writer expects to draw entirely from his own mind and imagination all of the ideas needed for a piece of creative writing. Research helps him to acquire new ideas and resource materials, to catch fresh, penetrating insights, and to discover dynamic relationships between the theme of his assignment and the interests and needs of his readers.

Four principles offer guidance in research for curriculum writing:

The first of these is *begin early*. Most writing assignments are made several months in advance of their deadline date. Experienced writers usually begin work immediately. This makes it possible for them to master thoroughly the

themes assigned to them and to accumulate a wealth of
ideas and resource materials. They do not expect to use all
of the material they assemble, but an abundance of material makes possible discriminating selectivity in the final
choice of ideas, facts, and illustrations.

A second important principle of research is *be thorough*.
Go to the best original sources dealing with the theme of
your assignment. If you are preparing a series of Sunday
school lessons, you will want to study carefully the Bible
material itself, the best commentaries dealing with your
assigned passages, and other books on related subjects. Serious study, through books and other sources, also should be
given to the interests and needs of the age group for whom
you are to write. Seek in your research to understand the
authors' central ideas; the practice of extracting brief passages from their context may lead to a misrepresentation of
facts. Objectivity is an important characteristic of effective
research. Seek to study with an open mind all sides of a
controversial question.

Another basic principle of research is *record accurately*.
One of the most successful plans for recording the results
of research is the use of 3 x 5 index cards. Place at the top
of the card the name of the author and the theme of the
passage or idea. Beneath this write out clearly the idea or
exact statement. If it is a direct quotation, be certain to
transcribe the passage exactly as it appears in the original.
Include all of the idea or passage which you think you will
need; do not rely on your memory to provide later the context or the details of an idea or passage. At the bottom of
the card, record carefully the book title, name of author,
location and name of publisher, date of publication, and the
numbers of the pages from which you are quoting.

A final step in research is *organize carefully*. Arrange by
themes or subjects all of the cards on which information
has been recorded. These themes or subjects do not neces-

sarily represent the outline for your manuscript, but they will be invaluable to you when you reach the point of preparing your outline.

Perhaps you have heard of the Texas cowboy who is said to have jumped on his horse and dashed off in six directions at once. Through a failure to clarify their objective, many writers attempt an equally impossible undertaking.

One of the most important steps in preparing a curriculum-writing assignment is to determine exactly what you hope to accomplish. Frequently editors assign aims along with lesson or program topics. If an aim or aims are assigned, the writer should study them as carefully as if he were a navigator plotting his course. If they are not assigned, he should work out his own on the basis of the titles, Scripture material, and other information received with the assignment.

A writer's aim is a brief statement of the specific change which he would like his lesson or program to make in the lives of its readers. Usually aims for curriculum materials are stated in terms of helping readers to develop or to strengthen an attitude, an appreciation, a habit, or an understanding. Almost any good book on effective teaching will include a chapter on aims. Most of the principles discussed in these books are equally effective in writing curriculum materials.

Four tests, if applied seriously, will help a writer clarify and strengthen his aims. These tests are: (1) *Is it definite?* Does it indicate exactly what I hope will be accomplished in the lives of my readers? (2) *Is it worthy?* Is the accomplishment of this aim worth all of the time it will require of me and my readers? (3) *Is it related?* Is this aim related to the general objectives of the unit, course, and organization in which my materials will be used? (4) *Is it attainable?* Through this writing assignment can I expect to accomplish this aim with any reasonable degree of success?

Good aims contribute to the success of a writer in several ways. One of their greatest values is that they provide a sense of purpose and direction in writing. With an aim clearly in mind, the writer has a valid basis for selecting and rejecting ideas and materials. Finally, a good aim helps the writer to evaluate the success of his work.

With his aim clearly in mind, the writer's next step is to prepare a complete outline. This outline represents the framework around which he develops his manuscript. The more nearly complete the outline, the easier it will be later to write the manuscript.

Obviously, it would be impossible to suggest a type of framework equally suitable for all types of materials for each age group. Generally speaking, however, most outlines can be divided into the introduction, the development, and the conclusion. In each section the writer should seek to produce certain reactions in the thinking of his readers.

In the first section, or introduction, the writer should seek to attract the reader's attention and to focus his interest on the passage, problem, or topic to be studied. The use of brief illustrations, life-centered problems, provocative statements, stimulating questions, and unusual facts are some of the techniques used to attract the reader's interest. In selecting his attention-getter, the writer needs to be careful, however, to choose one which will direct the reader's interest to a study of the material to follow.

In the central section of his outline, the writer should seek to lead the reader in a thoughtful study of the assigned Scripture passage, topic, or problem. Some of the ways to guide readers in a study of a Scripture passage are the expository, textual, and topical methods. An explanation of these methods may be found in books on methods of effective Bible study.

Program topics (and topical Sunday school lessons) frequently are developed as logical steps in a central idea, as several expressions of a great truth, or as possible solutions to an important problem.

In the conclusion, the writer should seek to lead the reader to a definite decision or, at least, to a realization that a change has taken place in his thinking. The desired decision or change will be determined, of course, by the writer's aim. If his aim was to help the reader to develop or to strengthen a habit, the decision might be to resolve to use certain available opportunities, possibly ones discussed in the lesson or program, for strengthening the habit. If the writer's aim was to help the reader to gain a better understanding of an important truth, he may seek in the conclusion to help the reader realize that he has acquired new knowledge and that important changes have taken place in his thinking.

Written suggestions for putting into practice the principal truth of the lesson or program can be both helpful and dangerous. They are dangerous if they are too superficial or if they do not represent accurately the real heart of the truth that has been studied. They can be highly beneficial if they suggest opportunities for putting into practice in daily life the main idea or central truth of the lesson or program. For example, at the close of a lesson or program on race relations, the writer might suggest that the reader study his attitude each time he is associated with a member of another race during the following week to see if his attitude is consistent with the Christian principles discussed in the lesson.

The writer who is thorough in research and careful in outlining discovers the writing of his manuscript to be a pleasant and gratifying experience. Freed from the toil of discovering and organizing ideas and materials, he is able to devote major attention to those factors which give a manuscript the appearance of a finished literary product.

Readability is one such factor that deserves special attention and effort. During recent years intensive research has been devoted to the discovery of qualities which make copy more readable or easier to understand. Most experts agree that readable writing has at least three characteristics: (1) It contains words which can be understood easily by the average reader. (2) The *average* length of the sentences is approximately fifteen words. (3) There is an abundance of concrete (rather than abstract) conceptual expressions. For a discussion of these and other characteristics of readable writing, curriculum writers would do well to consult one or more books dealing exclusively with readability.

The use of fresh, appropriate illustrations also helps to bring your outline to life. A good illustration is a bridge that helps a reader to move in his thinking from an abstract truth to real life. Care should be taken, therefore, to select illustrations which present accurately the truth being discussed.

Occasionally a writer of curriculum materials asks, "How many drafts of my manuscript should I write?" The only reasonable answer is that one should write as many drafts as are needed to assure clarity of thought, logical development, and grammatical perfection. Thomas Gray is said to have written seventy-five drafts of his famous "Elegy in a Country Churchyard." This noble example of painstaking persistence should be an inspiration to every writer of religious curriculum materials.

What Are the Compensations?

Payment for the writing of curriculum materials usually is made on the basis of the total assignment. Thus differences in length make it impossible to state average rates per word or line. As an example of rates, however, one denominational publishing house pays $325 for a series of thirteen Sunday school lessons for adults, and $200 for the accompanying teaching procedures.

Actually, the greatest compensation for writing curriculum materials does not come in dollars and cents. It comes with the realization that one is influencing the spiritual development of thousands of persons in many sections of our nation and, perhaps, the world. In our day of strife, the curriculum writer points out the way of reconciliation to labor and management, majority and minority groups, and others who sometimes misunderstand each other. In our day of trouble, he offers encouraging counsel to the discouraged, distressed, and forsaken. In our day of confusion, he broadcasts to all who will read his words the glorious announcement that Jesus is "the way, the truth, and the life" (John 14:6).

The greatest compensation comes also in the deep satisfaction of working with and for God in extending his kingdom upon earth. Down through restless, turbulent centuries God has sought earnestly to enter with love and power into the sinful hearts of men. Curriculum writers have the deep satisfaction of being used by God in his redemptive mission.

Raymond M. Rigdon is editor-in-chief of Training Union lesson courses published by the Sunday School Board of the Southern Baptist Convention. His responsibilities include the direction of a program of training in curriculum writing for the approximately one hundred persons who contribute to the fifteen periodicals under his supervision. His graduate training includes study at Peabody College and Southern Baptist Seminary, where he

earned a doctor of theology degree with a major in religious education. Formerly a member of the Uniform Lesson Committee, his writings include Sunday school lessons,
teaching helps, program materials, and general articles for
various religious publications.

CHAPTER *Thirteen*

Juvenile Materials

HELEN E. HULL

A LIVELY INTEREST in non-fiction is not confined to adults. Librarians report that the interest of children in scientific and other non-fiction areas becomes evident now at a much earlier age than formerly, and continues, of course, up through the teens. This eager curiosity about all sorts of subjects has been stimulated both by stepped-up scientific and technical progress, and also by the educational trends in the public schools. Religious editors are alert to this trend and the Sunday school story papers provide a good market for many kinds of non-fiction. Some of this material is also being produced in book form by religious publishers.

Not all of it, however, can be classified as strictly religious. Much of it may relate only indirectly to the religious life of the child. This is due partly to a deliberate

173

attempt to guide the child's interests toward all wholesome activities. But it is also due to a lack of good material with a religious emphasis.

It is no trouble at all for a writer to become a deadly bore when writing for religious publications. Probably one reason is that certain taboos tend to force the writer into a groove both in vocabulary and in ideas. Don't misunderstand me. The taboos must be kept in mind if you are to sell your manuscript. But don't let them stifle your imagination.

Decide where you want to market your material. Then find out what causes that particular editor's hackles to rise, and avoid it like an H-bomb fallout. For instance, in the more conservative groups there are certain restrictions in the area of social activities which you would do well to keep in mind. Find out whether or not that particular group frowns upon dancing before you submit an article that mentions it as part of a social program.

If you plan to write daily devotional suggestions, it would be wise to acquaint yourself with the doctrinal beliefs of the group that edits the paper. But this doesn't mean that you have to use the trite phrases and stereotyped patterns into which all of this material has been molded for so long. A delightful book which may prick holes in your thinking and let the fresh breezes blow through is Claudia Lewis' *Writing for Young Children*.

Types Sought by Editors

Here are some types of non-fiction for which editors of religious publications are looking: the article, which may reach into any number of areas—hobbies, manners, how-to-do-its, ways to earn money, social projects, science, history, travel, and religious festivals; also devotional helps designed to develop an interest in Bible reading, books of prayers for children, photo-stories of teen-age projects, puzzles, Bible quizzes, games for shut-ins or for groups, and ideas for parties.

If you need to know what appeals to children within a certain age range, you can:

1. Slip into a public school classroom and observe what are being used as educational projects.

2. Visit the children's department of your public library. Get a librarian's list of books for the age level in which you are interested.

3. Read a book. Helpful ones in this connection are *What Books for Children?* by Josette Frank and *Children and Books* by May Hill Arbuthnot.

4. Attend, if one is near, one of the Children's Book Festivals held in spring and fall in various parts of the country. There you will find a wealth of information as to what interests children up and down the age range.

5. Use as another good source of information *Junior Reviewers* (241 Greenwood Street, Newton Centre, Mass.), a little magazine which, as the name implies, publishes the comments of children regarding the new books on the market. Needless to say, the comments are amazingly enlightening!

All of the above suggestions are but poor substitutes for the best method of all—first-hand contact with the children themselves.

Since juvenile materials vary greatly in form, no general instructions regarding their preparation can be given. So let's take them one at a time.

Articles

We will not discuss here the technical patterns for article writing, as that is done in Chapter 9. The structure of children's articles does not vary essentially from that of adult articles.

Choose those subjects which have freshness of appeal. There have been too many articles about stamp collecting, and too few about boys who have built their own workable telescopes; too many articles about how to make Mother's Day greetings, and too few about girls who have conquered a handicap; too many articles about how to build bird-houses, and too few about Negro children who have tried to find a place in a white community.

A good rule to follow in selecting a subject is this: Don't confine your writing to *things,* but write about *people* (or animals) *who are doing things.* There is a place, of course, for the purely factual article. But even this may be written with imagination and with some relation to *people.*

Take the *Saturday Evening Post* and analyze some of its articles. Observe that if a writer wants to tell about light-houses, he does not say that such-and-such a lighthouse is in a certain place, that it has served so many miles of coast-line for a certain period of time. Instead, he picks out William Jones, a lighthouse keeper, and centers the article around him and his activities. An amazing amount of information about lighthouses is injected into the article, but it is alive with human appeal.

Be sure, however, that you do not sacrifice accuracy in your desire to create interest.

For some reason, we have fewer articles submitted to us for our junior and junior high papers than for our college age and adult readers. Maybe it is because we are fussy. May I repeat: we do not like articles which sound as though they had been copied from an encyclopedia. Take nature articles, for instance. Usually they are written as purely factual material. But some months ago we greeted with delight a series of imaginative and charming articles about various animals told from the animal's viewpoint.

These were used in our paper for juniors (ages 9–12). One of them began like this:

> Deep in the depths of the Wonderland of Rocks, Bobby was born. The only home he ever knew was in the mountains that are called by an Indian name which sounds like "Cheery Cows."
>
> God used the sun, wind and time to shape the rocks of the Cheery Cow Mountains into the queerest shapes possible. He sent rain often and hollowed out basins to hold the water for His wild creatures. During the rain, Bobby's mother hid her kittens in a pocket of rock where the rain could not come.
>
> Bobby was a queer sort of kitten. He liked water; he even liked to dabble in it, and swim a little. That queer quirk was to save his life later. . . .

And again:

> The Gila Monster emerged slowly from his winter sleep. The spring sun was hot on his pink and black bead-like scales. He moved gratefully into the open where he could gain the warmth of the sands as well as the sun. His tail was shrunk to a mere memory of the rich pantry it had been when he went to sleep last fall. He must find something to eat that had come through the winter alive, for it was too early for the white-tailed doves and quail to lay eggs. . . . The God who made him the garbage collector of the desert helped him now to find food. . . .

These articles not only gave information about the wild creatures in a painless and enchanting way, but they helped the young reader to connect God with his creation. They had action and suspense.

For our teen-age paper we recently used a honey of an article entitled "A Simple Explanation of the H-Bomb," which started out:

> After you read this article, you will probably not be able to make an H-bomb by yourself. However, you should be able to astonish your father by explaining the H-bomb to him in such a way that he will actually understand your explanations. . . .

It was illustrated with line drawings in cartoon style, and pointed out in teen-age language and in concrete terms the difference between fission and fusion, and the principles behind the making of A-bombs and H-bombs.

Do you know any youngsters who are doing something unusual? We recently used an article for teen-agers about a boy who had built a mechanical man which actually washes dishes. Another article told about a couple of boys who are ham radio operators. And I saw one that I wish I might have used (someone scooped me!) about three youngsters, a girl and two boys, all around thirteen years of age, who had written, illustrated, and set the type for an unusually attractive advertising piece being used by a large printing press manufacturer.

Articles dealing with science, history, travel, handcrafts, personal conduct, religious festivals, art and music, may be written in such a way as to give the child a picture of what is happening in the world around him, and his relationship to it. He gets these things in school, of course. But there is an opportunity in religious publications to infuse the Christian viewpoint and philosophy into these same subjects— if the editor can find writers who will do it. Mostly he can't find them, and too often he uses the same type of material to be found in any secular publication, except that it is not as well written.

Josette Frank in *Your Child's Reading Today* says, "Books which deal with the penetrating problems or sensitive emotions have greater need of art and insight than those which remain on the placid surface of life." Yet it is in these very areas that skilled writing is hard to find.

Perhaps it is because a great many persons who submit material to the religious publications are beginning writers, hesitant to tackle subjects which get beneath the "placid surface of life." But with all the children in the country who face heartbreaking situations in homes broken by divorce, it seems too bad that we have never yet, for instance, received an article telling a child how to adjust to such a situation. If a religious paper has nothing to say to a child like that, should it resent the criticism that it is filled with namby-pamby nothings?

Personal conduct articles are a good means of presenting Christian ideals. Suggestions for summer or after-school jobs have great possibilities. Maybe the youngster hasn't thought of a job as a way of serving while he is earning money. Help him to start thinking in terms of service as well as of material gain.

Some editors like to have photographs submitted with the article, but only if they are sharp glossy prints that help tell the story. Other editors prefer to make their own arrangements for accompanying illustrations. Query the editor on this.

Features

DEVOTIONAL HELPS

It is an unusual day which brings any of this material to my desk, and yet it is the sort of copy we should like to use in both our junior and junior high papers.

Devotional helps are used both in story papers and in book form by religious publishers. Query the editor first on this material. Some editors prefer to have it staff written, and most of them have rather precise ideas as to what they can use.

Probably most writers hesitate to tackle this type of material for one of three reasons: (1) It is hard to explain abstract truth to children. (2) Considerable preparation and research is needed. (3) Knowledge of denominational beliefs is more vital here than in some other types of material.

First, let me explain what I mean by *devotional helps*. These may be divided roughly into three classifications:

1. *The short devotional meditation.* This may be written by using an anecdote as a springboard for the spiritual emphasis, or it may be handled in straight expository style. Use concrete rather than abstract expressions wherever possible. Confine the meditation to one idea. Don't ramble. Keep it brief.

2. *Books of prayers.* It is best to query the editor first on this type of material. He wants to work closely with both the writer and the artist.

3. *The daily devotional guide.* When a child is urged to make Bible reading a daily habit, he sits down and opens a book different from any other he has been using. He knows there are interesting stories in it, but where does he find them? He knows the Bible should tell him how to live, because his minister and his Sunday school teacher and his parents have told him so, but where will he find these rules for living? He knows it is a book which will help him gain a satisfying relationship to God, but how shall he go about finding it?

The books he uses in school are clearly and simply written, and they proceed in a straightforward manner from the beginning to the end. But not so with the Bible. The stories are not always arranged in any particular chronological order, and they are set down in the midst of other material which may be utterly bewildering to a child. The language is often obscure. Therefore, he needs guidance in his daily reading.

Probably the best way to approach the whole problem,

particularly for younger children, is to use some narrative portion of the Bible as a basis for reading. Then relate the Bible reading for that day to the child's own experience or problem, so that he will have something to take with him for the day. Give him an idea as to what God expects of him in a similar situation. Keep in mind the seasonal emphasis, and the activities that are usual at a particular time of year.

These devotional helps should be arranged in a series of short paragraphs for daily use—from fifty to one hundred words per daily paragraph. Give the Bible reference. You may even help the child locate it in his Bible. Then give such brief comment as you care to make, with a question or two to thrust the point home.

Frances Russell of the United Church of Canada has done an excellent job for the junior high group in her book *Seek and Find*. Here is an example of the way she has handled it:

> *Friday*. The disciples were Jews, and it was hard for them to realize that the Gentiles meant just as much to God as they did. The story of how Peter learned this is in Acts 10. Read what he says in verses 34 and 35. What about us? Do we honour some people and despise others? If so, what must we do? What shall we ask in our prayer? [1]

Someone needs to do an equally good job for smaller children (9–12 years of age).

If you have any new ideas for presenting this type of guidance to a child, don't feel you must necessarily stick to a stereotyped form. Just be sure your ideas are practical and on the child's level. Query the editor before going too far. You may save yourself much hard work.

[1] Frances Russell, *Seek and Find*. Used by permission of the author and the publisher.

PHOTO-STORIES

There will be more scope for features of this kind in the junior high group than in the lower age levels, simply because older children are doing more things that can provide source material for you. If you know about interesting projects in which younger children are engaged, you are fortunate.

A photo-story is, as you might assume, one told largely with the use of photographs, and will need *good* photographs as a foundation. If you can possibly provide 8 x 10 glossy prints, do so, although the 4 x 5 size will probably be acceptable. Avoid pictures which show too much evidence of posing. Be sure the photographs are clear and sharp.

Rely on your pictures to tell the story, so that whatever you need to say in explanation can be brief.

It might be well to study the photo-stories in *Life* or *Look* magazines to see how they are handled. Observe the subjects chosen, and the incidents selected to tell the story. Note the angles from which the pictures are taken, and see how unstudied and unposed most of them appear to be.

It is a good idea to send both vertical and horizontal photos, so that the editor will not be faced with too complex a layout problem. He wants to give variety to the finished page.

PARTY IDEAS

Sunday school classes are always looking for new ways to have fun together. If you work with children, you may have discovered some exciting and novel ideas for indoor parties or outdoor fun.

Give detailed information about the materials needed, recipes for refreshments, instructions for making party favors, and so on. An article of this kind should not be longer than about a thousand words, and some editors may prefer it shorter.

Both story papers and book publishers are possible markets.

GAMES AND PUZZLES

These are as varied as the ages and interests of children, and are published both in story papers and in book form. The only limit here is your own ingenuity. Avoid the commonplace, such as "Scrambled Bible plants" or "Guess who these Bible characters are." Make your games and puzzles "fun with a purpose." For good examples of "fun with a purpose" see *Highlights for Children*, a monthly magazine edited by Gary Cleveland Myers (37 E. Long St., Columbus, Ohio; editorial office, Honesdale, Pa.). These are among the contributions that have been used:

> A list of remarks headed "Signs of Good or Bad Manners?"
>
> A quiz entitled "Which of the Following are Paid for What They Do?" ending with the question, "What good things have you done without being paid?"
>
> A brief anecdote involving an ethical or moral decision by a child, entitled "What Would You Have Done?"
>
> A series of questions on the "whys" of rules, laws, and government.

Bible quizzes come under the heading of games and puzzles. Many are published in book form, but one publisher is producing Bible quiz pads, with sheets which may be torn out for use. The nondenominational publishers are a good market for this material, such as Standard Publishing Company, Cincinnati; Zondervan Publishing House; and Moody Press.

The materials discussed in this chapter are, in almost every instance, opportunities for the free lance writer. The only opportunities for staff people would be with publishers who produce large quantities of this material in book form for the religious bookstore trade.

Helen E. Hull is from Pennsylvania, although now residing in Indiana. Educated in the Keystone state, she later became secretary to Burges Johnson, the author and editor who also served as professor of journalism and creative writing at Syracuse University. Miss Hull took courses at the university as well. In 1937 she began work at the Free Methodist Publishing House in the Department of Sunday School Literature, as assistant editor of story papers at the headquarters in Winona Lake, Indiana. She has done layout and art work as well as having editorial responsibility for the papers, which carry much material for juveniles. Her own writing has appeared in *Primary World, Light and Life Evangel, Free Methodist,* and other publications.

CHAPTER *Fourteen*

Religious Biography

ROLAND H. BAINTON

IN MANY RESPECTS, religious biography is no different from any other kind of biography. The first question for any book is to determine for whom it is intended —for children, young people, college students, educated laymen, ministers, specialists? Obviously, the vocabulary, style, format, and selection depend on the answer. A book may, however, reach people on different levels provided the vocabulary is simple, the content profound or subtle. *Pilgrim's Progress* and *Alice in Wonderland* attract children through adventurous episodes or quaint situations, while adults are allured by allegory and deft nuances.

The next question is: who is going to pay for the book? If the general public, the price must be high enough to cover the costs of production in case the sale is small and low enough that it will not be too small. This may well mean curtailment of illustrations and technical apparatus. If the book is subsidized by the author, he scrutinizes every word to see whether it is indispensable—a wholesome exercise; but if the bill is met by a patron or a foundation, there may be latitude for the de luxe.

In approaching a subject for a biography one should inquire why he is significant and what one wishes primarily to convey through the study. The same individual may be approached from different angles. Erasmus, for example, has been included in "The Great Hollanders Series." A poorer choice could hardly have been made. Erasmus was indeed a Hollander but he never wrote in Dutch and prided himself on being a European. But a biographer who is commissioned to include him in such a series must of necessity unearth whatever there is to the point. Luther might more appropriately be treated as a great German. He loved his Germans and did much to fashion not only their language but also their behavior. Yet to treat Luther from this standpoint would be to miss the essential. He was above all else a man of religion.

Of course, religious biography has to center on religion, but even here there are choices. Is the man of chief importance as a mystic, an inspirational poet, a philanthropist, a missionary, an ecclesiastical statesman, or what not? And if he was several at once, where is the stress to be placed?

Master the Man

With the audience and the objectives in mind, let the author then master the man. In the case of a prolific figure about whom much has been written, this task may be one of many years. An author commissioned to do a biography for a series at a nontechnical level may have neither the time nor the tools. What then? Must the task be left only to the historical expert? Not necessarily. But experts must be consulted.

A life of Luther for young people once was submitted to me. I observed that the author had caused him to be called while a monk Brother Augustine. I pointed out that he was indeed an Augustinian monk but never was referred to other than as Brother Martin.

The author replied that some secondary work had so referred to him. I retorted that it did not matter what some secondary work had to say on the subject. What was the usage of the contemporary documents? The author was not in a position to consult these sources, which are in Latin and in German. My advice was in such a situation to apply to three or four specialists. If they were agreed, well and good. If they differed and gave their reasons, the author would have to evaluate the arguments. If they gave no reasons, there would have to be an arbitrary choice.

But this one point is plain: an author is not at liberty to pick and choose out of secondary biographies solely with an eye to the piquant and the dramatic, without regard to what is true. Nor is an author of even a popular biography to take the assignment lightly. Another person working on Luther came to me in a state of confusion saying that he was over-researched, having devoted to the task three months!

How to Start

When the material has been mastered, then comes the question of presentation. How does one start? No question is more difficult to answer. One may have to experiment with half a dozen different starts, and here it is helpful to try out the material on samples of the prospective audience. A biography, if possible, should be delivered repeatedly in the form of public lectures. After every such experience there is bound to be revision. A teacher can make a seminar into a guinea pig. When writing a church history for children, I read a chapter to our daughter, then twelve years old. She commented: "Daddy, you have stepped up the vocabulary. This chapter has no climax and reads like a reference book."

But, to return, where does one start? That may depend on the subject. If he is a widely known figure, one may perhaps begin with his infancy, particularly if the book is intended for children. In the case of George Washington, for example, one may bring in the cherry tree; for Franklin, the scene of the lad munching a loaf in the streets of Philadelphia while his future wife laughed at him through a window. But it will not do to start in this way with a little-known figure.

A friend of mine has been writing a book on Sebastian Franck, who was a mystic, a champion of religious liberty in the sixteenth century, a fascinating and profound figure, but obviously little known in the United States. My friend started off with Franck's childhood, referring to him by the diminutive for the name Sebastian, namely, Basti. Now who on earth in this country cares anything about little Basti? Somehow or other one must at the outset convey to the audience why this man is worth taking time for at all.

The author in our day has to fight for an audience. All of us are simply inundated with reading material; so much so that it has been said that the best way to keep a top secret would be to mimeograph it and send it by second class mail to the clergy. Nobody has time any more for the style of Sir Walter Scott, who would roam around in a forest for an hour without running into anybody. The question that must be answered is: why is the subject of this biography important? Then one must select some incident in his life which will bring immediately to the fore his central significance.

Suppose one were writing on Calvin, then one might start perhaps with his flight from Paris because of persecution or with his arrival in Basel and the writing of his *Institutes*. In the instance of Luther, the entry into the monastery or the decision to enter the monastery gets one under way at once. For Wesley, the early home training was so important that perhaps one should start with his mother and her household. There is no obvious formula. Decide on something and try it out.

The Body of the Biography

When one comes to deal with the body of the biography, the procedure varies in accord with the amount of material available. A life of the Apostle Paul presents a different problem from a life of Chrysostom, Augustine, Luther, Calvin, Knox, or Wesley. In the case of Paul, one must scrutinize microscopically every sentence and every word of the Epistles and of the Book of Acts. The sparse information has to be amplified through our general knowledge of the contemporary world. When it comes to the later figures, the problem is one of elimination. The works of Chrysostom in English translation run to fourteen volumes; of Augustine, there are eight. Luther's original works comprise eighty volumes, and Calvin's go beyond fifty. The biography of Calvin by Doumerge runs to six volumes, and MacKinnon has done four on Luther. A life in a single volume must cut drastically. The outstanding episodes, the essential ideas, the significant writings, these must be isolated for presentation. The number of contemporaries introduced must be handled with parsimony. A single individual may serve as the representative of a class.

In a life of Luther, Erasmus will do for the Humanists and Hutten for the German nationalists. The Roman Catholic opponents, however, cannot be so easily epitomized in a single individual, and in a biography one cannot be permitted the license of the Luther movie in which Cardinal

Cajetan is omitted entirely and some of his characteristics are transferred to Eck, who thus becomes a conflation of the polished, upright, erudite Catholic opponent of Luther.

This instance raises the further question of how great liberties may be taken in the interest of condensation and piquancy. If the sources contain a conversation in the third person, the biography may legitimately transpose it into the first person, but to construct conversations is rather too much. Sources may, however, be cut, spliced, and rearranged to get over the ideas of the subject in the briefest and most telling fashion. A footnote or a preface should explain the method.

Some authors try to let the subject tell his own story, and it is entirely possible to make biographies out of the letters of Erasmus, Luther, or Calvin. Yet doing so is to forswear the full utilization of our resources, because today we know more about the characters of the sixteenth century than they knew about themselves, since we have access to the correspondence of all their friends. If the subject of the study is permitted to tell his own story, it will not be adequately rounded.

Illustrations are difficult mainly on the score of expense. Unhappily today the highest craftsmanship of bookmaking and the graphic arts cannot be combined save in journals with a wide circulation or in books heavily subsidized. The cheapest form of illustration is the line drawing, and it looks best with the printed page. The woodcut is ideal. For the sake of having a larger number of illustrations, drawings can be made from paintings or photographs, and faint drawings may be done over again with heavier lines. Again details can be lifted out of illustrations. For example, take a scene of the last judgment, huddled with people like a village fair. In the corner is a tug of war of an angel and the devil over a soul. This detail by redrawing can be extracted and used by itself.

The deepest question is as to the attitude of the biographer to his subject. Shall he be cool, detached, objective, critical, debunking, or admiring, or even hagiographic? A middle ground is best. There must be sympathy. The biographer must so inject himself into the subject as to wish that he might act as nobly as his hero at his best, and to understand how he might act as despicably as his subject at his worst. For a time at least the author must almost become the subject, but even then, he must again stand off and endeavor to evaluate objectively. Judgments need not be obtruded. Ordinarily an epilogue will suffice. Let this point above all be remembered: there can be no satisfactory biography without fire, passion, sympathy, pathos, and affection.

Roland H. Bainton includes among his eleven books *Here I Stand*, a biography of Martin Luther, so widely read that it was issued in a pocket edition. Most of his other volumes also deal with the history of the Christian Church and particularly of the Protestant Reformation. Among them are a life of George Lincoln Burr, for many years a professor at Cornell University; *Hunted Heretic*, a life of Michael Servetus; *The Martin Luther Christmas Book*, *The Travail of Religious Liberty*, and *The Reformation of the Sixteenth Century*. Translations of several have been made into German, French, Italian, Spanish, Japanese, and Greek. An ordained Congregational minister, Dr. Bainton is an affiliated member of the Society of Friends. He has been a member of the Yale University faculty since 1919, rising from instructor in church history in 1920 to Titus Street Professor of Ecclesiastical History in 1936, the post he still holds.

CHAPTER *Fifteen*

Inspirational Books for Laymen

FRED D. WENTZEL

THE CHRISTIAN MOVEMENT, which began as an exciting adventure, tends constantly to become dull routine. The fires of enthusiasm and of devotion burn low and must be rekindled again and again. The exhilarating conflict with evil in ourselves and in the world slows down, and we must hear some new trumpet call to nerve us for the battle.

This change is no new thing. At the dawn of Christian history, James urges his fellow disciples not to be content with hearing the gospel and professing their faith, but to give themselves also to the brave business of ethical living. The Book of Revelation was meant to renew hope and courage in a dispirited minority facing persecution by a cruel and mighty empire.

In our own time, few characteristics of the church have caused so much concern as its lack of vitality and venturesomeness. Hence we have had such books as *The Lost Radiance of the Christian Religion* by L. P. Jacks; *A Call to What Is Vital* by Rufus Jones, and *Signs of Hope in a Century of Despair* by Elton Trueblood. We have also had a deluge of lesser books, mostly sentimental and theologically questionable, whose authors have too much counseled us to achieve peace of mind through a series of easy psychological maneuvers and through an attitude of irresponsibility toward the common good.

There can be no doubt that we are a generation in need of inspiration. Of course we need instruction and entertainment, but much of the instruction and entertainment we receive through books, music, art, motion pictures, television, sports, and travel does not seem to succeed in giving our lives meaning, or in lifting from us the despairs of our age, or in making us joyful, or in setting our hands hopefully to the tasks of the followers of Jesus in this atomic time.

After much reading and seeing and hearing and wandering, we are left desolate, our hearts are not in our prayers, our emotions are not robust and fiery enough to sustain us in purposeful effort. To use Trueblood's phrase, we are still in search of an "alternative to futility," some idea, some course of action capable of stirring us to the depths and empowering us to live significantly and triumphantly.

It is the function of an inspirational book to move us profoundly; to persuade us by reason clothed in emotion; to lead us to discover new power in our own natures, in the natural world, and in God; to "strengthen . . . the weak hands, and confirm the feeble knees." Some books that we should scarcely put into an inspirational classification appeal so powerfully to our emotions that they serve to renew our spirits.

Think, for instance, of *Cry, the Beloved Country* by Alan Paton and *Out of My Life and Thought* by Albert Schweitzer. One is a novel, pleading for humanity in race relations. The other is an autobiography, given primarily to the tracing of the progress of a fine mind from one grand religious concept to another. Who can read either book without exaltation of soul, without being confirmed in his belief in the dignity of man and in the grandeur of the Christian religion?

How to Write the Book

But suppose one sets out deliberately to inspire. How is he to write a book? Perhaps the first requirement is that the author himself has been caught up by a powerful idea, a dynamic personal experience, or an exalting incident or event in which he participated in reality or in imagination. In what other way can he be assured that his words will possess that emotional quality without which no breath of life can pass from one individual to another? Here lies the secret of effective preaching—not that the sermon is delivered in flawless language and with artistically proper intonations, but that the speaker describes something of significance that has gripped his own thought and captivated his allegiance. The same law applies to the writer of an inspirational book. He himself must burn with the fires that he seeks to kindle in his readers.

"Bear in mind," says Anton Chekhov in one of his letters, "that writers who are considered immortal or just plain good and who intoxicate us have one very important trait in common: they are going somewhere and call you with them; you sense, not with your mind but with all your being, that they have an aim."

If a writer has stood on a high mountain of emotion and conviction and wishes us to share the eminence with him, he should persuade us to make the journey by appealing to our minds as well as to our hearts. Religion is poorly served by authors who urge us to have faith without giving us cogent grounds for faith, who multiply instances of prayer magically answered, who promise us sure happiness in a world where sure happiness is an impossibility. The good inspirational book is rightly emotional in the sense that it moves us deeply, but it is also realistic and reasonable. It says to the reader, "Let us sing a new song"; it says also, "Come now, and let us reason together."

The style of inspirational writing is at its best when it is pictorial. That modern classic, *A Testament of Devotion* by Thomas R. Kelly, succeeds in being fascinating and winsome, although it deals with an abstract subject, partly because it is full of simile and metaphor, incident and historical reference. *The Power of Positive Thinking* by Norman Vincent Peale, though some think it lacking in robust theology and in sensitiveness to the ways in which personal fortunes are involved in social realities, has persuaded thousands of readers by its innumerable instances of persons who have presumably won this or that success by the kind of thinking that the author recommends. We are not greatly moved without "seeing," and an author enables us to see by painting word-pictures of one sort or another. Only thus can his dark abstractions be invested with light.

Some Examples for Study

For style, reasonableness, and high emotional quality, a prospective author does well to study such examples of inspirational writing as the following: the series by Elton Trueblood that began with *The Predicament of Modern Man* and which includes *Alternative to Futility, The Common Ventures of Life*, and *Your Other Vocation; Strengthening the Spiritual Life* by Nels F. S. Ferré; *Achieving Real Happiness* by Kenneth Hildebrand; *I Believe* and *About Myself*, both by Nevin C. Harner.

Denominational and other publishers of religious books

count themselves fortunate when material of such spiritual and literary distinction as these examples represent is submitted to them. It would scarcely be stretching the truth to say that the market for books of genuine inspirational stature is unlimited.

Let us examine a few books that have proved their worth, in order that we may discover what they try to say, how they are put together, and what are some of the reasons for their effectiveness. One of these books that appears most artless is *Let Us Have Faith* by Helen Keller. This volume was written during the Second World War. The author's purpose is made clear in the first sentences: "For those of us who mourn the wrecking of half a civilization and the noble values it gave us to serve it is hard to see good in the future. . . . But however dark the world may seem we have a light at our command. It is faith, and it is ours to do with as we will." [1] Chapter after chapter presents persuasive descriptions of what faith is and what it can do for men and for nations. The last two chapters are climactic—they command attention by their forceful insistence that faith is a responsibility for those who are alive to the elements of destiny in current events, and that the most essential function of America in our time is to be the torchbearer and defender of faith.

Needless to say, the power of this book lies chiefly in the fact that it reports imaginatively the personal experience of the author. This is Helen Keller, known and admired for her marvelous victory over physical limitations. She invites the reader to come with her to the high places where she herself has found meaning and victory. We know that she has worked her way "from doubt to truth as one who reaches a clearing through a thicket of brambles and thorns." But her book wins us also by a surprising evidence of knowledge about men and about history, and not least by its

[1] Helen Keller, *Let Us Have Faith* (New York: Doubleday, Doran & Co., 1940). Used by permission.

understanding reference to things that the author has never been able to see. "Though faith belongs to the future," she writes, "its energy irradiates the present, just as the green leaf pigment—the delicate link between the sun and life— permeates the vegetable world." [2]

Like Miss Keller's book, Nels Ferré's *Strengthening the Spiritual Life* [3] gains much of its authority from the fact that it obviously flows out of the experience of the author. This slender volume describes concrete "ways of personal, family, and group devotions," with an emphasis on family worship that is rare in devotional literature. It offers a "formula for spiritual success" to "all who need relief from worry, rest from work, and peace of heart for genuine well-being." What the formula means in personal devotions, in family devotions, and in daily living is described in detail.

One of the distinctive characteristics of this book that appeals to the thoughtful reader is what one might call social realism. The author recognizes that we are inescapably related to the life of the community, and that we cannot find fulfillment spiritually without a responsible participation in community redemption. "A rabid sectarian," he writes, "a racialist, a sectionalist, a nationalist shows by his fruits that his heart is full of something that is not Christianity."

Ferré's style is homely, friendly, unpretentious. He invites us to come into his home, and into his heart, and he deals with us as friend to friend. He talks sense. He does not get us lost in fine generalities, but keeps interpreting and illuminating what he says by frequent reference to what we know and what troubles us. Some books of this sort are hard to understand, and some present the spiritual life in terms of such lofty and mystical experience that we are

[2] *Ibid.*
[3] Nels F. S. Ferré, *Strengthening the Spiritual Life* (New York: Harper & Brothers, 1951).

awed and discouraged. This book inspires us to do better and more intelligently what we are already doing, and to undertake what we never had the courage or the wisdom to do before.

Achieving Real Happiness by Kenneth Hildebrand is deliberately aimed at a limited, though large, group—people who are "modern, urbane, competent, and probably successful by ordinary standards . . . above average in education and mental alertness." [4] It recommends the employment of both psychology and religion as resources for meeting the perplexities, fears, and frustrations with which such people commonly wage a losing battle. The author is a pastoral counselor, and as he writes he has "real persons" in mind, though he has "taken care to guard their anonymity."

This book is a well-reasoned, comprehensive discussion of the points at which the educated, "practical" man in our time misses the mark in his personal life, becomes the victim of moods, resentments, and anxieties, is overwhelmed by trouble and suffering, and discovers sooner or later that he is without health, without hope, and without joy. Such a book might easily be heavy and wearisome reading, but this one is not. The author attracts us with his analysis of the ills of mind and spirit, and assures our interest and our understanding by a liberal use of stories, incidents, and apt literary references and quotations. The result is that one makes a positive response; one is moved to say, "That is true," or "That I will do!"

The Development of a Book

No writing of my own has ever given me so much unalloyed joy as *Song of the Earth*.[5] It was the first book of

[4] Kenneth Hildebrand, *Achieving Real Happiness* (New York: Harper & Brothers, 1955).

[5] Fred D. Wentzel, *Song of the Earth* (Philadelphia: Christian Education Press, 1946).

a trilogy on rural life. Those that followed it dealt with worship and with recreation. I volunteered for this assignment gladly. It gave me an opportunity to formulate an inspiring idea that came to me long ago and has since been confirmed by personal experience on farms and in summer camps, and not least by the philosophy of "reverence for life" which Albert Schweitzer develops persuasively in his books. I had become deeply convinced that one of the causes of our modern sickness was our estrangement from the natural world, our thinking and living as if the earth and the sky and the sea did not exist, or as if they were all our enemies. I felt that what needed most to be done in order to bring more zest and significance to the country church was to encourage its leaders and its members to "come home" to the earth, to learn to know the natural order, not as a thing to be used, or as a monster to be feared, but as a friend to be loved.

In organizing the book, I tried first to present in pictorial language, and with whatever poetic power I could command, the idea of at-homeness with the earth. Then I briefly sketched the lives of three "brothers of the earth," Jesus of Nazareth, Francis of Assisi, and Carver of Tuskegee, fortifying what I wrote about them by quotations of their words, by several poems, and by an original hymn. I devoted a chapter to the "pageant of the seasons," spring, summer, autumn, winter. It seemed to me that I could contribute to the persuading of the reader by asking him to think about the "greatness of little things" in nature, and about the ways in which neighborliness between man and beast and between man and man could make country life rich, satisfying, and secure. I introduced a note of social realism by describing those who are "homeless on the earth," migrants, tenants, sharecroppers.

In the last chapter, "Spires Against Sky," I invited the reader to hear what I believed was the true and liberating gospel of the Christian Church with reference to the relation between human beings and the marvelous world that was created to be their home.

Throughout the book I made generous use of brief biblical quotations. I was amazed to find, particularly in the Old Testament and in the Gospels, a wealth and variety of references to the natural world, beautifully phrased and religiously oriented, of which I had not been aware.

It was plain to me from the beginning that for maximum effectiveness I must lean heavily on a large number of carefully selected photographs of nature and of rural living. More than a year was spent in consulting friends who knew how to take pictures and in examining hundreds of pictures from the files of professional photographers.

I profited greatly in the final editing of my manuscript from the comments and kindly criticisms of my son, my secretary, and half a dozen friends. In the writing of books I have found this an indispensable step. Discerning, sympathetic critics—and editors also—have helped me to straighten out my thinking, to improve a manuscript by changing the sequence of paragraphs or of chapters, and to clarify sentences that seemed clear enough to me when I wrote them but proved difficult or confusing to the reader.

Fred D. Wentzel, director of publications for the Board of Christian Education of the Evangelical and Reformed Church, is himself the author of several inspirational books for laymen—the subject of his chapter. *Song of the Earth,* whose genesis he describes, is the first of a trilogy. Dr. Wentzel, a graduate of Franklin and Marshall, Lancaster Theological Seminary, and Columbia, has been on the Albright College faculty, a rural pastor, and a worker with youth. He has been associated with Fellowship House, Philadelphia, since its beginning, serving as president of the board of directors since 1945. Among his other books are two of poetry, *To the Dogmatist* and *The Man of Labor and Other Poems;* three devotional books for youth, *Windows of Worship, Gates of Beauty,* and *Pathways of Prayer;* as well as *Epistle to White Christians, Once There Were Two Churches,* and *The High Cost of Democracy.*

CHAPTER Sixteen

Books of Sermons and Devotional Books

CLARENCE EDWARD MACARTNEY

THE CHIEF OBJECT in writing books of sermons is the same as that of preaching a sermon—to reveal divine truth and bring men to Christ. No better summary of the purpose of a published sermon can be stated than that which is to be found at the end of one of the world's most famous books, John's Gospel. There John, that apostle whom Jesus loved, tells us why he wrote his Gospel: "Many other signs truly did Jesus in the presence of his disciples, which are not written in this book; but these are written, that ye might believe that Jesus is the Christ, the Son of God; and that believing ye might have life through his name."

Another John, John Milton, beginning to write one of the greatest of religious books, *Paradise Lost*, was so stirred

by the lofty purpose of what he was going to write that he
began by invoking the aid of the Holy Spirit:

> And chiefly thou, O Spirit! that dost prefer
> Before all temples the upright heart and pure,
> Instruct me, for thou knowest;
> . . . What in me is dark
> Illumine! what is low raise and support!
> That to the height of this great argument
> I may assert eternal Providence,
> And justify the ways of God to men.

The first qualification, therefore, for the writing of a sermon is to be animated by a noble purpose.

One condition of writing an effective sermon is a clear
outline. The sermon is not a rhapsody, but is, or ought to
be, a unity, part fitting into part, one proposition following
another in logical sequence. After the outline should come
several rough drafts of the sermon before it is written, or dictated, in full. A temptation to which many writers yield is
to commit the sermon to final form on paper before the
author is ready for it. The old-time classic division—three
parts, like "all Gaul"—is still the best. Those who hear or
read like to know where the preacher is going, and see if
he gets there.

The preacher frequently is asked how long it takes to
write a sermon. Who can tell? The preparation for it may
go back more than half a century, to the days of his childhood; it may draw upon years of study and reading; on
rare occasions the sermon may come to the author almost
full grown, in what may seem to be a brief period. But
always there has been preparation, conscious or uncon-
scious.

"Reading," Bacon said, "maketh a full man." It is hard
to preach or to write out of a great emptiness. Out of nothing, nothing comes. Men have different tastes; but, as a rule,

historical, biographical, and autobiographical reading is the most profitable for the writer and preacher. It is well, too, to make notes on one's reading. To this end a file of subjects and references can be started; as the years pass by, material on divers subjects will accumulate.

The habit of some writers and preachers today of not using a text is to be deplored. It has distinct disadvantages, for it may create the impression that one has found a method superior to that of the preachers of all ages; it certainly does not help to fasten the subject in the mind of the hearer, and, worst of all, the "no text" method robs the preacher, at the very start, of that "Thus saith the Lord," which is a mighty help.

Although the author of books of sermons and of devotional books seeks to reach and help human hearts, men of all types and classes, he is not unmindful of the fact that a great many of his readers are ministers, Sunday school teachers, and Bible teachers, who read the book for suggestion and inspiration in their own field of work. And always there are others who seek help, comfort, and strength for life's daily battle.

The Writer's First Duty

The first duty of the preacher or writer of sermons is to set forth, explain, and proclaim the distinctive truths of the Christian faith. Paul, the greatest religious writer of all the ages as well as the greatest preacher, writing to his young disciple Timothy, spoke of the message he and Timothy had to give to the world as "the glorious gospel of the blessed God, which was committed to my trust."

Many sacred trusts are committed to men in their journey through life; but none so sacred as that which Christ commits to him who writes or speaks as Christ's messenger. It is his high privilege and solemn duty to proclaim the oracles of God and his wonderful plan for man's redemption, what the apostle speaks of as the "mystery of Christ"; not meaning that which is enigmatical, inexplicable, inscrutable, but that which was not known, and which could not be known, until God revealed it through Christ.

It goes without saying that both in the pulpit and in Christian literature there has been a great decline in doctrinal preaching, the declaration of what Dr. Thomas Chalmers, the famous Scottish preacher and mathematician, called the "grand particularities of the Christian faith." It was doctrinal preaching and teaching and writing which established the Christian religion in the world, and has kept it there.

Undoubtedly, one of the chief reasons for the present-day rise and flourishing of so many new and strange sects, with some Christian truths emphasized and others grossly perverted, has been the subsidence of biblical and doctrinal teaching in the older churches. The preacher or writer of a sermon which strikes the great chords of our faith will speak of God the Father, God the Son, God the Holy Spirit, the Soul, Sin, Redemption, Repentance, Faith, Immortality, and the ultimate and glorious triumph of Christ and his Church.

Today there is much preaching of what is spoken of as the "Social Gospel." The gospel has, indeed, social implications, and sermons ought to make this clear and press home upon men's conscience their social obligations. But this is no substitute for the revealed truths of Christianity, or for a true Christian experience. Norman Thomas, ofttimes candidate for the Presidency on the Socialist ticket, and himself for a brief period a minister, speaking once to a gathering of ministers, said: "For the minister a social conscience and some humanitarian enthusiasm are no substitute for a living message about a God whose love and power he has found not only his peace, but also his ground

of hope for the victory of the kingdom of God and peace
for all mankind."

Types of Sermons

An interesting and helpful type of sermon is the biographical. The list of books published today shows beyond
any doubt that men are interested in biography. And where
can we find such biography as in the Bible? To a large degree, it is a biographical book. In the Old Testament we
have the biographies of the patriarchs, the prophets, the
judges, the kings, the reformers, the warriors. In the Psalms
and Job there is not only biography but also autobiography;
and in the New Testament we have the biographies of
Jesus, the Twelve Apostles, and of Paul. Even a doctrinal
sermon can be well presented with a Bible character for a
foil and background. For example, Abraham and Faith,
Joseph and Providence, the Woman of Tekoah and the
Atonement. There is not an experience of the soul of man,
not a doubt, not a fear, not a temptation, not a sorrow, a
sin, a joy, a hope, or a triumph over adversity and death,
which cannot be taught by letting a Bible character do the
preaching.

Then there is the field of history and biography outside
the Bible: great theologians, like Augustine, and that wonderful piece of autobiography, his "Confessions"; the Reformers—Calvin, Luther, Knox; the great preachers—golden-
mouthed Chrysostom, Wesley, Whitefield, Spurgeon,
Beecher.

Another kind of sermon is what may be called a Sermon
from Life; that is, a sermon based on some incident of pastoral experience—never, however, violating the trust of the
minister's confessional. Such sermons deal with temptation,
sin, sorrow, disappointment, forgiveness, the passing opportunity, and turning points in life.

There is also the Devotional Sermon. It might be a sermon on prayer, on comfort in affliction, for there are always broken hearts; or a sermon on that almost lost chord of preaching and religious books, the joys of the life hereafter. After preaching some time ago on the subject of immortality, I met with a group of ministers whose churches had united for the week's Lenten meetings. The subject of the sermon was discussed, and, to my surprise, most of those present said that not for a long time had they preached a sermon on Heaven and the Life Everlasting.

The written sermon, as well as the spoken sermon, ought to have windows—that is, illustrations. The feathers on an arrow are not, as some think, just a decoration. They give balance and lift to the arrow and help it to find the target. The illustrations in the sermon are like feathers for the arrow. Nothing is worse than a poor, trivial illustration; nothing better than a good one. The purpose of the illustration is not only to make the truth clear but to adorn it, to make it attractive to those who hear or read. Bible biography is the best source for the sermon's illustrations. Outside the Bible, the field of illustration is wide: history, nature, mythology, philosophy; current events, too, provided the preacher and writer does not sink to the level of a mere news commentator. Whether it be a spoken or a written sermon, personal illustrations should be few, for the oft exposed personality of the preacher and author is apt to become commonplace and tiresome.

Quite often the weakest parts of the sermon are its introduction and its conclusion. A well-chosen illustration may stir the attention of the hearer or reader at the beginning of the sermon, and a good illustration at the conclusion of the sermon may sum up the message and apply it. It is well to remember that the greatest sermon ever preached, the Sermon on the Mount, comes to a close with an illustration —the two houses, one built on the sand and the other built

on the rock. Nothing could be less interesting, less calcu-
lated to catch the attention, than words about the context,
or different meanings given to the text.

One of the great preachers of St. Paul's in London, Can-
non Liddon, had a sermon, "The First Five Minutes after
Death." He tells of a retired colonel who had served in the
Indian Army. On rare occasions his friends would persuade
him to relate some of his experiences. After he had held
them spellbound one evening, he paused for a moment, and
then added, "I expect to see something far more thrilling
than I have seen yet." His hearers were surprised, and won-
dered what it might be, for he was past seventy and no
longer active. After another pause he said, "I mean the first
five minutes after death." After the same manner, there are
illustrations which arrest and hold the attention at the beginning of the sermon.

Napoleon once said that men of imagination rule the
world. However that may be, the sermon affords a rich
opportunity for sanctified imagination. Take, for example,
the matchless parable of the Lost Son. Jesus told of the welcome home the prodigal received; but the journey home he
leaves to our imagination. Why not fill it in? Describe the
long, hard journey; how now and then he became discouraged, and was tempted to give up the effort; how he asked
in vain for food in the towns where, on his outward journey, he had wasted his substance in riotous living; how he
stopped dead in his track once, and, leaning on his staff,
said to himself, "What if Father is dead? Then my elder
brother will set the dogs on me." Yet always he repeated
the resolve with which he had started, "I will arise, and go
unto my father." And so he reached home.

There can be no objection, either, to imagining what
Paul and Peter had to say to each other when Paul went to
Jerusalem and spent those "fifteen days with Peter." If wisely
done, a sermon on Heaven will be made real and winsome

by an occasional excursion into it on the wings of imagination.

One of the chief faults of spoken or written published sermons is overmuch quotation. Someone counted the quotations used in an able and scholarly address at the inauguration of a professor in one of the seminaries, and discovered that a large portion of the address was made up of quotations. They were all apposite and well chosen; but those who hear or read sermons prefer to know what the preacher himself has to say on the subject.

Many successful books of sermons are made up of sermons preached in a series. The Ten Commandments, the Lord's Prayer, the Lamb of God, lend themselves to serial treatment. A series on Temptation, Repentance, Prayer, Conversion, is always timely. Here again one can make good use of the Bible characters. There are single characters, too, in the Bible on whom a series of sermons can be preached: Abraham, Joseph, Moses, Elijah, David, Peter, and Paul. Such a series will awaken to noble music all the great chords of the Christian faith.

Like that Syrian bowman, whose arrow laid Ahab low, the preacher, God's bowman, "draws a bow at a venture." Yet he must do so with the prayer and confidence that his arrow will find some divinely appointed target; will convict the sinner, warn the tempted, comfort the brokenhearted, cheer the lonely, bring the wanderer home, and thus add another note to the music of heaven.

Devotional Books

In writing a devotional book, the author must bear in mind that such a book is written for those who may be advanced Christians. It may be one for family worship, now, unhappily, almost extinct, but once, and can be again, a blessed source of Christian influence. A book of this nature has passages of the Bible to be read aloud; perhaps also comments thereon, and brief prayers.

Then there are the devotional books for personal use. Such a book may be made up of prayers only; or prayers with a verse of Scripture. Probably the most useful kind of devotional book is what might be called a Calendar Devotion Book; that is, a prayer, a thought for the day, and a verse from the Bible. The best form for such a book is one which has a verse from the Bible at the head of the page, followed by a short comment upon or explanation of the verse or passage. As a rule, only one particular thought should be emphasized. On one page there should be a morning devotion, say for January 1, and on the opposite page an evening devotion. A good example of this is the still widely used *Morning and Evening Daily Readings* by the famous English preacher, Charles H. Spurgeon. In such books it is important that the print be not too small. This is a blemish in many devotional books.

In addition to devotional books such as are described above, there are many popular compilations of prayers, poetry, and prose passages.

Publication and Writing of Sermons

The writer must bear in mind that perhaps nine out of every ten persons who buy a volume of sermons are ministers themselves. Thus a successful author of published sermons has a great field of influence, especially upon young ministers. When he preaches in his pulpit the minister speaks to his own congregation, but if only a thousand copies of his book of sermons are purchased and read by ministers, he may preach to a thousand congregations.

In the sermon as preached and spoken there will be some things which ought to be deleted when the sermon is printed, particularly allusions to local events and current happenings. This does not mean that all such allusions should disappear from the printed sermon, but that there are many events to which reference is effective at the time and place the sermon is preached but not afterwards. It is well to remember, however, that since the majority of the readers of a printed sermon are ministers, the more the printed sermon retains of the form and spirit of the spoken sermon, the more acceptable it will be to the reader.

The style and the method of preachers vary, and for that reason there will be some sermons which require drastic changes before being printed, while others can be printed almost as they were spoken. My own printed and published sermons—and I mention myself only because I understand that what is desired in this chapter is something based on personal experience—through the years have appeared with almost no changes from the sermon as written, dictated, and preached.

Serial Preaching and the Printed Sermon

The question is sometimes asked, "Are series of pulpit sermons suitable for a book of sermons?" The answer is yes, if the sermons have real merit. A series stands a better chance of success than a book of unrelated sermons, without any common theme. The alert and hard-working preacher always is looking for a good series on biblical characters; the great personalities of church history; the Apostles' Creed, the Parables, the Lord's Prayer, the Miracles, and the events of our Lord's Passion and Crucifixion.

Although it may not in some cases be necessary to make many changes in the manuscript of the sermon before it is suitable for publication, nevertheless the preparation of a sermon for printing gives the preacher an opportunity to put more work and more prayer on the sermon, deleting what was weak and ineffective, adding some new thought, or clarifying what was not clear. The more work the writer puts on the preparation of the sermon, both for the pulpit and for the book, the better the sermon will be.

In Philadelphia, when I was at the Arch Street Presbyterian Church, there was an able, evangelical, and successful preacher at the Arch Street Methodist Church, four blocks below my church. This minister once said to a fellow preacher: "What do you do with your old sermons?"

He answered: "What do you do with yours?"

"When I get home on Sunday night," he said, "I turn both of the sermons for the day over and write on the back of them, 'Ye must be born again.'"

Not in jest, but in all reverence, the sermon that is going to be preached again, from the pulpit or from the printed page, must be revitalized and, in that sense, "born again."

It goes without saying that for his own honor and safety, the writer of printed sermons must be meticulous in the use he makes of other men's thoughts and forms of speech. If a preacher is a plagiarist, or a semi-plagiarist, it would be well for him not to publish his sermons, for his sin "is sure to find him out."

––––––––––––––––

Clarence Edward Macartney's books of sermons are among the most widely read in the United States. Author of more than fifty books, most of them volumes of sermons, but some in the field of history, especially the period of Lincoln and the Civil War, he is also a pastor of long experience. He has been pastor of three Presbyterian churches: First Presbyterian in Paterson, New Jersey, Arch Street in Philadelphia, and the historic First Presbyterian Church of Pittsburgh, where he served for twenty-six years, retiring in 1953. In 1924 he was elected moderator of the General

Assembly of the Presbyterian Church, U.S.A., one of the youngest men ever to be chosen for that office. A frequent lecturer in colleges and seminaries, he now resides in his boyhood home, Fern Cliffe, on the campus of Geneva College, where his father was a professor.

Writing Religious Material for Audio-Visual Use

CHAPTER *Seventeen*

Religious Radio

HENRY B. ADAMS

THERE IS hardly a more versatile medium than radio, yet fully three out of five religious programs are no more than a service of worship originating from studio or sanctuary. Unfortunately, such programs are about as popular with the average listener as the church services he does not attend. Such programs do not use writers, but the rest of religious broadcasting does need good writers and in some cases will employ them.

What Is Religious Radio Writing?

Talks of all kinds predominate in religious radio. The number of religious news programs is increasing. Religious interviews, round tables, and quiz shows are another important sector. Drama and music fill out the roster of program types now in use.

The writer finds his place in this field where the medium poses almost impossible demands upon the religious leaders who work in it. The pastor or church executive who delivers news on the air may not have the writing skill or the time to gather his materials. Pastors would like to present a brief daily thought-for-the-day, but the pressure of preparing 240 scripts a year is staggering. Drama is a specialized field. Few local persons are qualified to prepare such programs and compete with the best that networks offer. Music constitutes more than half of all radio time, and sacred music needs specialized treatment.

Except at the highest national level, budgets are almost nonexistent and permit only men who combine writing and production skills. If the writer can perform in the program, too, so much the better.

What then do writers sell? For national programs, writers are employed almost exclusively for broadcasts of dramatic material. At the local level, employment is usually confined to programs sold by the writer-producer to some church group or sponsor.

On the whole, writing for religious radio must be gratis for the present. Almost every professional radio writer has built his reputation through long years of voluntary writing with only an occasional fee. Only a handful of church councils now have any budget for broadcasting at all. Only a few sponsors are ready to gamble advertising money on religious programs. But the field is growing. Serious writers who make their work available can create a demand.

Trends in Religious Radio Writing

In its application to the Federal Communications Commission for a license, a station promises to provide a specified per cent of its broadcast time for public service programs, including religion. Free time for religion is generally given for programs provided by the representatives of the major faiths.

The station promises to give free time for public service, but it must pay for its operation from the sale of time to advertisers. Religious programs for which time charges are paid appear on the log as public service but also bring revenue. Programs on free time bring none.

A problem appears here. Paid religious programs represent only the groups with the biggest checkbooks—hardly a representative system and hardly serving the best public interest. The code of the American Association of Radio and Television Broadcasters recognizes the problem and recommends against the sale of time for religious purposes.

For many years, this policy of "no-sale for religion" prevailed in most of the nation's large stations and all the networks. But with television competition, radio networks and large independent stations are reconsidering. A new era seems to be emerging.

In spite of the reluctance of most advertisers to sponsor religious programs, advertiser-sponsored religion on the air is increasing. Religion is becoming popular everywhere, and advertisers are beginning to capitalize on it.

The growth of sponsorship also threatens to jeopardize free time. Managements are reluctant to give time free if it can be sold to a sponsor for the same kind of program content. This situation raises serious problems for religion, but promises more job opportunities for writers.

Religious broadcasts under advertiser-sponsorship are less likely to be representative of common Christian convictions than if they were produced by the churches. But there may be compensations. If professional writers take seriously their moral obligation to bespeak the main line of

Christian faith, losses at one point may be offset by gains at another.

What Is Most Needed and Valuable

Six kinds of writing are needed most in religious radio. I cannot say which is most important, but here they are in the order of their potential for sponsorship:

1. The daily devotional thought-for-the-day needs a writer but is least likely to employ one. It is a natural vehicle for a pastor, but he needs a writer because he is already too busy. The very element which makes this program type effective—constant brief repetition—is what keeps the local pastor from attempting it: five scripts or more a week! Yet it can be a powerful influence.

2. The religious news program is far more important than most church broadcasters realize. The average devoted Christian often feels alone in his faith. He is surprised when he discovers that many of those who work with him in the same business share his faith but never express it. They, too, are unaware of the greatness of the world-wide Christian community. A religious news show underscores it.

For such a program, resource material is vital. Two major syndicates supply world-wide coverage on a subscription basis. This material should be edited locally, and gathering and writing local news is an additional chore. When someone is employed on a program of this kind he is almost always a combination newscaster, writer, and producer.

Newscasting is factual reporting, so it is possible to get sponsorship. Opinions expressed are not necessarily the opinions of the advertiser. The sponsor merely renders a public service and presents his own message at the beginning and end.

3. Drama and documentary writing offer even larger

opportunities. Volunteer writers are hard to get and often incompetent, yet drama is a powerful tool for religion. Only first broadcast rights for a script need be sold; good drama has a permanent value.

At present, there is in the country no large depository of dramatic radio scripts for religion. There may be a market for this kind of material, but it has not been cultivated. My own correspondence with firms such as Samuel French indicates publishers are interested in religious radio drama. They now publish almost nothing of this kind; scripts available through denominational offices are so poor as to be unusable.

Biography is the best beginning. There are innumerable stories of great souls who have given leadership to the Christian faith. Some enterprising writer will prepare a series of scripts, and a publisher will distribute it. Such efforts will stimulate other efforts and result in more drama programming and a greater demand for writers.

4. Sacred music programs may not be as widely used, but they offer opportunity for the writer who combines several skills. Sacred music is the least controversial of the materials religion uses.

The biggest hurdle is the music itself. Live musicians are expensive, if good, and probably beyond the budget of local advertisers. But with enough recorded music—and there is a growing amount of this—a local show is reasonably possible.

There are even possibilities of syndication. Programs may be transcribed and released on a per-use lease, or scripts distributed for a fee. Scripts should indicate the records needed, exact play-times, copy for an announcer to read, and all details that will simplify production in the local station.

5. The woman's show is another program opportunity with religious significance. Local stations know women's

interests and produce programs for them, but the combination of these special interests with religious overtones is almost never seen.

The average housewife's concerns lend themselves to religious emphasis: child training, cooking, home decoration, community service. A program of practical suggestions could have real significance, even though few would suspect it was religious. A part of child training is teaching him to pray, encouraging awareness of the reality of God. Cooking, decorating, and routine housekeeping tasks can become part of a woman's opportunity to shape the lives in her home and create Christian personalities. It ought to be a practical program with spiritual overtones.

Probably this is a woman's job. She writes for herself, appears in the program, and manages the operation. Drawing in a sponsor's message is not difficult. Any of a dozen businesses are concerned with the housewife's work.

6. The book review show is peculiarly fitted for sponsorship. Publishers supply free copies of new books to the writer. He can cover three of them each week, one in a major review and two in minor ones. Almost any important city has a bookstore able to sponsor such a program. And it can be religiously significant if it occasionally covers outstanding religious books.

Sources of Material

So you want to try your hand? Then let's get down to details. You can't write about religion unless you have first-hand experience of it. Religion is part of the inner personal life. Explore it. Don't be a detached observer. You must understand it as do the people who devote themselves to it.

Then, look around you. Grist for your mill is in every daily experience: at the corner grocery, on the bus, over the telephone. Cultivate your powers of observation.

Whatever your subject, you should know its literature. If you write a music program, you will find help in the *Handbook to the Hymnal*, published by Westminster Press. Consult a religious library or bookstore for such materials.

If you want methods of child training in prayer or worship, don't forget the resources of Christian education. Study church school curriculum materials as well as publications for parents and teachers.

Read novels and short stories, too. The experience of some fictional character stimulates your own thinking along parallel lines. Read the Bible; it's a rich resource for your use. And if you write drama, you need to know the biographies of great religious leaders. Church history becomes important here, also. What these men did cannot be understood without a knowledge of their times.

Now, suppose you have an assignment: to prepare a five-minute devotional talk each day, five times a week for six months. Finding that many different ideas is a job in itself. We'll call the program "Today's Word." Each script will have a particular word around which its ideas revolve. One day it will be "arrow"; the next, "rudder"; and the third, "horn."

To simplify writing, you need a format or pattern as familiar as your living room rug. For example, let's develop "Today's Word" in this way: (1) discuss present usage of the word, (2) tell how the word is used in a particular Bible passage, (3) make a practical application, and (4) sum it up and repeat a special biblical text with the word in it.

Now make up a list of words. A concordance classifies the words in the Bible and lists where each word is used. Pick out twenty-five or thirty special words as a beginning. A dictionary or encyclopedia gives background on present-day English usage. Find some application worth thinking about that rises from this usage, and then begin to write.

Let's try the same process with a program of practical help for the housewife. Don't try it unless you can put your hands on a variety of practical household hints. These are published in magazines and newspapers all over the nation.

Work out a format, into which you can fit materials each week. Settle on the kind of religious help you want to give. Then run down books and pamphlets with suggestions you can use. Question successful women who have solved these problems themselves. You may decide that an interview with some of these women would be a useful part of the program itself. You can see this is logically a job for a woman writer.

How to Start, Develop, and End

If you're going to write for radio, cultivate an aural style designed for the ear. Study the next three paragraphs; they illustrate what I mean.

Keep your sentences short. Try to *average* fourteen words or less. Don't worry about the look of the copy on the page. It's designed for the ear, not the eye. Divide compound sentences into separate sentences, even though you may begin with a conjunction. The grammarians may frown, but forget them.

Use one-syllable words as much as you can. You'll avoid the gadgets on words we call affixes. They slow down understanding. Use lots of personal references, too. Talk to people as you would in conversation. Don't be impersonal. By all means use as many active and live verbs as you can. Avoid passive, infinitive, and other inactive forms of the verb.

Don't be afraid of contractions, either. Broken sentences are the way we think and talk. You don't want to sound literary unless it's for effect. So, talk your material into the typewriter.

Rudolf Flesch in *The Art of Plain Talk* has some tests you can apply to your writing. What he describes as "standard" readability is only standard for the eye. "Fairly easy" is standard level of comprehension for the ear.

The next step is to determine your target. Write out your aims and objectives in sentences of not more than eight or ten words each. Who are the people you want to reach? Formulate a profile of the average listener. What are his religious beliefs, his personal tastes, his standards?

After that, draft a format. How will you open, what will you do in the body, and how will you close? The opening is vital. You can lose an audience before it discovers that your presentation of religion is more appealing than the average. It may help to begin with a "hook" that arrests listener attention and suggests where the program is going. News programs do it with quick headlines before the title and first commercial. In drama, it may be a quick thirty-second vignette to arouse interest.

Study your closing, too. Many a program starts strong but peters out. For news you'll need a strong closing story or a chuckle. In a talk it may be story material with a punch and application. In a music show it certainly means a climactic number.

Next, lay out the series. Outline at least thirteen weeks before you begin to write the first script. Do the subjects for each really cover the field? Do they connect? Are they dated, or can you use the scripts at some other time with equal value?

Now, you can write. Follow the accepted form for radio scripts found in standard texts. Remember that lower-case letters are used for things to be said aloud, and capitals are for instructions and information *not* to be said aloud.

Special Problems

Preachers are reluctant to have someone write their sermons for them. Their people are not likely to tolerate it, either. So if you do persuade a clergyman to let you help him, write what he can honestly say. Don't write, "I know a man who said to his wife . . ." Have him say, "Let me tell you about a man who said to his wife . . ."

The prejudice against ghost writing may be avoided if the writer is classified as a production assistant. The minister adapts what the writer has written by a modest amount of pencil editing and "makes it his own."

Sponsorship for religion has its problems, too. Men are identified by their jobs. The minister is associated with his church. No matter how he may try, he can never be completely free of denominational brands. So the sponsor of his program risks the danger of losing the support of people of some other communion. A layman is identified by his job, not by his church. On the air he has no special labels, and an advertiser finds his program less controversial.

A third problem might be described as "gaining breadth by losing depth." Religious broadcasting is a broad spectrum. At one end it makes direct appeals to men's souls, and at the other end it merges with the cultural. In between is a broad field offering many different approaches to men's minds and hearts.

Radio is a mass entertainment medium. Even religious radio must be entertainment with spiritual overtones. It may not have the depth of many church services, but it can reach many the church could not touch. Writers constantly wrestle with differences in point of view, here, among those for whom they work. Many do not see that radio accomplishes by popular repetition and mass coverage what other media accomplish by limited appeal and incisive depth.

Writing Possibilities

There is little opportunity for a radio writer in a staff position. Most such posts are administrative. More opportunities are open to the free lance writer.

A few national agencies commission writers to prepare program series. These are only in New York and Hollywood. Syndication offers additional opportunity. Program materials and scripts of merit can be distributed by a number of agencies. A few agencies have sprung up within the past few years solely for this purpose.

But probably your most profitable opportunity as a free lance writer is in packaging programs. It is not big pay, but it represents at least an opportunity to recover some money from the experience. Programs with religious overtones can be sold to a church group or to an advertiser-sponsor. You may have to learn production know-how, performing skill, and double in every capacity. But persistence and skill patiently developed will pave the way.

What has been said is not intended to be discouraging. The situation is changing. It is no longer what it was even five years ago. Opportunities are growing, and it is important that writers see that what they do now may speed the growth of opportunity in the future.

Professional skills have not been commonplace in religious radio, which may account for its lack of popularity in the past. Now there is a growing interest in religion throughout the nation and the world. And radio is reflecting it. If religious radio can grow in the caliber of its content and production, it will have a place of permanence in the life of the nation. This depends largely upon people of skill and ability giving themselves to it. At first it may call for voluntary assistance without compensation. But it will inevitably lead in time to job opportunities.

Henry B. Adams is assistant professor of speech and broadcasting at San Francisco Theological Seminary and a member of the Presbyterian National Department of Radio and Television. He is founder and president of Church Broadcasting Associates, producers and distributors of religious radio and television resources and programs, one of the nation's principal sources of syndicated religious news for radio. He is a Presbyterian Church in the U.S.A. minister.

CHAPTER *Eighteen*

Religious Television

CHARLES H. SCHMITZ

A LITTLE BOY and a little girl entered some plants in a flower show. When the prizes were given out, the little boy won first prize. The girl came home crying, and said to her mother, "All I got was horrible mention!" We want to write for television so as not to invite "horrible mention." We will then need to develop a growing understanding of, and appreciation of, this miracle of communication.

The Nature of Television

Television has seriously affected the life of the home, the public school, the motion picture theater, the national political scene, and the church. Television is a unique art form, different from anything else we know.

Note well the distinctive nature of television. It is not radio. Radio is sound alone; television is sound plus sight. Radio reaches for the ears alone; television reaches primarily for the eyes. Radio encourages the use of the imagination; television restricts the imagination. Radio listeners may give it divided attention; television asks for fuller attention.

Television is not the theater. The theater audience pays to get in; television is free. The theater serves a crowd; television is beamed to the single viewer, or two or three viewers at home. The theater's audience sees and hears from the orchestra seats or the balcony; television viewers see and hear at close range. In television, the viewer has a seat on the stage. The theater's audience can never see important details, but viewers of television may see nervous fingers at close-up. The possibilities of the television camera have not yet been fully explored.

Television is not motion pictures, although motion picture film is used. The motion picture screen is measured in feet; in television the measurement is in inches. The size of the screen affects program content. Motion pictures are generally prepared to be viewed by a group who have dressed up to go out and who have paid admission. The television program usually is viewed by one or two or three persons, relaxed, dressed in comfort, and at ease in the home. The motion picture theater audience generally stays through the whole program to get its money's worth; the television audience turns to other available choices quickly when interest lags.

Television has in its very nature many interesting facets. Consider its immediacy; instantaneous sight plus instantaneous sound by means of which the viewer can see what is happening right now many miles away. Consider its spontaneity: a dancer may fall, an actor may miss a cue, an animal may misbehave on camera—anything can happen; it is unpredictable—and that adds to its interest. Errors in television are not usually edited out as they are in motion pictures. Television has tremendous human interest: it is a personality medium in which people interest people. Consider its intimacy and informality: no room for starchy preachers, but where warmth and friendliness and humor add up. The television viewer is to be thought of as being as close as the camera itself. Television calls for *interesting* action: not a minister fingering his watch or examining his notes or reading a sermon—such actions repel. Interesting action is the kind that truly communicates, that moves the viewer to do something.

In keeping with the nature of television, there are a number of program possibilities for religion. There is *the informal devotional program* to provide a spiritual lift. The telecasting of *special religious events* such as Easter, Christmas, national conventions—these have a place on the air. Competent teachers who have mastered the visual as well as the aural method of teaching may *teach the Bible:* its history, stories, geography, and characters. *Religious newscasting, panel discussions, youth forums, interviews,* are other additional program possibilities for television. In the area of evangelism, others may be won to the faith with special programs employing visual aids as Jesus did, using the seed, the coin, and so forth.

The nature of television suggests program titles that are short and attention-compelling. Only the best telegenic talent obtainable should be used. Techniques that are creative and imaginative need to be employed. Programming should be based on reality—real people in real situations meeting real needs. Only as the nature of television is understood can we think of writing with any degree of effectiveness.

We may be familiar with certain types of writing and so falsely assume we can write for television. The minister who writes his sermon each week for *pulpit presentation* is writing for a sympathetic, like-minded, captive audience which may be seated in a setting of stained glass windows, altar, cross, candlesticks, and a colorful robed choir. Consciously or unconsciously, the minister in his sermon preparation is using crowd psychology beamed to a congregation some of whom may be as much as a city block away from him in the back pew.

The religious leader who writes a book may use *the literary style* of writing, meaning long, involved sentences with many dependent clauses. His writing may reflect the writing of theologians whose style may be called the "referral" style of writing, that is, if the reader cannot understand it the first time, he can read it over again. The literary style is also called writing with "a second chance." Writing for radio or television is writing with only a single opportunity to be understood—no "referral," no "second chance" is possible.

The clergyman who writes for *radio* should be writing for the ears alone. In writing for radio, we deal with a medium of sound altogether; therefore the attempt is made to reach all the senses *only* through the ears. This is called the aural style of writing. Such writing should recognize that the ears generally do not "remember" too well; that the ears lend themselves to the imagination; that the ears believe more than the eyes believe.

When it comes to writing for *television*, however, the accent is on the visual—the eyes have it! Writing for television should seek to make the faith real through sight. Sound is there only for support. Writing for television at its best keeps the eyes of the viewer open to every visual effect. The ideal religious program for television should communicate a spiritual quality even when the sound is turned down. To transmit deep convictions visually is not easy—but this is writing for television. Write through the camera's eye. This is writing with purpose.

The Television Viewer

Who can possibly describe with accuracy the television audience? It defies analysis and description. Nevertheless, some general statements about television viewers can be made. Certainly here is a potential mixed audience of the religious and the nonreligious, the dechurched and the unchurched, the troubled and the untroubled, the friendly and the hostile, the young and the old. In the audience are persons from all walks of life—dishwashers, executives, common laborers, housewives, secretaries, educators, politicians, statesmen, technicians, doctors, lawyers, merchantmen, the jobless, the retired, and many, many others. In the audience are found college and seminary graduates, and also the illiterate, lovers of high brow music and lovers of jazz, people of all races, climates, religions, people with common tastes, and people with unusual tastes.

Most viewers are at home, although some may be found in taverns, others in hotel rooms, or institutions. The viewers at home may face all kinds of interruptions: the doorbell may ring, the baby may cry, the telephone may need to be answered. The television writer needs always to remember the circumstances of reception, and so to write that even in the face of interruptions, the program will make sense. It is necessary to keep in mind the individuals who tune in late after the program has started—in this respect, it is good to "give the score of the game" repeatedly just for the late tuners-in. The viewers at home are generally close to the TV receiver, so that eye contact is important. The TV camera represents the eye of the viewer at home and should be so treated. There is no "back pew" in television. This means that in writing for television, the details may create profound impressions, worthy or unworthy.

Television magnifies the situation and gives the viewer a seat close to the broadcaster.

The television viewer is a kind of moving target. He is not necessarily a continuing "member of the congregation." The total audience for any program in television is variable; it changes from day to day. It is not static. The television audience is not like a classroom audience, wherein the pupils are the same from day to day and where the teacher may have a tightly knit course, completing today's lecture tomorrow. It is unwise in television to say, "Now remember I said to you yesterday," because today's audience is not identical with yesterday's. If the program is appealing, the number of viewers will increase. The population of a given community, too, may be on the increase or decrease. The number of television sets in use is not constant either. So then, in writing for television or radio, we write toward a moving target.

Some things about the likes and dislikes of the viewers should be understood. Viewers are generally not interested in the problems of the broadcaster. They want straight talk kept at a minimum. Music is preferred to talk. Viewers want to understand effortlessly—they will not strain themselves while the preacher seeks to make a fine theological point. They like to have their curiosity aroused. They prefer a screen that is not all cluttered up. Viewers dislike statistics, theological jargon, new words, regional words or phrases—anything that blocks understanding. The television audience expects the broadcaster to know what it wants through knowing what it is.

The writer for television programs must constantly discipline himself in asking how this will look on the screen, not how it will look in the TV studio. What the electronic eyes of television can or cannot see is something quite different from what human eyes can and cannot see. Judgment is generally made on a basis of how this looks to our *eyes*, whereas final judgment must depend upon how this looks to the eyes of the television camera. For example, in the area of color, straight blacks and whites beside each other are to be avoided because of their sharp contrast. The writer will need to have some knowledge of what the camera can and cannot accept.

Television viewers usually want to be entertained; they do not care to be educated directly. The entertainment value of the program creates receptivity. Only when the attention of the audience has been gained can the television writer expect to communicate his faith. The *religious* value of the script may depend for its impact upon its *entertainment* value. The one need not necessarily be divorced from the other. Ministers, priests, and rabbis may well consider that religious faith at its best is not something ugly and repulsive, but rather something warm, friendly, and attractive. This it must be for the television writer.

Of one thing we may be sure: the television viewer is not like the religious leader. Jesus upon one occasion placed a child before him and said, "of such is the kingdom of heaven." In our communication techniques, we tend to place a college and seminary trained clergyman in the center of things and infer that "of such is the kingdom of heaven!"

Churchmen are in no sense ever to consider themselves representative listeners or viewers, for they have peculiar tastes and unusual interests. They tend to evaluate programs by their own point of view. They select program ideas on a basis of what *they* like. Ministers have been known to make an attempt to appeal to the dechurched or the unchurched with the broadcasting of a church service! The church service is put on the air because that is what the minister likes. The clergyman forgets that the dechurched and the unchurched have already rejected the church service, else they would be there. So the minister is using a type of program the folks have stayed away from, just to win them! The religious leader seldom sees himself as laymen see him. Should the religious leader ever write a television script, he is likely to write something that may be described as being written by a preacher for a preacher, but not for the people.

He who writes for television must always and in all ways have the viewer in mind. The viewer generally is an ordinary person at home. He is relaxed. He has turned the television receiver on for something interesting to him. Ordinarily, he is in no mood for pomp and ceremony, for starch and dignity, for that refrigerated, embalmed kind of religious presentation. He wants life and he wants it abundantly, coming to him through this tool of communication called television.

Sustaining Interest

To capture attention at the beginning of a religious television program is not enough. Interest must be sustained throughout the program if it is to be effective. But how does one sustain interest in a religious television program?

To *present great truths in a fresh way* is to help sustain interest. Religion has developed through the centuries a traditional habit of presenting great truths and convictions with the same identical words and phrases. It becomes to many people a kind of religious "spot announcement," repeated so often that it loses its meaning both for those who are repeating it and for those who listen to it. Sometimes the words that are used are no longer in the vocabulary of the people. Words like "vouchsafe," "sufferance," "governance," "supplication," "unfeignedly," "fellowship," are not in the vocabulary of the ordinary man, woman, or child. Yet religious leaders persist in using outmoded words.

As an illustration, consider the communion service. About

twenty years ago it was most impolite to talk about blood in a mixed group. It just wasn't done, but how times have changed! Now we give blood, store blood, type blood, sell blood, ship blood, have blood banks, and announcements about the giving of blood are a daily occurrence. To share one's life through the giving of blood is real to thousands of people today. The story of Calvary and the Lord's Supper is not a remote event of nineteen centuries ago without meaning for life today. Why not give it fresh meaning by making that great event in history pertinent to life today? All the great truths of the church have meaning for life right now. Present great truths in a fresh way!

To *provide action and movement* in writing for television is another way to hold interest. Watch the television screen and note that there is a visual change about every twenty seconds. Where the broadcaster himself does not provide movement, the cameras do by dollying in or out, panning left or right, or just switching cameras. The best visual aids in television are those with movement. Motion picture producers see to it that the audience is given a terrific jolt every seven or eight minutes in order to carry the interest of the audience. A great internationally famous statesman, who has received any number of awards for the excellence of his work, writes only while he walks, dictating to a secretary while walking in order to put movement and pacing into his writing. Movement is necessary in writing for television.

Another step in sustaining interest in writing for television is to *write from life to life and not from book to book*. The tendency among some religious leaders is to use lengthy quotations. They are habitual readers and so want to share what they have read. Quotations can become boring because they are another person's thought expressed in his way. When quotations are read, they may sound like a collection of words, not thoughts. Far better it is to write from life to life. Life invites life. To have shared what one is talking about is to give it great communicative value.

In writing so as to hold interest, there are several other considerations. Wherever possible, use living words that through their very sound explain their own meaning, words like "smooth" and "lull." Avoid vague generalities, be concrete, avoid flat claims. Have no loose ends to writing. Never kill spontaneity. Above all, write toward the people, not toward the minority of minorities with your tastes and interests.

Simplicity in Style

A clergyman may have a vocabulary of 50,000 words —Shakespeare managed with only 20,000! According to the 1950 census, the average education in the United States is just nine years of schooling. To write exclusively for college graduates as one prepares a television program would be a big mistake. Most individuals in this country have never finished high school. This is not to say that they are stupid; it is simply to say that they may have a limited vocabulary. Bear this in mind when writing for religious TV.

Never equate an extensive vocabulary with intelligence, nor a limited vocabulary with ignorance. In New York City are a number of individuals with exceptionally large vocabularies—but *that is all they have!* On the other hand, quite a number of individuals listed in *Who's Who* have limited vocabularies. Some very wise persons cannot command a great many words. One reason we have needed a New Revised Standard Version of the Bible is that the scholars of other centuries were utterly wrong in assuming that the manuscripts at their disposal were written in classical Greek—the Greek of the scholars, of the philosophers, of the classroom. They found out that the manuscripts were written in the everyday Greek of the child, the housewife, the carpenter. There is no place for seminary class-room English on radio or television.

Not only is simplicity in terms of vocabulary necessary, but also simplicity in terms of sentence structure. Use short sentences. Contractions are convincing. Brief and timely illustrations taken out of the contemporary scene—these are effective. Poetry is to be avoided unless the script is being written for an exceptional, professional broadcaster.

The top executive of one of the nation's great television manufacturing plants addressed a group of religious leaders. He told them that in his factory he had a number of different departments, among them science and sales. Each disliked the other. The men in the science department were called "the long-haired boys." As technicians, they knew what every tube and every wire in the television cameras or receivers were for. In the other department the salesmen knew only the outside of the television camera and receivers—what they looked like and how they performed. The salesmen knew that on the receiving sets, one knob was to turn the set on and increase the volume, the other knob was to select the stations, but about the inside of the sets they knew nothing.

"Now who do you think," said the top executive to these ministers, "writes the ads that interest buyers in television cameras and receivers—not the scientists because *they know too much* that would be uninteresting and dull. The job of selling," he continued, "is given to the salesmen who know little about the inside of TV equipment."

Nothing more was said, but these religious leaders caught on to the fact that their extensive knowledge of theology, of biblical history, of a specialized vocabulary—all these became a barrier to effective communication. That is why laymen rather than ministers often do a better job of winning folk to the faith.

Write in simple terms when you write for religious television. "Let your words be for children, while your thoughts are for men." One may be profound with a simple vocabulary.

Memory Impact

To be a successful, effective writer for religious television programming is to understand how memory works. To write and produce programs that are fleeting, that bounce off the mind, is to write superficially. Religious television programs should reflect a depth of thinking and a breadth of understanding. We need to write to where *people live*, so that when they see and hear they say to themselves, "This is me!"

Memory is impressed when it sees programs that strike the experiences that are found in memory. Too often writers work on the fringes of life—they should work at the core. Because there are experiences common to many, we should engage these rather than spending such talent as we may possess upon the unique, unusual experiences limited to a few. Television reaches millions of people. It is a mass means of communication. It is not a telephone by which we may contact the other "twin" with an experience similar to our own.

Memory is impressed not only when we write to where people live, but also when we *repeat*. Repetition is one of the most successful clues to memory impact. To say something once on the air is not enough. We may well learn from commercial spot announcements the value of repetition—mentioning the name of the item for sale again and again so that memory will retain it. Listeners may not like repetition, but they do recall the product advertised. By repetition *we do not mean to say it word for word again and again*. Just as there are *Four Gospels*, each presenting the same Person but with somewhat different approaches, so the faith we possess needs to be put on the air again and again and again and again with different fresh approaches.

Memory works favorably when in the words of Plato, "Beauty of style and harmony and grace and good rhythm depend on *simplicity*." Memory cannot hold theological jargon nor the gobbledygook of some educators. Involved writing is poor writing.

An aid to memory is to *demonstrate and describe* (wherever possible) at the same time. Try to "show how" while you "tell how," thinking in pictures more than in words. If it is possible to make a comparison between use and non-use, that helps the viewer to *see* the difference, registering upon his memory.

If you want to be remembered, *say it briefly*. If you want to be forgotten, take a long time to say it. The only monument to a speech we know of is to Lincoln's Gettysburg Address.

To *summarize* is another way to contribute to memory impact. To show what has been shown, to pull the program together at the end, is to make it more effective.

Time and Timing

How far is a minute? To a cripple shuffling along, a minute means only a few feet. To a man traveling in a horse and buggy, a minute can mean a block. To a person riding in an automobile, a minute may mean a mile. To a pilot in a plane, a minute can mean a distance of five miles. But to a broadcaster, a minute means most of all—a possible contact with thousands of people. Millions of dollars worth of TV one-minute-and-twenty-second spot announcements are sold every year. They reach far into a viewer's mind and way of life.

Time is of the essence in broadcasting. To refuse, abuse, misuse, or confuse time is to commit the unpardonable sin.

Radio and television tell the truth about time. *This fact is the most difficult one for religious leaders to understand.*

A broadcasting station manager told us about the minister who was to go on the air at nine in the morning. He showed up at five minutes after nine. The station refused to let him go on the air—so he fretted and stormed and threatened. What this minister needed to learn was simply *how to tell time*, because how can you "redeem the time" unless you can tell it! Radio and television tell the truth about time—the program begins when they say it does and ends when they say it does.

Develop a delicate sense of timing, as a baseball player does for a slow or a fast ball; as a comedian does in his delayed reaction to an insult; as an evangelist does who knows just when to extend the altar call—not a moment before and not a moment after.

Spend a minimum of time on introductions—the credit lines are usually uninteresting and dull. It is most necessary to begin interestingly with a hook to capture attention. The audience must be won immediately.

Allow time in the script for camera changes or scene changes. Allow time for movement of the participants.

Write toward the time of day and day of the week the program is to be on the air. We are different people at different times of the day and on different days of the week. Study TV programming in the morning and at night and note the difference. At night, our defenses are down. Study TV programming Sunday afternoon and Monday afternoon and note the difference. Certain audiences may be reached better at some time than at others. To ignore the time element is to miss a real opportunity.

The Canadian Broadcasting Corporation has put out what it calls "The CBC Chart of Happy Living" prepared by the National Committee for Mental Hygiene of Canada. The chart points out the needs from the preschool level to later maturity and on. It lists the intellectual, emotional, social, and physical needs through all the different age levels.[1] Should you wish to write for an audience of a specific age level, have their hungers in mind and write through them —do not set them aside.

Study Jesus

Religious leaders in their writing have followed the methods and techniques of the Apostle Paul, rather than those of Jesus. Religious leaders have forgotten that individuals fell asleep under Paul's methods of communication—*but no one ever fell asleep while Jesus communicated*. In fact, Jesus brought the dead back to life again through his words. Follow Paul's theology if you wish, but not his methods and techniques of communication. If you follow Paul in your writing for television, you will fail. If you study the techniques of Jesus and follow him, you will succeed.

Jesus made truth come to life. Jesus used the known to direct minds and hearts toward the unknown. Jesus communicated not as do mailmen who deliver sealed letters with sealed lips to people for whom they have no concern. Jesus communicated not as telephone operators may, who speak coldly in terms of numbers to people they do not care about. Jesus did not communicate as so many television announcers do, speaking in glowing terms and demonstrating products they themselves never use. Rather, Jesus communicated as a prophet telling forth the truth courageously. Jesus communicated as a witness does, speaking from life to life. Jesus communicated as the Savior of the world, sacrificially giving himself for his convictions. Jesus made the truth come to life—that is television writing at its best.

[1] This chart has been reproduced in *Broadcasting Religion* (New York: National Council of Churches, 1954), pp. 58–59.

Jesus showed how to live more than he told how to live. Study him.

The thoughts of Jesus were crisp, not soft. When he talked about faith, it was something to possess, not to let go. When he spoke of hope, it was something to lighten life, not smother it. When he thought of love, it was something full bodied, not emaciated. Study him.

Charles H. Schmitz, director of broadcast training, Broadcasting and Film Commission of the National Council of Churches, is an American Baptist Convention minister. Educated at the University of Omaha and Colgate-Rochester Divinity School, he has done additional study at Crozer and Presbyterian Theological Seminaries. The Rev. Mr. Schmitz has been chairman of the radio and television committee of his denomination; member of the program committee of the Protestant Radio Commission; chairman, radio and television committee of the New York State Council of Churches, and staff member of the annual religious radio workshop of the Radio Commission. For five years he had daily as well as weekly devotional broadcasts in Syracuse, New York, and has taken part in many religious radio and television workshops. Author of three widely used pamphlets in religious radio, he has written articles on the subject for *Crozer Quarterly* and *Christian Century Pulpit*. His books include *Windows Toward God*, *Broadcasting Religion*, and *Religious Television Program Ideas*.

CHAPTER *Nineteen*

Writing for Films

HENRY ENDRESS

GUTHRIE MC CLINTIC, one of America's leading play directors, was interviewed in Paris by Art Buchwald, of the New York *Herald Tribune*, about the respective roles of playwrights, actors, and directors in the theater.

"The three important parts of the theater," he said, "are, first, the play—nobody can survive if it's a bad play—then the actors, and then the director."

It's true of motion pictures as well.

A film is no better than its script. A good film was never produced from a bad script.

Nobody deliberately writes a bad script and nobody deliberately produces a bad film. The nightmare of every producer is that his judgment in evaluating a script may fail him. So, in an attempt to avoid such catastrophies, the commercial producer surrounds himself with first-rate writers, and, naturally, top talent in the other specialized fields in making a motion picture. But no matter how hard you try, you never see quite what you expect. A film is the work of many men. It is the result of many judgments, and what's more, many circumstances beyond your control.

Film magnates delegate a special expert to sit alone in a projection room, well before release date, and to look, with cold objectivity, at the work of other men and to determine what footage should be cut, what more should be added, and what scenes should be changed. Nevertheless, when the first screening of the finished film is held, there come those clammy silences when projection room lights go on again, and finally those kindly spoken words of condemnation: "George, the color's great!" . . . or, "That one scene with the girl on the bridge justifies the whole picture. You'll get comment on that, George!"

George, being no novice, knows exactly what they mean. He knows what is wrong. His cast, camera work, sets, and editing are fine, but he had a bad script. And he knows that a bad script never made a good film. George, however, has bounce. He goes home, weeps with his wife, works out a fool-proof rationalization of why the picture is good and why it will "go." Next day he returns to the office with a headful of ideas and enthusiasm for "one of the biggest exploitation jobs in film history." He intended to make a good film and now will make the best of it.

I believe the church film producer has a double nightmare. His subject is highly specialized, often basically unpictorial, and, unfortunately, stories of Christian faith prepared by competent, understanding scriptwriters are harder to come by. Craftsmen who know and have experienced the Christian faith apparently are not numerous. When the staff producer of one denomination obtains a budget for a film, there usually is frantic telephoning to his counterpart in other denominations with the question: "Frank, can you suggest a good scriptwriter?"

Craftsmen Are Needed

The scarcity of competent, experienced, and dedicated craftsmen in the field of scriptwriting is serious. It is a situation, however, for which the church itself is quite responsible. The pietists, unfortunately, years ago turned the church away from the use of the film in its teaching and preaching. They condemned the God-given medium when they should have grasped the opportunity and used it in His name.

Enlightened men are leading the church beyond narrow prejudice to the proper use of theater and cinema arts for God's will and purpose. Today more and more artists, actors, and writers are being drawn into the church and are dedicating life and work to the preaching of the gospel. The Christian Stewardship movements in the evangelical churches and the Christopher movement in the Roman Catholic Church are increasingly influential in this area. Talented men and women now discover that they are not forced into stifling, conventional molds when they work in and for the church. There opens up to them new freedom and power—and an opportunity to write about issues that matter most.

The religious film producer, until recently, has not enjoyed the benefit of professional film talent around him. He has had to check his scripts with other churchmen who did not know the medium. They evaluated a script as they would a sermon, or they judged it by whether or not it mentioned their favorite church cause or all the causes of the church. And nonprofessionals invariably want to add more scenes and dialogue when, only too frequently, the script needs cutting and sharpening.

When a church producer has finished an unsatisfactory film, there is rarely a turning back. His budget is depleted and it might well take the action of another church convention to get additional money to make improvements. And the convention undoubtedly would want to see the film first!

Even a TV producer is in a better spot; his bad show is only seen once. The churchman's film, on the other hand, makes the rounds of churches for years, and unfavorable comments continue to haunt him.

Religious drama is coming back and is making its impact in theatrical production, motion pictures, radio, and television. The annual Passion plays, from Hollywood and Oklahoma to church halls everywhere, gain mounting support. Wittenberg College, Springfield, Ohio, has appointed a director of religious drama to its faculty and has built up an impressive library of religious films. Other church colleges are experimenting with film production. The Lutheran Church–Missouri Synod has scored a most impressive record with drama for television. At this writing, the "This Is the Life" series of more than fifty films is drawing to a close. The series will now go on within a new format.

It is notable that churches and their boards and institutions are no longer satisfied with anything less than top talent in these fields. They are committed to the fact that these works, too, are "offerings" and that Jesus Christ deserves nothing less than the best in technical and artistic talent.

The Early Religious Film

Not too long ago, most church films were produced without any professional talent or script at all. In those days it was standard practice to send missionaries out to India, Africa, and the Far East with a 16mm. camera, a box of raw film, and the instruction, "Shoot film and send it back home for church members to see what their offerings are

accomplishing." And so devoted pastors, with no understanding of the medium, no previous experience, nor even a
story-line, went out as the Lord's cameramen and produced
a film as they did their missionary work in jungles and
mountain areas. They shot thousands of feet of film and
rushed them back home to be developed, edited (by a
board secretary), and shown in church halls.

The faithful parishioners arrived to see "a great mission
film out of the heart of Africa," but they usually were
bored—and appalled—by a choppy, badly photographed,
pointless motion picture of people staring into a camera
lens. Occasionally there was drama: a missionary and native
helpers wobbled across a rope bridge strung across a deep
gorge. This sequence was repeated so often in a certain
film that one person called out, "I hope the bridge breaks
and the cameraman's on it."

The happy ending to this story is slightly different.

Foreign mission boards, by and large, have abandoned
this type of production. They now use professional scriptwriters and producers because they know such films hurt,
rather than help, the work of the church. Religion is no excuse for poor quality, and a bad film does not convince
church members that the work of Jesus Christ is the most
important thing in their lives. To bring an audience back
for another religious film, the church must offer something
which can compete with the high technical standards of the
film they can see in the theater down the street.

The big change in church production standards began
when Dr. James K. Friedrich, an Episcopalian clergyman,
organized Cathedral Films in Hollywood. His first intent
was to produce Christian films for theaters. This aim is just
now being achieved through his major Century Films production, *Day of Triumph*. From 1938 to 1954, his efforts
were centered in producing teaching and promotional films
for the church. Around him he drew a corps of equally

committed co-workers of professionals, executives, writers, directors, and actors. They produced biblical and modern stories that became increasingly better as larger budgets became available and as they gained production experience and a deeper understanding of the use of audio-visual aids in the church.

Christian churches, Roman Catholic as well as Protestant, owe a debt of gratitude to pioneers James K. Friedrich and John T. Coyle of Cathedral Films. They provided us all with basic libraries of Christian films, and whatever has been accomplished by the rest of us, who have either worked with Cathedral Films or have not, we must acknowledge that we learned from their achievements and their mistakes. And we have been motivated by their faith in the medium and their effective experimentation with it.

It was from these men that I first received fundamentals in preparing motion picture scripts. Dr. Friedrich was the idea man and producer. Jack Coyle was the director and the relentless taskmaster who never drew a line through my paragraphs but, rather, shattered them with a question or comment. My long dissertations on "what it could be" and "how it could be played" always were cut short by Coyle like this:

"In one sentence, tell me what your aim is in this film. . . ."

"In one sentence, tell me the theme. . . ."

"In one sentence, tell me the story. . . ."

And if I couldn't do that, Coyle answered: "That proves your aim isn't clear, your thinking is fuzzy, and your story is too complicated."

Development of a Film

There was writing and rewriting until it was clearly set down on paper, in three simple sentences, exactly what we were aiming to do. For the film *Like a Mighty Army*, for example, we wrote:

> AIM: to show what a congregation of Christians will do in evangelism and stewardship when they are shaken out of their self-satisfaction and lethargy by the gospel of Jesus Christ.
>
> THEME: that a congregation, as well as the individual Christian, is a steward of the gospel and, through love and gratitude to God for his great blessings, must share it with others.

The story-line could not be developed until a real research job had been done. Since evangelism, stewardship, and home mission development were to be stressed, a careful study was made of case histories of several congregations with records, good and bad, in these areas of work. Material was culled from books and reports and lengthy interviews were held with board executives, mission developers, and pastors. Most valuable, too, was our file of good stories from congregations, gathered in field trips, from correspondence, and through feature stories in *The Lutheran*.

Mountains of resource material grew and were adapted, revised, or discarded in the lengthy process. Once materials were together, the story was plotted out in graph form; then as a test of where we were going, the story-line was written in the one sentence Jack Coyle demanded:

> STORY: through the relentless prodding by a young councilman, the Harrison City congregation rose out of lethargy, and with new vision, conducted a survey of East Harrison, helped to plant a new mission there, and gave generous offerings, and even some of its members, to aid the new church with a vigorous start.

Our next step was to expand our graph, plotting out the details of the story. Each sequence and scene had to take the story one step closer to the climax. If it did not, it was considered extraneous and was dropped. There were several drafts before a satisfactory outline was finished. Then came the expanded treatment (synopsis) with many snatches of dialogue and direction, and finally the first version of the script. After a half-dozen revisions, and after general agreement by church offices and the producing company, we worked for several days to break the manuscript down into a shooting script with camera movements and stage directions.

Preparing the "Luther" Script

A more complicated and exciting job was the preparation of the script for the motion picture *Martin Luther*, a joint project of virtually all Lutherans in America. It was determined that this film had to meet technical standards of the best that came out of Hollywood and, at the same time, that it must achieve a penetrating understanding of a man's Christian faith and a spiritual depth seldom before reached in the cinematic arts.

Integrity and authenticity were watchwords and so, after consultation with numerous producers in America and Europe, Louis De Rochemont Associates of New York, the creators of *The March of Time* and specialists in on-location, true-life dramas, were engaged for the project. God's hand, evident again and again, was in De Rochemont's selection of Lothar Wolff to serve as a co-writer and executive producer.

Wolff and Allan Sloane spent months in research, studying books of German and American church historians, both Roman Catholic and Protestant. With the aid of a church committee of seven—consisting of theologians, historians, and church film producers—they carefully plotted out the story, checking so carefully that, again and again, even original documents were studied and retranslated by the committee.

Sloane had a most useful way of cataloging the facts of Luther's life and the specific reference data. He typed the material in chronological order—from Luther's birth to death—on 8½ x 11 sheets which he then Scotch-taped together and rolled up in a scroll for easy reference.

When a question arose about where Luther was and what he did on a certain date, Sloane "rolled along" down the dated paragraphs of the scroll and reported the facts. What was his authority for this information? He could give that speedily and accurately, too.

Sloane's first draft of the script—a document with the power and poetry of a Shakespearian play—was set aside and a fresh start was made because it was evident that a birth-to-death Luther story would become overly long and weaker than a film story that had sharp limits on what it tried to do. After many story conferences it was determined that the film should be limited to religious issues and that the Martin Luther story should be told from the point where his search for peace with God sent him into the monastery and ending at the climactic events of Augsburg.

Lothar Wolff insisted, over and over again, that "you can't present every detail of a man's life—especially Luther's life—in a film story." The parade of unsuccessful biographical films bears testimony to that. Thus, within the limits set, and with aims and audience clearly in mind, script writing proceeded through one revision after another.

The mark of an amateur is that he is satisfied with the first or second writing. Perfection demands patience, and good writing is a matter of writing and writing and writing. James Shute, one of America's top writers for documentary films, tells me he often reworks a single paragraph for a couple of hours—and then rewrites the next day again.

There certainly was nothing unprofessional about the

Luther script. It went through *thirteen versions* before all experts—church and film—were satisfied and the picture was shot and edited. During that period, not only Wolff and Sloane but all seven members of our script committee had a real hand in writing and rewriting. And it is true that such revisions and changes do not always come naturally or happily.

At one point (around version No. 5), a feeling of satisfaction about the script enveloped certain board members. "We are nearly ready to shoot," they said. "No!" insisted another group of board members. "We're not satisfied as yet. Let's test this script out on some of the top people in the industry." And so copies were sent to Dore Schary of MGM, Kenneth MacGowan of the Cinema Arts Department of UCLA, Carol Reed in London, and others, for reactions. Criticisms and suggestions were received—and another version was prepared.

Wolff and Sloane had their ups and downs, too—as might well be expected when two men of talent and enthusiasm collaborate. More than once Sloane jammed his cigarette stub into an ashtray and stamped down Madison Avenue to my office to say, "Wolff is impossible!" Yet, after a bull session over a cup of coffee, Allan Sloane, revived and refreshed, galloped back up the street to Lothar Wolff's office or apartment and they began again, stauncher friends, to take another "whack at it."

Allan's favorite scene, which "held the whole picture together," no longer seemed so important. And Lothar, in the meantime, had found some of Allan's poetic thrusts more acceptable. And so scriptwriting went on.

In the middle of shooting, on the basis of script No. 13 (unrevised standard version), it was Louis De Rochemont who held forth in the Wiesbaden film studio restaurant and declared, with the sound of the Lord thundering out of a darkened sky, "That Luther so far doesn't come off as hu-

man as he really was. . . . Where are the touches of joy?
. . . Where is the warmth? . . . Where is the humor?" Louis,
no mean writer himself, has a sixth sense about scripts.

It was my lot to rush down to the studio floor and ask
film director Irving Pichel to shoot the parsonage scene
of the Luther family over again, "giving it the warmth,
the love, and the 'gentle' touch Luther had for Katie and
the children." Many directors would have thrown me out,
but friend Pichel patiently restaged a couple of scenes and
Luther's warmth and love did come through in a grand
way.

During production, Messrs. Wolff, Pichel, Dr. Oswald
C. J. Hoffmann of the Lutheran Church–Missouri Synod,
and I argued one midnight about a much-needed revision
of the final scene of the picture. We shot one version and
found it simply didn't "jell." With irritation and vigor I
declared that, in this scene, Luther had to say something of
spiritual significance, not only to the members of his congregation who stood before him, but to Christians of all
time! Dr. Hoffmann took the assignment to rewrite and,
after study and work that took him into the early hours of
the morning, he walked into breakfast with new stage directions and the prayer of thanksgiving to be spoken by
Luther at the altar of his church when he hears the trium-
phant news of Augsburg. This became the final ending to
the picture.

It is in such anguish, pain, joy, and friendships that scripts
are written and motion pictures are made.

Scriptwriting for the Luther film was unique in that so
many men of different backgrounds and callings—some
total novices in film work—worked so harmoniously and
productively together. Scriptwriters and producers generally believe sponsors and technical advisers are more hin-
drance than help, but, in the case of our working committee
of nine, teamwork was achieved. There was mutual respect

for the other man's talent and knowledge (films, theology, or history) and authority was delegated so that, after all the discussion was over, decisions could be made on the spot by two or three persons.

A scriptwriter working for a church will find it normal procedure to deal with a committee rather than a single individual with full authority. To get the job done, however, it is vital for the committee, once policy has been set, to appoint one or two representatives who can work with the writer and producer with power of decision.

Wolff reminded writers and sponsors again and again that we were working in a visual medium. Authentic action, accurate Luther speeches, the theological arguments, and the words from original documents—all were important; but in film production the vital question is, "How will it look on the screen?" To put something on the screen is no mean job when one is dealing with spiritual struggles and theological conflicts!

Such an assignment tests the creative imagination, resourcefulness, and ingenuity of any writer. What does one hear as Luther debates with Eck in Leipzig? Will the rapid-fire dialogue have meaning for a twentieth century lay audience as these theologians battle over great concepts concerning man and God, man and church, and man and salvation? Can this dialogue resound in simple language, yet convey the depth and significance of the historic controversy that brought the label of "Saxon Hus" upon Luther? But, what is even more important, can we see it on the screen?

Talents of scriptwriter, producer, and director joined in making this scene memorable. The intensity of the argument and the scene itself deepened as camera movement and precise editing brought the faces of Luther and Eck into tighter and tighter close-ups. Finally the fullface of

Luther fills the screen as he declares: "Heresy? So be it—it is still the truth!"

The writers and director, dealing not only with words but with a vision of what transpired in a room, in the hearts and in the faces of men, rose to real heights in cinematic arts at this point. It was realism that dealt not with the obvious, but dug into the depths of conviction. There was no effort for cheap simplification. The sequence goes to the core of the matter and shakes the audience because of it.

The effective use of the close-up and the drama of the face were used by scriptwriter and director, too, with most effective result in the Wittenberg scene when Luther explains to Staupitz, "Man needs only Jesus Christ," and in the high moment of the trial before the Diet of Worms.

In plotting sequences and writing dialogue, the film writer bears in mind that he is *painting* rather than photographing with a camera. He is not concerned about showing all details of life, related and unrelated, but, instead, strives to give the essence of the situation. He brings into sharp focus what is important in fact and feeling, and leaves out that which is unessential to the forward drive of the story.

Just as the sixteenth century costumes were stylized so actors did not get lost in beards and robes of Luther's day, so language must be stylized to bring characters into sharper focus. Rambling dialogue brings a film to a dead stop, or, at least, slows its pace.

The Problem of Language

Debate always arises about use of ecclesiastical language, particularly in modern religious films. Again and again, as we attempt to have pastors and laymen discuss matters of faith in screen plays, we are told that "they just don't talk that way." What these critics really mean is that they haven't often listened in or participated in religious discussions and the whole matter sounds strange when they suddenly are confronted with such a scene on the screen.

Language understood by a general audience is certainly the aim, but it is also clear, if we wish to discuss great concepts of religious faith with clarity and definition, some religious terminology must be used—and audiences must learn to understand it if they don't expect to be complete religious illiterates. The clichés of old barrel sermons are out, of course; we are talking here about the essential and necessary vocabulary of Christian understanding. Men may allude to the Scriptures and even quote without sounding like freaks. The films *Martin Luther* and *A Man Called Peter*, to name just a couple, are convincing examples of that.

What about the writers and opportunities for them in the religious and commercial fields? Scriptwriting is a craft and proficiency comes as a result of training and plenty of experience in writing, writing, writing, writing. Some writers can do this as an avocation. But the most effective writers are those who devote their lives to it and work with and for the church producers.

The best in the field are those who have received special training or those who have served years of apprenticeship under hard taskmasters in the school of practical experience. To have the advantage of formal instruction at a university or training school is ideal and every professional will recommend it heartily; many will insist upon it because super-professionals always insist upon higher standards for their successors than they set up for themselves.

Many of our best writers, among them some who insist you need formal training, are self-taught and became experts through self-discipline and experience. A good number of them are ex-newspapermen, publicity boys, and story writers who got into the field quite by accident. Because of initiative in making the most of talent and opportunity, they are writing some of our best screen plays. It is exciting to watch men of talent, without benefit of much training, make good in their respective fields and "stump the experts." And it helps keep the super-professionals humble.

Most important of all, it helps bring about a free development of new talent willing to launch out in areas of experimentation. And that's good for any profession!

Generally, when denominations search out scriptwriters, volunteers arrive to offer their services. Many are well-meaning churchmen and women who have written pamphlets and study books and enthusiastically look for the opportunity to try a hand at writing a film story. Most have had no previous experience with cinematic arts and, at best, may simply provide leads for good stories. Yet, for a few, this is the start of a new career.

Church executives themselves, in desperation, launch out into scriptwriting to make sure they "get what they want" in Christian emphasis—with varying results in the art of the cinema. Some—talented, teachable, and motivated by responsibility—do a commendable job, at least as collaborators.

Roman Catholic churchmen wisely encourage their members to develop talent and offer them first-rate courses at Fordham University. Arthur DeBra, New York community service representative of the Motion Picture Association, reports Fordham graduates already are making a mark in Hollywood. He urges other denominations to give their talented young people similar encouragement and training.

Kenneth MacGowan, head of the cinema arts department at the University of California, Los Angeles, offers effective training on the borders of the world's film capital.

Columbia University and Fordham are worthy choices in the East.

A bibliography of helpful books is included for this chapter. The writer should not limit himself to how-to-do-it books, but must, above all, understand the medium from the point of view of actor, director, and producer as well as the writer. Most fruitful of all is to study the work of others by seeing films and by reading scripts.

The Market Situation

The market for selling motion picture scripts is more limited and not as easily reached as the markets for other forms of writing. Producers usually engage writers to prepare manuscripts after they themselves select their subject or story. As a matter of fact, they are extremely hesitant in reading scripts brought in on speculation, for they fear the legal difficulties that often arise over "stolen ideas."

We, in our Lutheran film work, have adopted the industry's policy of not reading scripts unless the authors work through recognized agents or, more typical, unless they sign advance releases which protect the producer against further liability. In either case there is opened the opportunity for negotiation, in good faith, where material is used.

Lutheran Film Associates is reading treatments and scripts but it is interested, primarily, in subjects related to the Lutheran Church. The Stewardship Department centers its work on the subject of Christian stewardship. The Broadcasting and Film Commission of the National Council of the Churches of Christ in the U.S.A., producing films under the co-sponsorship of co-operating Protestant denominations, has a broader range of subjects.

Cathedral Films of Burbank, California, and Family Films of Beverly Hills, California, specialize in religious films and are reading scripts prepared on a speculation basis. Lutheran

Television Productions, the agency of the Lutheran Church —Missouri Synod, producing the "This Is the Life" series for release on television and, subsequently, through Concordia Films, St. Louis, for 16mm. church showings, is watching for good story ideas and scripts.

The success of *Martin Luther*, Twentieth Century-Fox's *A Man Called Peter*, and Century Films' *Day of Triumph* may well lead to more such theatrical productions. A trend may well be under way and your script may be—in subject, in synopsis, or in script form—what they are looking for. The best way to catch attention and sell is to publish your story as a featurette in a magazine or as a novel. A good story, with some promotion behind it, may bring a buyer.

Television opens new opportunities, since its aims and problems in dramatic presentation are quite like those in motion pictures. Experience in video can be a step to the film world—particularly if one gets out of the television capitals like New York and Hollywood and joins the staff of a hinterland station where television has not become "big business." In such a situation a creative writer, with initiative and no allergy toward hard work, can test ideas with great freedom. He finds that no patterns are frozen and jobs have not been rigidly classified and, therefore, the writer can get a full range of experience as a "Jack-of-all-trades," from idea man to producer.

Radio itself should not be overlooked. It is split wide open again for fresh ideas and new patterns of programming in its effort to survive. Even in the big cities, radio executives now are listening carefully to the nonprofessionals as well as the professionals for material that will draw and hold audiences.

Such experience plus talent and training are basic, but most important of all is *to have something to say* . . . on controversial issues . . . on human problems . . . about faith.

Since commercial film makers have been preoccupied

with "wowing" audiences, most of them have failed to realize that it is possible both to entertain and to say something in the same film. Some have few convictions to express, but among many who do have them, there is an eerie silence; they do not express themselves because they fear bans and boycotts. Cinema arts, as a result, have not made their much-needed contribution to America's free exchange of ideas. *Lost Boundaries* and *Martin Luther*, both produced by Louis De Rochemont Associates, by the way, are among notable exceptions.

Church film producers have expressed convictions, but not enough of us have come to grips with what is vital in the Christian faith. We've been too busy promoting or ladling out rather thin soup. A few secularists, engaged to help churches produce films, have convinced some that we must "sneak in the Christian emphasis without anybody noticing." The result is that in many church films, you really don't notice the Christian emphasis because it simply isn't there; instead there is advice on how to be happy and successful and appreciated—"pink pills for pale people" stuff.

When we, and commercial producers as well, get below the surface to the depths of what makes men tick, we'll discover drama that excites and has meaning. When we stop prostituting Bible stories with such grotesque offerings as *The Prodigal*, we'll discover the power and significance of God's message to man. When we have the courage to express convictions openly and sincerely, we'll arrive at a new era in cinema arts, and at adult rather than adolescent democracy.

A key person is the evangelical Christian writer who feels compelled to bear witness to God's truth, using all the talent, training, experience, energy, opportunity, and faith that God has given him.

Henry Endress, as executive secretary of Lutheran Church Productions, served as an associate producer and a writer for the theatrical success *Martin Luther*, produced by Louis De Rochemont Associates. A newspaper man, public relations director, and fund-raising counselor, he got his first taste of film production in the Wagner Lutheran College film *Movie Bugs*, in 1936. As the secretary for Stewardship of the United Lutheran Church in America, he made—and wrote most of the scripts for—seven films. Used often as a consultant on scripts and editing by other churches and commercial producers, he was working on two new films when he wrote the chapter for this book. In 1954, Dr. Endress was named "Lutheran of the Year" by the Federation of Lutheran Clubs.

Appendices

Appendices

Markets

ANY STANDARD MANUSCRIPT MARKET GUIDE, such as *The Writer's Market*, issued every few years by *Writer's Digest* magazine, or *Writer's Handbook*, published at longer intervals by The Writer, Inc., can guide the religious writer to the principal markets for his material, whether it be for secular or religious outlets.

This appendix is not so much an attempt to provide numerous specific market facts, which are rapidly outdated anyway, as to discuss markets and name some typical places to send material.

Names and addresses of religious publications appear not only in the two handbooks already mentioned but also in the *Yearbook of American Churches* (and similar volumes for other countries); the *Literary Market Place*, especially on books; Ayer's *Directory of Newspapers and Periodicals*, also an annual; the *Catholic Press Directory;* and in the various magazines for writers, particularly *Author and Journalist.* See especially "Protestant Press Market Letter" by Edith Tiller Osteyee, in the June and July, 1955, issues of *Writer's Digest.*

Comments and lists appear here by chapters. Most of the material was prepared by the authors of the various chapters.

CHAPTERS 1 AND 2

Marketing information is not required of these chapters; note that Chapter 2, however, discusses problems of marketing typescripts.

CHAPTER 3. THE NOVEL AND RELIGION

Mrs. Banning's comment is: "Any of the leading publishers would be interested in a novel which deals with religious forces. None would reject it willingly if it had sufficient merit. But a publisher might reject a good novel because his list already included books which had similar trends, so one rejection should never be considered conclusive."

The *Literary Market Place*, an annual directory used mainly by the book publishing industry, carries a list of all reputable U.S. publishers, including a separate table of those that publish religious books.

CHAPTER 4. GIVING THE SHORT STORY MEANING

Professor Root provided a detailed list, much of which has value in other chapters and will be referred to for them. His list is of course selective. Additional publications can be found in *The Writer's Market* and the *Writer's Handbook*, each of which may be supplemented by newer information announced in the various writers' magazines.

American Baptist Publishing Society, 1701 Chestnut St., Philadelphia 3, Pa. Publications using short stories include *Young People* (for 18 and over; about 3,000 words); *Teens* (for high school age; about 2,000), and *Story World* (under 9; 500–700). ½–¾¢ a word; after acceptance.

Augustana Book Concern; copy should be sent to Deloris Kanten, Editor, Parish Education Department, Augustana Lutheran Church, 2445 Park Ave., Minneapolis 4, Minn. Publications include *Teen Talk* (teen-agers, 1,500–3,000 words); *Junior Life* (sub-teens, 600–800); and *'Til 8 Stories* (about 300).

Christian Advocate, 740 Rush St., Chicago 11, Ill. General Methodist magazine, using human interest fiction with religious slant. To 2,500 words. 1½¢ and up; acceptance.

Christian Board of Publication, Disciples of Christ, Beaumont and Pine Blvd., Box 179, St. Louis 3, Mo. Publications include *Vision*, "a magazine for today's youth" in teens (about 2,000 words), and *Storyland* (up to nine; to 1,000). 1/3–½¢.

Christian Herald, 27 E. 39th St., New York 16, N.Y. Wholesome adult stories. Up to 3,500 words. $35 to $150; acceptance.

Christian Life, 434 S. Wabash Ave., Chicago 5, Ill. Adult Evangelical Protestant. Uses short stories of 700 and 2,500 words. 1¢ up; publication.

Christian Youth, 1816 Chestnut St., Philadelphia 3, Pa. Published by American Sunday School Union. Short fiction in two sections: for teen-agers (about 2,000 words) and "for younger readers" (about 800).

Church of England in Canada (General Board of Religious Education), 600 Jarvis St., Toronto, Ont., Canada. Publications include *The Adventurer* and *The Young Soldier and Crusader*. Teen-agers; 2,000–2,500 words.

David C. Cook Publishing Co., Elgin, Ill. Uses short stories in several publications, including *Little Learners* (4 to 6; 350–400); *Sunday Digest* (adults; about 1,800); and *Sunday Pix* (teen-agers; up to 1,000). 2¢; acceptance.

Extension, 1307 S. Wabash Ave., Chicago 5, Ill. Published by Catholic Church Extension Society. Uses considerable adult fiction; 2,000–3,000 words.

Gospel Trumpet Co. (Publication Board of the Church of God), 1303 E. Fifth St., Anderson, Ind. Publications include *Youth* (young people; up to 2,500 words); *Friendways* (boys and girls; about 1,000); and *Stories for Children* (primary; 300–400 words).

Light and Life Press, Winona Lake, Ind. Publications include *Evangel* (young adults; to 3,000 words); *Teen Time* (2,000–2,500); *Story Trails* (boys and girls; 1,000); and *Primary World* (300).

Methodist Church Editorial Division, 810 Broadway, Nashville 2, Tenn. Publications include *Classmate* (young adults; 3,500–4,500 words); *Twelve/Fifteen* (young teens; 3,000–3,500); *Trails for Juniors* (to 2,000); and *Pictures and Stories* (primary; 1,000–1,200). Syndicates some material to other publications, author sharing. 1½¢; acceptance.

Nazarene Publishing House, 2923 Troost Ave., Box 527, Kansas

City 41, Mo. Publications include *Junior Joys* (9 to 11; 1,000 words) and *Sunshine* (under 9; to 500).

One, 57 E. Main St., Columbus 15, Ohio. A Lutheran "magazine for Christian youth." High teens; 2,500 words. About 1¢; acceptance.

Otterbein Press, Dayton 2, Ohio. Evangelical United Brethren house. Publications include *Friends* (junior high; to 2,500 words); *Boys and Girls* (9 to 11; 1,500); and *Children's Stories* (primary; about 300–500). About ½¢; acceptance. This house is associated with the Evangelical Press, Third and Reily Streets, Harrisburg, Pa., whose publications include *Builders* (young adults; to 3,000 words).

Presbyterian Church in the U.S. (Board of Christian Education), 8 N. Sixth St., Richmond 9, Va. Publications include *Onward* (teens; 2,000 words); *Junior Life* (9 to 11; 1,000); and *Story Hour* (primary; to 500).

Presbyterian Story Papers, Witherspoon Building, Philadelphia 7, Pa. Board of Christian Education, Presbyterian Church in the U.S.A. Publications include *Forward* (18 to 23; about 3,000 words); *Venture* (12 to 15; 1,500–2,500); *Trailblazer* (9 to 11; 1,000–1,800); and *Stories* (6 to 8; 400–1,000). Stories purchased are widely republished. Emphasis on realistic characters and character-building. ½¢ and up; acceptance.

The Sign, National Catholic Magazine, Union City, N.J. Adult magazine of Passionist Fathers. To 4,500 words. 3¢; acceptance.

Southern Baptist Convention (Sunday School Board), 127 Ninth Ave., North, Nashville 3, Tenn. Publications include *Upward* (teens; about 3,000 words); *The Sentinel* (9 to 13; about 1,600); and *Storytime* (primary; 500–800).

United Church Publishing House and Baptist Publications Committee of Canada, 299 Queen Street, West, Toronto 2B, Ont., Canada. Publications include *Onward* (young adults); *The Canadian Girl* (teen girls; to 3,000 words); *The Canadian Boy* (teen boys; to 3,000); *The Explorer* (boys and girls, 9 to 11; about 1,500); and *Story Hour* (primary; about 500).

United Presbyterian Church (Board of Christian Education), 209 Ninth St., Pittsburgh, Pa. Publications include *Pilot* for junior high young people; 1,500–2,500 words. Rates vary.

World Over, A Magazine for Boys and Girls, 1776 Broadway, New York 19, N.Y. Jewish Education Committee. Stories of Jewish interest for 9 to 12 age; 600–1,200 words. 3¢.

Youth, 1505 Race St., Philadelphia 2, Pa. Teen-age pocket magazine of Evangelical and Reformed Church. Willing to use controversial topics, modern settings, real-life situations involving newspaper boys, 4-H clubs, teen cliques, etc. Hero should solve own problems. High school age; about 2,000 words. ½¢; acceptance.

CHAPTER 5. THE RELIGIOUS DRAMA

The two largest publishers of plays for amateurs are the Walter H. Baker Company of Boston and Samuel French, Inc., of New York. If a play has proved successful in a local community, both these publishers are interested in reading the manuscript. In addition to these major companies, the Friendship Press, the publishing division of the Joint Commission on Missionary Education of the National Council of the Churches of Christ in the U.S.A., 257 Fourth Ave., New York 10, N.Y., is interested in plays on missionary themes.

Few magazines are in the market for plays of this kind. The *International Journal of Religious Education*, 79 E. Adams St., Chicago 3, Ill., is almost alone in its use of plays.

The denominational publishers are printing very few plays but it would be well to keep in touch with the major ones for special projects and for plays used for specific emphases.

Book publishers ordinarily do not publish single plays unless the play has been a success on Broadway. But good plays can find publishers if the authors will get productions so that the script is tested and reveals if it has possibilities of being used by other groups. Many short plays have found a publisher in collections or in anthologies. Production gets the name of a play known, and editors are likely to be attracted to plays that have been tried out.

CHAPTER 6. RELIGIOUS POETRY

"The publications of the various denominations," Dr. Harkness observed, "are a market for religious verse." Their names and addresses may be found in the *Yearbook of American Churches* and other common sources. Other publications, such as *Christian Herald* and *Christian Century*, which do not have denominational ties, are excellent outlets also. The smaller secular local newspapers print religious poetry of certain types; at Christmas and Easter religious poetry is acceptable also to the large national secular periodicals and papers. Several dozen poetry magazines also are a market but are unenthusiastic about religious verse.

Virtually all books of poetry are published at a loss in the United States; only the work of the most renowned poets, such as Frost and Sandburg, sell enough copies to bring the publishers a profit. Good religious verse fares even worse unless it becomes part of a study course which promotes sales of books in large quantities. Yet a few publishing houses, for altruistic reasons or to gain prestige, are willing to bring out collections of high-quality religious verse. Religious publishing houses are as cautious as the general publishers.

Most poems published in the periodical and newspaper press bring no financial return to the author; a few periodicals pay $1 to $5 for a poem, or pay in extra copies of the publication, subscriptions, books, and other merchandise; some pay 10, 20, 25, or 50 cents and occasionally higher per line. Poetry magazines often run contests and pay a prize winner as much as $50.

CHAPTER 7. RELIGION IS NEWS

Most religious news is written by staff members of newspapers, magazines, radio stations, news services, or other organized news gatherers. Little such news is marketed on a free lance basis, as are articles and stories of religion.

A free lance religious writer who has a big story can sell it to the larger local newspapers, such agencies as the Associated Press, United Press, International News Service, and other secular transmitting services. Spectacular as well as unspectacular news is desired also by Religious News Service, the only interfaith news agency, which has its headquarters at 43 W. 57th St., New York 19, N.Y. The National Catholic Welfare Conference Press Department, 1312 Massachusetts Ave., N.W., Washington 5, D.C., handles some news but mainly feature material of interest to Catholics. Payment usually is on an outright basis.

CHAPTER 8. PUBLICIZING RELIGION

Publicity material always is free to the publication that consents to print it or the station that agrees to broadcast or telecast it. Religious writers with high-powered ideas may be able to sell their wares to the directors of offices of public relations and publicity for denominations or interdenominational organizations, or to the commercial agencies that do business on a contract basis.

Most publicity material of any sort is prepared at headquarters, so to speak. A news writer for a large local church writes from the standpoint of the institution (too often to the exclusion of the public's or the publisher's or broadcaster's angle) and thus has copy to give away rather than sell. Since marketing a manuscript is more than selling it for money but also includes publishing it even without return to the author, the writer whose material is used, whether paid for or not, has accomplished his goal, if that goal is to appear in print. Payment in coin of the realm is not involved.

CHAPTER 9. THE RELIGIOUS FEATURE ARTICLE

Most of the publications in Professor Root's and Miss Hull's lists (Chapters 4 and 13) are interested in the religious feature and article. Mr. Everett discusses market possibilities in his chapter, indicating that the denominational as well as all other religious publications, with the possible exception of the scholarly journal, are interested in such material. The journal is looking for articles of its own type, however, and is a market in a special way. The religious press pays the usual rates for such material: $5 to $300 for an article, depending upon the publication and its circulation, with most payments closer to $25.

Secular newspapers, news agencies, and specialized news services (see market notes for Chapter 7) are receptive. Small-town weeklies print such features eagerly but pay nothing as a rule. Small dailies pay from $5 to $10 a column; metropolitan papers $15 to $25 a column.

Usually extra amounts are paid for photographs, ranging from $1 to $5 for each print. Most features and many articles call for illustrations; their marketing is handicapped without them, especially in secular newspapers and large national secular magazines.

CHAPTER 10. EDITORIAL WRITING ABOUT RELIGION

For all practical purposes, there is no free lance market for the religious editorial. Staff members of religious publications write them for their papers and magazines. A secular publication seeking to editorialize gives the assignment, usually, to some interested member of the editorial board, to the church or religious news editor, or, but rarely, to a teacher of religion or some other churchman in the community. A religious writer desiring to write editorials, nevertheless, does better to try to interest an editor in an editorial column. The column, in some of its forms, is closely related to the editorial. Witness Simeon Stylites in the *Christian Century*. When thus contributed, these essays are paid for either at a flat rate or at the usual space rates, which vary by publication.

CHAPTER 11. REVIEWS AND CRITICISM

Dr. Garrison considers the matter of publication in his chapter. To that comment can be added the statement that many denominational publications are glad to have authoritative reviews of books not already covered, provided they have space for the review. A few pay space rates for such copy.

Critical comment on other than books, such as reviews of religious drama, art, films, and music, is better offered as a critical article than as a formal review. If accepted, it probably will be paid for at the usual rates for article material.

Most critical writing in the press brings little financial return. Book reviewers generally get the book in exchange for the review, only the writers for the big national publications being paid cash in addition. Reviews of a religious art show can be exchanged for tickets to the exhibit, and so on through the other arts.

CHAPTER 12. CURRICULUM MATERIALS

Dr. Rigdon's list is of certain denominational offices that use, generally by assignment, curriculum materials of the sort he describes in his chapter. To these might be added, from *The Writer's Market*, the names of the several nondenominational or commercial firms that publish curriculum materials independently, such as the David C. Cook Company, Elgin, Illinois.

A recent survey, Dr. Rigdon explained, conducted in connection with the preparation of this book, revealed that virtually all religious curriculum materials are prepared on assignment basis only. Several suggestions for securing an assignment are made in the chapter on writing curriculum materials. Names and addresses of leading publishers of religious curriculum materials are as follows:

American Baptist Publication Society, American Baptist Convention, 1701 Chestnut St., Philadelphia 3, Pa.

Board of Parish Education, American Lutheran Church, 57 E. Main Street, Columbus 15, Ohio.

Baptist Publications Committee of Canada, Baptist Federation of Canada, 299 Queen Street, West, Toronto 2B, Ont., Canada.

Board of Christian Education, Church of God, 1303 E. Fifth St., Anderson, Ind.

Department of Church Schools, and Nazarene Publishing House (Beacon Hill Press), Church of the Nazarene, 2923 Troost Ave., Box 527, Kansas City 41, Mo.

Board of Publication and Christian Education, Cumberland Presbyterian Church, Box 5535, Memphis 4, Tenn.

Christian Board of Publication, Disciples of Christ, Beaumont and Pine Blvd., Box 179, St. Louis 3, Mo.

Board of Christian Education and Publication, Evangelical and Reformed Church, 1505 Race St., Philadelphia 2, Pa., and 1724 Chouteau Ave., St. Louis 3, Mo.

Board of Christian Education, Evangelical United Brethren Church, 1900 Knott Building, Dayton 2, Ohio.

Editorial Division, Board of Education, The Methodist Church, Methodist Publishing House, 810 Broadway, Nashville 2, Tenn.

Board of Christian Education, Presbyterian Church in the U.S., Presbyterian Building, 8 N. Sixth Street, Richmond 9, Va.

Board of Christian Education, Presbyterian Church in the U.S.A., Witherspoon Building, Philadelphia 7, Pa.

Department of Christian Education of the National Council, and Seabury Press, Protestant Episcopal Church, 28 Havemeyer Place, Greenwich, Conn.

Baptist Sunday School Board, Southern Baptist Convention, 127 Ninth Ave., North, Nashville 3, Tenn.

Board of Christian Education, United Church of Canada, 299 Queen Street, West, Toronto 2B, Ont., Canada.

Board of Parish Education, United Lutheran Church in America, 1228 Spruce St., Philadelphia 7, Pa.

Board of Christian Education, United Presbyterian Church of North America, 209 Ninth St., Pittsburgh 22, Pa.

CHAPTER 13. JUVENILE MATERIALS

(See also the list for Chapter 4.)

PERIODICALS

Boys and Girls, Otterbein Press, Dayton 2, Ohio. A weekly for juniors. Uses short articles on history, nature, biography, inventions, things to do and make, etc. Photographs and puzzles. Length: 300–500 words. Low payment; acceptance.

Canadian Boy and *Canadian Girl*, Room 520, 299 Queen St., Toronto 2B, Ont., Canada. A weekly for intermediates. Uses articles, photo-stories, puzzles, quizzes. 500 words.

Children's Friend, 425 S. Fourth St., Minneapolis 15, Minn. A weekly for children 8 to 12. Brief articles. Photographs. ¼¢; acceptance.

Friends, 1724 Chouteau Ave., St. Louis 3, Mo. A weekly for children under 9. Uses brief articles with or without photographs or illustrations. ¼¢ and up; acceptance.

Juniors, 1701 Chestnut St., Philadelphia 3, Pa. A weekly for boys and girls 9 to 11. Uses illustrated articles. Length: 600–800 words. Approximately $4.50 per thousand; acceptance.

My Counsellor, 434 S. Wabash Ave., Chicago 5, Ill. A weekly for boys and girls 9 to 13. Articles, biographical, personal experience, religious projects. Length: 1,500–1,700 words. 1½¢ and up; month following acceptance.

Pilot, 209 Ninth St., Pittsburgh 22, Pa. A weekly for junior high age. Uses articles on various subjects. Length: 1,500 words. No fixed rates.

Sentinel, 127 Ninth Ave., North, Nashville 3, Tenn. A weekly for boys and girls 9 to 13. Uses brief informational and travel articles, with or without illustrations. Length: 500–800 words. ½¢; 16th of each month.

Stories, 930 Witherspoon Building, Philadelphia 7, Pa. A weekly for boys and girls 6 to 8. Uses short articles on things to make and do. Length: 200–500 words. ½¢ and up; acceptance.

Storytime, 127 Ninth Ave., North, Nashville 3, Tenn. A weekly for children 4 to 8. Uses brief articles about things to make, such as games and toys, and gifts for parents. ½¢; 16th of each month.

Story Trails, Winona Lake, Ind. A weekly for boys and girls 9 to 12. Uses brief articles, how-to-do-its, nature, behavior, hobbies. Photographs. Length: 1,000 words maximum. 1¢; acceptance.

Story World, 1701 Chestnut St., Philadelphia 3, Pa. A weekly for children under 9. Uses brief articles, illustrated, telling things to make or do. Length: 200–400 words. $7.50 per thousand; acceptance.

Straight, Hamilton Ave. at 8100, Cincinnati 31, Ohio. A weekly for boys and girls 12 to 16. Uses news of teen-agers who have made special accomplishment in any field, unusual hobbies, money-making activities, photographs of teen-age projects, puzzles, quizzes. Length: 500–800 words. Between ⅓¢ and ½¢; 15th of month following acceptance.

Teens, 1701 Chestnut St., Philadelphia 3, Pa. A weekly for boys and girls 13 to 17. Uses features on science, religion, how-to-make, vocations, hobbies; articles on boys who have been outstanding in some field such as sports, hobbies, school, part-time jobs. Length: 850 words. Photographs. $5 and up for features with photograph; $4 for articles.

Teen Time, Winona Lake, Ind. A weekly for boys and girls 13 to 16. Uses articles on subjects ranging from hobby and recreational ideas to young people's service projects and Bible study clubs. Photographs. Length: 1,000–1,500 words maximum; filler articles, 200–500. 1¢; acceptance.

Trailblazer, 930 Witherspoon Bldg., Philadelphia 7, Pa. A weekly for boys and girls 9 to 11. Uses articles on handcraft, nature, hobbies, church projects, sports; also puzzles, activity games, quizzes. Photographs. Length: 200–1,000 words. ½¢ and up; acceptance.

Trails for Juniors, 810 Broadway, Nashville 2, Tenn. A weekly for boys and girls 9 to 12. Special articles on assignment. 1½¢ and up; acceptance.

Twelve/Fifteen, 810 Broadway, Nashville 2, Tenn. A weekly for boys and girls 12 to 15. Uses articles—no encyclopedic rewrites. Photographs. 1½¢; acceptance.

Upward, 127 Ninth Ave., North, Nashville 3, Tenn. A weekly for boys and girls 13 to 16. Uses articles, informational, personality, guidance, etc. Photographs. Length: to 1,500 words.

Venture, 930 Witherspoon Bldg., Philadelphia 7, Pa. A weekly for boys and girls 12 to 15. Articles on individual or group hobbies, handcrafts, sports, science, church projects, nature, history, travel, vocations, biography, cooking, good manners. Puzzles, quizzes, games, party plans, occasionally. Length: 500–1,000 words. ½¢ and up; acceptance.

Vision, Beaumont and Pine Blvd., St. Louis 3, Mo. A weekly for boys and girls 12 to 18. Articles on current interests, relating current happenings to teen-agers. Interested in finding young writers. Length: Under 2,000 words. ½¢ for prose; $3 and up for photographs.

BOOK PUBLISHERS

Abingdon Press, 810 Broadway, Nashville 2, Tenn., and 150 Fifth Avenue, New York 11, N.Y. Picture books, read-aloud books, easy-to-read books, religious books, nature and recreational books. No illustrations. Royalty basis.

Wm. B. Eerdmans Publishing Co., 255 Jefferson Ave., S.E., Grand Rapids 3, Mich. Publishes books of games and other types of recreation, Bible story books, illustrated books on church and world history. Length: 15,000–30,000 words. Royalty basis.

Moody Press, 820 N. LaSalle St., Chicago 10, Ill. Publishes in book form Bible quizzes, Bible games, devotions for children, cookbooks for children with devotional material, picture books for small children. Royalty basis.

Zondervan Publishing House, 1415 Lake Drive, S.E., Grand Rapids 6, Mich. Uses books of games, oral and visual quizzes and puzzles, devotional materials, craft and hobby books, etiquette helps, and cookbooks. Average length: 8,500 words. Royalty basis.

CHAPTER 14. RELIGIOUS BIOGRAPHY

No publisher of religious books specializes particularly in biography. All are interested in good work in this field. The denominational houses, to be sure, are commonly interested particularly in biographies of the founders or prominent representatives of their churches. In the case of John Knox or John Calvin, one might seek a publisher in the Westminster Press or the John Knox Press. For the Wesley brothers, one would turn naturally to the Abingdon Press. For Luther or Melanchthon, one thinks of the Lutheran publishing houses, such as the Muhlenberg Press, the Augustana Press, and the Concordia. In the case of religious liberals such as Erasmus, William Ellery Channing, Theodore Parker, or Albert Schweitzer, one would turn appropriately to the Beacon Press. There are numerous Roman Catholic houses as well, such as Sheed & Ward.

The lines, however, are not sharply drawn. For example, the Methodist publishing house—the Abingdon Press—has brought out three studies of Luther, perhaps as a debt of honor, since Wesley was converted during the reading of Luther's preface to the Epistle to the Romans. The nondenominational publishing houses such as Harper's, Scribner's, Macmillan, and the like are always open to any good work in this field.

The university presses have been founded in order to bring out works of a more erudite character, but inasmuch as the majority of these presses are not adequately financed, they have to cater to books capable of reaching a wider audience. In consequence, the university presses tend to enter the same fields as the general non-denominational publishing houses. Notably, the Oxford University Press is in this category. A number of the university presses have published works in the field. The Yale University Press, for example, has brought out a life of Swedenborg; the Duke University Press, of Harriet Beecher Stowe; and the Harvard University Press, of Eleanor of Aquitaine, though perhaps she does not precisely rate a place among religious biographies.

CHAPTER 15. INSPIRATIONAL BOOKS FOR LAYMEN

Abingdon Press and Revell probably publish more inspirational books than other publishers, percentage-wise, but the market is about the same with all religious publishers and secular houses with religious departments. That statement holds for manuscripts of dignity and soundness, as over against manuscripts of the superficial, sentimental sort. The general practice of publishers is to offer standard royalty contracts, providing a 10 per cent royalty. A word about quotations, which are so freely used in these books: the important thing is to rely on them sparingly, to be careful in selection so that the quotation is clearly related to the author's own thought and not simply dragged in for supposed effect, and to make sure that one has the proper source and permission to use the quote.

CHAPTER 16. BOOKS OF SERMONS AND DEVOTIONAL BOOKS

All religious publishing houses and all secular houses with religious book departments are logical outlets for sermon books and devotional book manuscripts. For many years it has been the practice of a denominational publishing firm to give preference to the sermon collections of its own clergy, but no house would turn down an excellent collection offered by a writer belonging to another denomination unless, of course, it could not tolerate his views. Some of the most widely used and read sermon collections in print are issued by secular houses, notably Doubleday, Macmillan, and Harper's. The *Literary Market Place* is the standard source for lists of such publishers as well as religious houses. This directory is published each July by R. R. Bowker Co., New York. Standard book agreements are entered into, as a rule, for both collections of sermons and devotional books. Writers who contribute one or two sermons to anthologies of such writings generally are paid a flat sum or share in the royalties.

CHAPTER 17. RELIGIOUS RADIO

Broadcasting and Film Commission, 220 Fifth Avenue, New York 1, N.Y., an agency of the National Council of Churches, buys dramatic radio scripts for seasonal occasions, biblical, historical, or contemporary. Length: 15 or 30 minutes. $100 to $250 each on acceptance. Buys appropriate complete programs and program series of all kinds, any standard length. Payment negotiated.

Church Broadcasting Associates, P.O. Box 186, San Anselmo, Calif., an independent producer and distributor of religious news, five-minute devotional talks, dramatic scripts, transcribed programs for church groups and advertiser-sponsors, both radio and television. Payment by royalty.

CHAPTER 18. RELIGIOUS TELEVISION

Broadcasting and Film Commission, National Council of Churches, 220 Fifth Avenue, New York 1, N.Y., considers *network quality* dramatic religious television scripts. Needs vary from time to time. Write to find out what present needs may be.

The radio and television departments of the denominations and communions also are a possible market. Write to discover their present requirements. Consult *Yearbook of American Churches*, edited by Benson Y. Landis, and published by the National Council, for names and addresses.

CHAPTER 19. WRITING FOR FILMS

Broadcasting and Film Commission, National Council of Churches, 220 Fifth Avenue, New York 1, N.Y. Agency of participating denominations producing films on a co-operative basis.

Cathedral Films, 140 N. Hollywood Way, Burbank, Calif., a nonprofit company producing films for the church.

Concordia Films, 3558 S. Jefferson, St. Louis 18, Mo., a production and distribution agency of the Lutheran Church–Missouri Synod.

Family Films, 8840 W. Olympic Blvd., Beverly Hills, Calif., a commercial firm producing films for the church.

Louis De Rochemont Associates, 380 Madison Avenue, New York 19, N.Y. A commercial firm producing theatrical and sponsored films.

Lutheran Film Associates, Inc., 35 W. 45th Street, New York 19, N.Y. A sister organization of Lutheran Church Productions, maker of the *Martin Luther* film.

ADDITIONAL MARKET DATA

ADDITIONAL MARKET DATA

ADDITIONAL MARKET DATA

ADDITIONAL MARKET DATA

ADDITIONAL MARKET DATA

APPENDIX *II*

For Further Reading

Books ABOUT religious writing are few. As one of the authors of this book observed, that is exactly why *Writing for the Religious Market* is needed. Writers must rely on secular books for further technical aid; since the fundamental principles apply to all specialties, this situation is satisfactory in so far as books are available at all. Although an extensive literature of religious writing is unnecessary, some additional specialized volumes would be welcome. Here, then, is an assignment for religious writers themselves.

For the convenience of the users, the reading list is arranged by chapters, with a minimum of duplication. Because few of the religious writing books are devoted to one specialty, readers will find themselves relying heavily upon those noted for Chapter 1, for their content applies to many aspects of religious writing. Most of these readings were selected by the respective authors of the chapters.

For a more specialized and more nearly complete bibliography, readers are referred to the editor's *The Journalist's Bookshelf*, the sixth edition of which was published in 1955 by Quill and Scroll Foundation, 111 W. Jackson Boulevard, Chicago 4, Ill. This book contains an annotated list covering most U.S. books on journalism.

CHAPTER 1. WHAT IS RELIGIOUS WRITING?

Abrams, Ray H. *Organized Religion in the United States*. Philadelphia: American Academy of Political and Social Science, 1948.

Browne, Benjamin P., Editor. *Christian Journalism for Today*. Philadelphia: Judson Press, 1952. Revised, 1954.

Osteyee, Edith Tiller. *Writing for Christian Publications*. Philadelphia: Judson Press, 1953.

Vittoria, Theodore J., Editor. *The Catholic Voice*. New York: Society of St. Paul, 1949.

Wolseley, Roland E. *Careers in Religious Journalism*. New York: Association Press, 1955.

————. *Interpreting the Church Through Press and Radio*. Philadelphia: Muhlenberg Press, 1951.

CHAPTER 2. THE PRACTICAL SIDE

Bennett, Arnold. *The Truth About an Author*. New York: Doran, 1911.

Bower, Warren, Editor. *How to Write for Pleasure and Profit*. Philadelphia: Lippincott, 1951.

Brande, Dorothea. *Becoming a Writer*. New York: Harcourt, Brace, 1934.

Brickell, Herschel, Editor. *Writers on Writing*. New York: Doubleday, 1949.

Brittain, Vera. *On Being an Author*. New York: Macmillan, 1948.

Campbell, Walter C. *Writing Non-Fiction*. Boston: The Writer, Inc., 1949.

Fisher, Vardis. *God or Caesar?* Caldwell, Idaho: Caxton, 1953.

Kearney, Paul W. *Free-Lance Writing for a Living*. New York: McKay, 1953.

Lewis, Maxine. *The Magic Key to Successful Writing*. New York: Prentice-Hall, 1955.

Maugham, W. Somerset. *The Summing Up*. New York: Garden City Books, 1940.

Munson, Gorham. *The Written Word*. New York: Creative Age Press, 1949.

————. *The Writer's Workshop Companion*. New York: Farrar, Straus and Young, 1951.

Piercy, Josephine I., Editor. *Modern Writers at Work*. New York: Macmillan, 1930.

Roberts, Kenneth. *I Wanted to Write*. New York: Doubleday, 1949.

Wittenberg, Philip. *The Protection and Marketing of Literary Property*. New York: Messner, 1937.

CHAPTER 3. THE NOVEL AND RELIGION

Mrs. Banning submitted the following titles, writing: "The books pertaining to this subject that would be most useful to the novelist are not studies of technique, few of which exist in this field, but those novels that have dealt with religious problems and forces, and in greatly varying degree won recognition as successful books." (Editor's Note: Mrs. Banning did not place her own book first; but I have rearranged them alphabetically).

Banning, Margaret Culkin. *Fallen Away*. New York: Harper, 1952.

Cather, Willa. *Death Comes to the Archbishop*. New York: Knopf, 1951.

Douglas, Lloyd. *The Robe*. Boston: Houghton Mifflin, 1942.

Faulkner, William. *A Fable*. New York: Random House, 1954.

Greene, Graham. *The Heart of the Matter*. New York: Viking, 1946.

Hardy, Thomas. *Jude the Obscure*. New York: Harper, 1905.

Lewis, Sinclair. *Elmer Gantry*. New York: Harcourt, Brace, 1927.

Paton, Alan. *Too Late the Phalarope*. New York: Scribner, 1953.

Robinson, Henry Morton. *The Cardinal*. New York: Simon and Schuster, 1950.

Smith, Sheila Kay. *A View from the Parsonage*. New York: Harper, 1954.

Waugh, Evelyn. *Brideshead Revisited*. Boston: Little, Brown, 1955.

Among the few technical books on the novel are these:

Comfort, Alexander. *The Novel and Our Time*. London: Phoenix House, 1948.

Daiches, David. *The Novel and the Modern World*. Chicago: University of Chicago Press, 1939.

James, Henry. *The Art of the Novel*. New York: Scribner, 1934.

Keyes, Frances Parkinson. *The Cost of a Best Seller*. New York: Messner, 1950.

McHugh, Vincent. *Primer of the Novel*. New York: Random House, 1950.

O'Hara, Mary. *Novel-in-the-Making*. New York: McKay, 1954.
Orvis, Mary Burchard. *The Art of Writing Fiction*. New York: Prentice-Hall, 1948.

CHAPTER 4. GIVING THE SHORT STORY MEANING

Elwood, Maren. *Characters Make Your Story*. Boston: Houghton Mifflin, 1942.
————. *Write the Short Short*. Boston: The Writer, Inc., 1947.
Gilkes, Lillian, and Bower, Warren. *Short Story Craft*. New York: Macmillan, 1949.
Kamerman, Sylvia E., Editor. *Writing the Short Short Story*. Boston: The Writer, Inc., 1942.
Kempton, Kenneth Payson. *The Short Story*. Cambridge: Harvard University Press, 1947.
Mowery, William Byron. *Professional Short-Story Writing*. New York: Crowell, 1953.
O'Faolain, Sean. *The Short Story*. New York: Devin-Adair, 1951.
Summers, Richard. *Craft of the Short Story*. New York: Rinehart, 1948.
Ware, Edmund, and Bailey, Robeson. *From Fact to Fiction*. New York: Appleton-Century, 1946.
Whitney, Phyllis A. *Writing Juvenile Fiction*. Boston: The Writer, Inc., 1947.

CHAPTER 5. THE RELIGIOUS DRAMA

Archer, William. *Play-Making, A Manual of Craftsmanship*. Boston: Small, Maynard, 1912.
Baker, George Pierce. *Dramatic Technique*. Boston: Houghton Mifflin, 1919.
Bentley, Eric. *The Playwright as Thinker*. New York: Meridian Books, 1955.
Ehrensperger, Harold. *Conscience on Stage*. Nashville, Tenn.: Abingdon-Cokesbury, 1947.
Eliot, T. S. *Poetry and Drama*. London: Faber & Faber, undated.
Gallaway, Marian. *Constructing a Play*. New York: Prentice-Hall, 1950.
Kerr, Walter. *How Not to Write a Play*. New York: Simon and Schuster, 1955.

Lawson, John Howard. *Theory and Technique of Playwriting and Screenwriting.* New York: Putnam, 1949.

Matthews, Brander. *The Principles of Playmaking.* New York: Scribner, 1919.

Wilde, Percival. *The Craftsmanship of the One-act Play.* Boston: Little, Brown, 1928.

See also the files of *The Drama Magazine* and the original *Theatre Arts.*

CHAPTER 6. RELIGIOUS POETRY

Alden, Raymond M. *English Verse: specimens illustrating its principles and history.* New York: Holt, 1903.

Andrews, Clarence E. *The Writing and Reading of Verse.* New York and London: Appleton, 1918.

Cane, Melville. *Making a Poem.* New York: Harcourt, Brace, 1953.

Carruth, William H. *Verse Writing.* New York: Macmillan, 1917.

Coblentz, Stanton A. *An Editor Looks at Poetry.* Mill Valley, Calif.: The Wings Press, 1947.

Lewis, Charlton M. *The Principles of English Verse.* New York: Holt, 1906.

Matthews, Brander. *A Study of Versification.* Boston: Houghton Mifflin, 1911.

Stewart, George R. *The Technique of English Verse.* New York: Holt, 1930.

CHAPTER 7. RELIGION IS NEWS

Brodie, W. Austin. *Keeping Your Church in the News.* Westwood, N. J.: Revell, 1942.

Bush, W. Chilton. *The Art of News Communication.* New York: Appleton-Century-Crofts, 1954.

Campbell, Laurence R., and Wolseley, Roland E. *Newsmen at Work.* Boston: Houghton Mifflin, 1949.

Charnley, Mitchell V. *News by Radio.* New York: Macmillan, 1949.

MacDougall, Curtis D. *Interpretative Reporting.* New York: Macmillan, 1948.

Norton, William Bernard. *Church and Newspaper.* New York: Macmillan, 1930.

Warren, Carl. *Modern News Reporting*. New York: Harper, 1951.
————. *Radio News Writing and Editing*. New York: Harper, 1948.
Wolseley, Roland E. *Interpreting the Church Through Press and Radio*. Philadelphia: Muhlenberg Press, 1951.

CHAPTER 8. PUBLICIZING RELIGION

Four books on the list for Chapter 7, those by Brodie, Campbell and Wolseley, MacDougall, and Wolseley, are recommended by Miss Smith, as well as:

Baus, Herbert M. *Publicity, How to Plan, Produce and Place It*. New York: Harper, 1942.
Harral, Stewart. *Patterns of Publicity Copy*. Norman, Okla.: University of Oklahoma Press, 1950.
————. *Public Relations for Churches*. Nashville, Tenn.: Abingdon-Cokesbury, 1945.
Hushaw, Charles C., and Sutcliffe, Richart T. *Telling the Good News*. Philadelphia: United Lutheran Church Publication House, 1954.
Johnson, Stanley, and Harriss, Julian. *The Complete Reporter*. New York: Macmillan, 1945.
Ramsberger, Jack. *How to Make Publicity Work*. New York: Reynal, 1948.
Stuber, Stanley I. *Public Relations Manual for Churches*. New York: Doubleday, 1951.

CHAPTER 9. THE RELIGIOUS FEATURE ARTICLE

Bailey, Robeson. *Techniques in Article-Writing*. New York: Appleton-Century, 1947.
Bird, George L. *Article Writing and Marketing*. New York: Rinehart, 1956. Revised Edition.
Brennecke, Ernest J., and Clark, Donald L. *Magazine Article Writing*. New York: Macmillan, 1942. Revised Edition.
Gundell, Glenn, Editor. *Writing—From Idea to Printed Page*. New York: Doubleday, 1949.
Harrington, H. F., and Watson, Elmo Scott. *Modern Feature Writing*. New York: Harper, 1935.

Kearney, Paul W. *Free-Lance Writing for a Living*. New York: McKay, 1953.

Lederer, William J. *Spare-Time Article Writing for Money*. New York: Norton, 1954.

Patterson, Helen M. *Writing and Selling Feature Articles*. New York: Prentice-Hall, 1949. Second Edition.

Reddick, DeWitt C. *Modern Feature Writing*. New York: Harper, 1949.

Steigleman, Walter A. *Writing the Feature Article*. New York: Macmillan, 1950.

CHAPTER 10. EDITORIAL WRITING ABOUT RELIGION

Bush, Chilton R. *Editorial Thinking and Writing*. New York: Appleton, 1932.

Jones, Robert W. *The Editorial Page*. New York: Crowell, 1930.

Spencer, M. Lyle. *Editorial Writing*. Boston: Houghton Mifflin, 1924.

Waldrop, A. Gayle. *Editor and Editorial Writer*. New York: Rinehart, 1955. Revised Edition.

CHAPTER 11. REVIEWS AND CRITICISM

Note: Because Dr. Garrison has restricted this chapter to reviews and criticism of religious books and the amount of critical writing on religious art, drama, and music is small, this reading list covers chiefly treatment of books.

Drewry, John E. *Book Reviewing*. Boston: The Writer, Inc., 1945.

Gard, Wayne. *Book Reviewing*. New York: Knopf, 1927.

Gardiner, Harold C. *Tenets for Readers and Reviewers*. New York: America Press, 1944.

Greene, Theodore M. *The Arts and the Art of Criticism*. Princeton, N.J.: Princeton University Press, 1940.

Jones, Llewellyn. *How to Criticize Books*. New York: Norton, 1928.

Smith, S. Stephenson. *The Craft of the Critic*. New York: Crowell, 1931.

CHAPTER 12. CURRICULUM MATERIALS

Alberty, Harold. *Reorganizing the High-School Curriculum.* New York: Macmillan, 1950.

Caswell, Hollis L., and Campbell, Doak S. *Curriculum Development.* New York: American Book, 1935.

Eavey, C. B. *Principles of Teaching for Christian Teachers.* Grand Rapids, Mich.: Zondervan, 1940.

Flesch, Rudolf F. *The Art of Readable Writing.* New York: Harper, 1949.

Gwynn, J. Minor. *Curriculum Principles and Social Trends.* New York: Macmillan, 1950.

Lankard, Frank G. *A History of the American Sunday School Curriculum.* Nashville, Tenn.: Abingdon, 1927.

Myers, A. J. William. *Teaching Religion Creatively.* Westwood, N.J.: Revell, 1932.

Smart, James D. *The Teaching Ministry of the Church.* Philadelphia: Westminster Press, 1954.

Special Committee on the Curriculum Guide, Division of Christian Education. *A Guide for Curriculum in Christian Education.* Chicago: National Council of the Churches of Christ in the U.S.A., 1955.

Vieth, Paul H. *The Church and Christian Education.* St. Louis: Bethany Press, 1947.

CHAPTER 13. JUVENILE MATERIALS

Arbuthnot, May Hill. *Children and Books.* Chicago: Scott, Foresman, 1947.

Berry, Erick, and Best, Herbert. *Writing for Children.* New York: Viking, 1954.

Colby, Jean Poindexter. *The Children's Book Field.* New York: Pelligrini & Cudahy, 1952.

Eaton, Anne Thaxter, Editor. *Treasure for the Taking.* New York: Viking, 1946.

Ferris, Helen, Editor. *Writing Books for Boys and Girls.* New York: Doubleday, 1952.

Frank, Josette. *What Books for Children?* New York: Doubleday, 1937.

————. *Your Child's Reading Today.* New York: Doubleday, 1954.

Lederer, William J. *Spare-Time Article Writing for Money*. New York: Norton, 1954.

Lewis, Claudia. *Writing for Young Children*. New York: Simon and Schuster, 1954.

Robinson, Mabel Louise. *Writing for Young People*. New York: Nelson, 1950.

Russell, Frances. *Seek and Find*. Toronto: Dent, 1955.

CHAPTER 14. RELIGIOUS BIOGRAPHY

Beckwith, J. A., and Cope, G. G., Editors. *Contemporary American Biography*. New York: Harper, 1941.

Bowen, Catherine Drinker. *The Writing of Biography*. Boston: The Writer, Inc., 1951.

Bradford, Gamaliel. *Biography and the Human Heart*. Boston: Houghton Mifflin, 1932.

Nicolson, Harold. *The Development of English Biography*. London: Hogarth, 1933.

CHAPTER 15. INSPIRATIONAL BOOKS FOR LAYMEN

Dr. Wentzel suggests source books primarily, since there are none devoted to the writing of such volumes as concern his chapter.

Cecil, Lord David, Editor. *Oxford Book of Christian Verse*. Oxford, Eng.: Clarendon Press, 1940.

Clark, Thomas Curtis, and Gillespie, Esther A., Compilers. *1,000 Quotable Poems*. Chicago: Willett, Clark, 1937.

Osteyee, Edith Tiller. *Writing for Christian Publications*. Philadelphia: Judson Press, 1953.

Untermeyer, Louis, Editor. *A Treasury of Great Poems, English and American*. New York: Simon and Schuster, 1942.

CHAPTER 16. BOOKS OF SERMONS AND DEVOTIONAL BOOKS

BOOKS OF SERMONS

Editor's Note: Dr. Macartney's books were included only after repeated pleas by the editor that he list them.

Black, Hugh. *The Mystery of Preaching*. Westwood, N. J.: Revell, 1924.

Brodus, John A. *Preparation and Delivery of Sermons*. New York: Armstrong, 1901.

Brooks, Phillips. *Lectures on Preaching*. Yale Lectures. New York: Dutton, 1877.

Burrell, David. *The Sermon, Its Construction and Delivery*. Westwood, N.J.: Revell, 1913.

Forsythe, P. T. *Positive Preaching and The Modern Mind*. Yale Lectures. New York: Armstrong, 1901.

Horne, Charles S. *The Romance of Preaching*. Westwood, N.J.: Revell, 1914.

Jeffs, H. *The Art of Sermon Illustration*. Westwood, N.J.: Revell, undated.

Kennard, J. Spencer. *Psychic Power in Preaching*. Philadelphia: Jacobs, 1901.

Macartney, Clarence Edward. *Bible Character Sermons, Mountains and Mountain Men*. Nashville, Tenn.: Abingdon, 1950.

———. *Chariots of Fire*. Nashville, Tenn.: Abingdon, 1951.

———. *Great Women of the Bible*. Nashville, Tenn.: Abingdon, 1942.

———. *Macartney's Illustrations*. Nashville, Tenn.: Abingdon, 1945.

———. *Preaching Without Notes*. Nashville, Tenn.: Abingdon, 1946.

———. *The Sons of Thunder*. Stone Lectures at Princeton Seminary. Westwood, N.J.: Revell, 1929.

McDowell, William. *Good Ministers of Jesus Christ*. Nashville, Tenn.: Abingdon, 1917.

Smith, David. *The Art of Preaching*. London: Hodder & Stoughton, undated.

DEVOTIONAL BOOKS

Augustine, Saint. *Confessions of St. Augustine*. London: Methuen, 1897.

Beecher, Henry Ward. *Prayers from Plymouth Pulpit*. New York: Scribner, 1867.

Gore, Charles. *Prayer and the Lord's Prayer*. New York: Harper, 1947.

Johnson, Samuel. *Samuel Johnson's Prayers*. New York: Harper, 1947.

Macartney, Clarence Edward. *The Lord's Prayer.* Westwood, N.J.: Revell, 1947.
———. *Wrestlers with God.* New York: Smith, 1930.
Prayers Ancient and Modern. A compilation. Boston: Little, Brown, 1912.
Spurgeon, Charles H. *Morning and Evening Daily Readings.* London: Marshall, Morgan & Scott, undated.
Thomas a Kempis. *The Imitation of Christ.* Many editions.

CHAPTER 17. RELIGIOUS RADIO

Barnouw, Erik. *Handbook of Radio Writing.* Boston: Little, Brown, 1947.
Brooks, William F. *Radio News Writing.* New York: McGraw-Hill, 1948.
Crews, Albert. *Professional Radio Writing.* Boston: Houghton Mifflin, 1946.
Flesch, Rudolf. *The Art of Plain Talk.* New York: Harper, 1946.
Griswold, C. T., and Schmitz, C. H., Editors. *Broadcasting Religion.* New York: National Council of the Churches of Christ in the U.S.A., 1954.
Parker, E., Inman, E., and Snyder, R. *Religious Radio.* New York: Harper, 1948.
Wishengrad, Morton. *Eternal Light.* New York: Crown, 1947.

CHAPTER 18. RELIGIOUS TELEVISION

To Mr. Adams' selection of books by Flesch and by Griswold and Schmitz, for Chapter 17, Mr. Schmitz adds:

Bretz, Rudy. *Techniques of Television Production.* New York: McGraw-Hill, 1953.
Greene, Robert S. *Television Writing.* New York: Harper, 1952.
Schmitz, Charles H. *Windows Toward God.* Nashville, Tenn.: Abingdon-Cokesbury, 1950.
Stasheff, Edward, and Bretz, Rudy. *The Television Program.* New York: Wyn, 1951.
Television Production Techniques by Experts. New York: National Council of the Churches of Christ in the U.S.A., 1953.

CHAPTER 19. WRITING FOR FILMS

Chekhov, Michael. *To the Actor*. New York: Harper, 1953.

Egri, Lajos. *The Art of Dramatic Writing*. New York: Simon and Schuster, 1946.

Eisenstein, Sergei M. *The Film Sense*. New York: Harcourt, Brace, 1942.

Grierson, John. *Grierson on Documentary*. New York: Harcourt, Brace, 1947.

Herman, Lewis. *A Practical Manual of Screen Playwriting*. Cleveland, Ohio: World, 1952.

Lawson, John Howard. *Theory and Technique of Playwriting and Screenwriting*. New York: Putnam, 1949.

Lindgren, Ernest. *The Art of the Film*. London: Allen & Unwin, 1948.

Manvell, Roger. *Film*. London: Penguin Books, 1946; also *The Cinema* (annual). London: Pelican Books.

National Board of Review of Motion Pictures. *Films in Review* Magazine. New York.

Polti, Georges. *The Thirty-Six Dramatic Situations*. Boston: The Writer, Inc., 1945.

Van Druten, John. *Playwright at Work*. New York: Harper, 1953.

Index

Index